Building on her previous works on Sophocles and Aeschylus, Shirley Darcus Sullivan takes an in-depth look at Euripides' use of psychological terms – *phrēn*, *nous*, *prapides*, *thumos*, *kardia*, *kear*, and *psychē* – and compares his usage to that of both earlier and contemporary poets, notably Aeschylus and Sophocles.

Sullivan discusses each term separately, gathering them from Euripides' seventeen extant tragedies and from fragments of other plays. She begins with a broad look at how both earlier and contemporary poets used the various terms, moving on to a detailed discussion of Euripides' own usage, from his most often used *phrēn* to his new use of *psychē*.

Euripides' Use of Psychological Terminology will be of interest to scholars of classics, in particular those in fifth-century Greek classics, as well as to those interested in psychology and its presentation in ancient literature.

SHIRLEY DARCUS SULLIVAN is professor of classics at the University of British Columbia.

Euripides' Use
of Psychological
Terminology

SHIRLEY DARCUS SULLIVAN

McGill-Queen's University Press
Montreal & Kingston · London · Ithaca

© McGill-Queen's University Press 2000
ISBN 0-7735-2051-1

Legal deposit second quarter 2000
Bibliothèque nationale du Québec

Printed in Canada on acid-free paper

McGill-Queen's University Press acknowledges the financial
support of the Government of Canada through the Book
Publishing Industry Development Program (BPIDP) for its
activities. We also acknowledge the support of the Canada
Council for the Arts for our publishing program.

Canadian Cataloguing in Publication Data

Sullivan, Shirley Darcus, 1945–
　　Euripides' use of psychological terminology
　　Includes bibliographical references and index.
　　ISBN 0-7735-2051-1
　　1. Euripides – Language.　2. Psychology in literature.
　　I. Title.
　　PA3978.S84 2000　882'.01　C99-901380-7

This book was typeset by Typo Litho Composition Inc.
in 10/12 Times.

For Mary

Mater Thesauri Cordis

Contents

Tables

Preface

The dramatist Euripides (c. 484–406 B.C.) wrote a very large number of tragedies of which we have sixteen complete tragedies as well as the *Alcestis*, substituted for a satyr play but largely tragic in nature. We possess also a very large number of fragments from other plays. In these seventeen dramas and fragments there appear seven psychological terms: *phrēn*, *nous*, *prapides*, *thumos*, *kardia*, *kear*, and *psychē*. These will form the subject of the present work. It will examine how Euripides uses these terms, studying how his references either resemble those of contemporary poets or differ from them. It will illustrate also where and how Euripides refers to psychological terminology in ways both like and unlike those of Aeschylus and Sophocles.

Since most of the plays cannot be firmly dated, all the plays will be treated in the various chapters in alphabetical order. The book will first discuss psychological terminology in general in Euripides (chapter 1). It will then examine each psychic term separately (chapters 2–8). The book will conclude with an overview of Euripides' use of psychological terms (chapter 9). The focus of this study will be on how traditional or new Euripides' usage of these terms was. The book, therefore, will concentrate on the analysis of psychological terms. Its scope will prevent extensive discussion of scholarly debate in the interpretation of various passages, especially since these rarely relate to the meaning of psychological terms.

READERSHIP

This study is intended primarily for the reader interested in both Euripides and in fifth-century Greek tragedy. It should also be of interest to anyone studying the ways in which the early Greeks viewed psychological activity. Euripides' usage will be compared to that of poets from Homer down to Pindar and Bacchylides (c. 750–440 B.C.). It will be compared also to that of Aeschylus (525–456 B.C.) and Sophocles (479–406 B.C.).

The book is meant for both the specialist and the non-specialist. All passages are presented in translation for the reader who may not know Greek. For those who do know Greek, frequent quotations from the text have been given. All the psychic terms are always given in transliterated form.

BIBLIOGRAPHY AND TRANSLATIONS

The Bibliography lists all the texts consulted and indicates those whose numbering is followed (marking these with an [N]). For Euripides the three volumes of the text edited by J. Diggle are used. For the fragments all are taken from the second edition of Nauck with the addition of two fragments from a recent papyrus as edited in C. Collard, M.J. Cropp, and K.H. Lee, *Selected Fragmentary Plays*, vol. I. All line-numberings are according to these editions. In both the Bibliography and the Notes the abbreviations of journals follow for the most part those found in *L'Année philologique*. Authors listed in the bibliography are mentioned in the notes by name and short title only.

The Bibliography is extensive, listing all the books that treat different aspects of Euripidean tragedy. Since books that specifically examine psychological terms in Euripides are very few, these other studies provide important background material for the current study.

The translation of the Greek passages is my own. This translation tends to be as literal as possible in order to clarify the exact use of the various psychic terms.

The study will show what Euripides' use of psychic terms was like. Often it is traditional; often it is new. It is hoped that this examination of his usage will contribute in some way to an understanding of his tragedies as a whole.

Acknowledgments

My thanks to the Social Sciences and Humanities Research Council of Canada for the research grant that generously supported this project. My thanks also to the University of British Columbia for the Humanities Research Grant that likewise supported this research.

For the encouragement and support of my colleagues at the University of British Columbia, I express my appreciation. To Arden Williams, who worked with great care and diligence on entering the manuscript on to the computer, I give my warmest thanks.

I thank the anonymous reader for McGill-Queen's University Press for a detailed and helpful report. To Joan McGilvray and Susan Kent Davidson of McGill-Queen's University Press I express my thanks for the careful editing of my manuscript and enthusiastic support of this work.

Euripides: Psychological Terminology in the Plays

1 Introduction

GENERAL AIM

This study will discuss how Euripides (c. 484–406 B.C.) refers to psychological terminology. Its specific aim is to illustrate how his usage of psychic terms resembles that of earlier and contemporary poets and also Aeschylus and Sophocles and how it differs from it. These poets will include Homer, Hesiod, the lyric and elegiac poets, Pindar and Bacchylides. Comparison will also be made with the *Homeric Hymns*. The book will not compare Euripides' usage with that of the Presocratics, the fifth-century historians, other tragedians of the fifth century, or writers of comedy. A comparison of Euripides with prose usage of the fifth century would be valuable, as also would one with comedy, but both would greatly lengthen the current study. Such comparisons would validly be the subject of another work. Earlier poets were, of course, writing epic, lyric, elegy, or victory odes, not tragedy. Euripides' specific use of the genre of tragedy will be kept in mind as the various instances of terms are discussed. The use by Aeschylus and Sophocles of the same genre makes their references to psychic terms of especial interest as we study those of Euripides.

In the case of Euripides we possess sixteen complete tragedies as well as the *Alcestis*, substituted for a satyr play but tragic in nature. We have too the *Cyclops*, a satyr play, and the *Rhesus*, whose authority is generally rejected.[1] The *Cyclops* will not be treated because it does not fit into the genre of tragedy. It would be more appropriately studied with fifth-century comedy, which would be, as suggested above, a valuable separate study.

The dates of most of the tragedies are not known.[2] We can place the *Alcestis* in 438 B.C., the *Medea* in 431, the *Hippolytus* in 428, the *Trojan Women* in

415, the *Helen* in 412, and the *Orestes* in 408 with some certainty. We know that the *Iphigenia at Aulis* and the *Bacchae* were put on after Euripides' death in 406. For the other plays the dates are conjectured.

Scholars agree on a relative chronology of the plays, and this is reflected in the order of the plays presented in the Oxford text. In the case of the fragments the dates of certain plays are known. Our knowledge of these plays, however, is not firm enough to allow a discussion of a variation or development of the usage of psychic terms by Euripides himself. Instead, we will study his overall usage.

Since this is so, in our treatment we shall simply place the plays in alphabetical order. All fragments we shall treat after the plays (with their titles, when known, given).

Our evidence of Euripides is essentially fragmentary in nature, especially when compared to all the plays that have been lost. Since this is the case, we shall refer with caution to "Euripidean usage." We speak only within the context of the evidence we now possess. Yet, in the case of Euripides more than with Aeschylus and Sophocles, our evidence is abundant enough for us to form clear impressions about his use of psychic terms and, in particular, to observe how traditional or new it is.

BACKGROUND ON THE PSYCHIC TERMS

The nature of psychological terminology has been much discussed both by other scholars[3] and by myself.[4] With regard to tragedy I have recently completed *Aeschylus' Use of Psychological Terminology: Traditional and New* and *Sophocles' Use of Psychological Terminology: Old and New*. In both these studies background was presented on the general nature of psychic terms in early Greek poets because an understanding of it proves to be a necessary prelude to the study of it in a later author. This is the case also with Euripides. Background material was presented fully in the study of Aeschylus referred to above, and less fully in that of Sophocles.

In order that this background information be accessible in the current book, a summary is here presented. The following are suggestions, based on scholarly interpretations, of the ways in which psychic terms in early Greek poetry appear to be best understood.

1 Psychic terms designate entities that comprise aspects both "physical" and "psychological." We moderns separate categories such as "concrete" and "abstract," "physical" and "psychological," whereas the early Greeks do not.

2 The expression "psychic entities" appears to describe well what psychic terms designate. "Psychic" emphasizes the psychological aspects which they display. "Entity" suggests a separate identifiable presence within the

person. This entity appears to be distinct both from the person and from other such entities within. These "psychic entities" can act themselves, be acted upon by the person, or be affected by outside forces. They can be locations where a person acts, means someone uses, or accompaniments to someone's activities.

3 These psychic entities have a broad range of function, including aspects that we moderns tend to separate out. They can be agent (for example, "that which feels"), function (for example, "process of feeling"), and result (for example, "feelings"). In a single use of one of these terms we may find also, in a fused presence, aspects that we term "intellectual," "emotional," "volitional," "moral," and even, on occasion, "physical." In light of this fused presence, categories termed "predominantly intellectual" or "predominantly emotional" will be used; it will be remembered that other aspects may also be present.

4 There are eight psychic terms that appear in early Greek literature: *phrēn*, *nous* (*noos*), *prapides*, *thumos*, *kardia*, *kear* (*kēr*), *ētor*, and *psychē*. Euripides, in the tragedies that we have, makes references to seven of these, excluding *ētor*. The number of psychic terms itself tells us that psychological activity was seen as a "multiple" activity, carried on by several different psychic entities. This book will examine the seven psychic terms that Euripides uses. Cognate words (verbs, adverbs, adjectives, and nouns) are important and are listed in Appendix D. An analysis of them would greatly lengthen the current study and merits instead a separate study.

5 Regarding this number of psychic entities we may ask: did the early Greeks have a notion of "self" that would act as a centre of psychological activity? If so, how did it relate to the psychic entities within? The answers to these questions are difficult to give; these questions themselves are ones that have been much discussed.[5] The view that seems best to present the situation in early Greek literature is that the early Greeks did not have a carefully worked-out concept of "self" but did clearly possess some ill-defined notion of a "self." People saw themselves as separate individuals. They also saw themselves as made up of psychic entities which could differ in their nature in different people. People likewise saw themselves as being distinct from these psychic entities within. Thus we appear to have the situation of people, aware in an ill-defined manner of their individuality, observing psychic entities within themselves functioning in a variety of ways. Depending upon how these psychic entities functioned and how a person related to them, certain behaviour became manifest. Such behaviour made one person differ from another. Person and psychic entity remained distinct. Persons saw themselves as being apart from their psychic entities, but from moment to moment behaviour reflected the activity both of person and of psychic entities.

6 Over time one psychic entity, *psychē*, gradually comes to signify the seat of a person's thought, emotion, and will.[6] This term in Homer and Hesiod signifies simply the "breath that gives life." In the lyric and elegiac poets it begins to act as a seat of emotion within the person. In Sophocles and Euripides we see evidence of its increasing role as a psychological agent within the living person. The two tragedians mark an important stage in the appearance of *psychē* in the role of the seat of personality or "self."

7 On the one hand, the psychic entities are often very alike and share in many similar functions. On the other, they can be quite distinct from one another. *Nous*, for example, displays characteristics not shared by *phrēn* and *thumos*. *Phrēn* likewise differs from *thumos*. Even the terms for "heart" – *kardia, kear, ētor* – have distinct traits. Psychic entities thus, even though often alike, do not appear to be simply interchangeable.

8 In different contexts, why does a poet mention one term rather than another? Certainly in this regard the importance of metre cannot be denied. But passages suggest again and again that even within the restrictions imposed by metre a conscious choice of one term rather than another has occurred.[7] Distinctive traits appear to have been associated with the various entities, ones that made the appearance of some entity in a particular context especially appropriate.

9 Themes of early poetry clearly influence the frequency of the mention of psychic terms and the terms themselves that are chosen. In the case of Aeschylus, Sophocles, and Euripides this proves true in relation to their various dramas. The restrictive force of theme makes caution in generalizing about the range of function of the psychic entities necessary.

10 What we learn of psychic terms in early Greek poetry, Aeschylus, Sophocles, and Euripides will not necessarily tell us much about their usage in the spoken language of the time. In the case of all three dramatists the structure of tragedy clearly affected what terms they used. Particular themes probably influenced which terms they thought appropriate. We may correctly suppose that these dramatists used the familiar since they had to make themselves understood. We may look also for the new, for they would probably wish to challenge their audiences with fresh language and images.

EXISTING SCHOLARSHIP ON PSYCHIC TERMS IN EURIPIDES

On psychological terminology in Euripides himself we have one important study, that of Meissner. Other works, treating psychic terms in Greek tragedy in general, also refer to his usage.

B. Meissner, *Mythisches und Rationales in der Psychologie der euripideischen Tragödie* (Göttingen 1951). In this dissertation Meissner discusses early uses of psychic terms in which he sees both physical and psychological aspects as being present. He refers to this usage as "mythisches" (4–7). He suggests that by the fifth century the psychological aspect had become uppermost in certain terms, especially in *phrēn* and *kardia* (47–76, 107–25). With regard to this psychological aspect, it became in some cases more specific, being what he terms "rationales." This change occurs especially with *phrēn* (76–97) and sometimes with *psychē* (65–8).

Meissner argues also that *psychē* becomes a psychological agent in the living person, resembling other psychic entities in the roles they had in the person while alive. He further suggests that both *kardia* and *psychē* can, on occasion, be considered as representing persons themselves, especially in the case of direct address to these psychic entities (60–76, 107–25).

Meissner offers valuable interpretations of individual passages in Euripides, treating in detail occurrences of the various terms. His treatment of *psychē* shows in particular new ways in which Euripides refers to this term. Meissner suggests a stronger movement from "mythisches" to "rationales" than the present work will describe. Our study will, in contrast, argue for the frequent presence still in Euripides of traditional usage, that is, of the "mythisches" which Meissner believes is, to a large degree, no longer evident. The present work will propose that Euripides uses psychic terms, especially *phrēn*, *thumos*, *nous*, and *kardia*, much in the way that earlier poets and also Aeschylus and Sophocles do. Like Sophocles, Euripides introduces new uses of *psychē*, but even with this term many references, it seems, resemble those found earlier. Euripides' usage is wide-ranging. It comprehends the old and the new. Its chief feature appears not to be a change in emphasis, such as Meissner supposes, but a rich range of usage, broader than that found earlier but none the less inclusive of it.

T.B.L. Webster, "Some Psychological Terms in Greek Tragedy," *JHS* 77 (1957), 149–54. Webster suggests four basic meanings of psychic terms: "part of the body," "psychological agent," "psychological process," "result of psychological process" (149). These meanings are not distinct but merge into one another. Even though there is a great overlap in function, psychic terms may still have distinctive traits (154). Webster discusses various passages from all three tragedians, offering valuable interpretations, especially with regard to *psychē*.

D. Claus, *Toward the Soul: An Inquiry into the Meaning of Psychē before Plato* (New Haven 1981). Claus principally treats the nature of *psychē* but discusses as well other psychic terms. With regard to drama he focuses mostly upon *psychē*. He refers to passages from all three tragedies and does not focus on Euripides. He argues that *psychē* had a basic meaning of "life-force," which to a large extent continued in fifth century usage. The view of *psychē* suggested in this present work will differ; chapters 7 and 8 will discuss our interpretation of this term.

F. Solmsen, *"Phrēn, Kardia, Psychē* in Greek Tragedy," *Studies Woodbury* (Chico, Calif. 1984), 265–74. Solmsen discusses different passages in Euripides, offering brief but interesting interpretations.

R. Padel, *In and Out of Mind: Greek Images of the Tragic Self* (Princeton 1992). Padel has an important chapter on "Innards" in which she details the inner nature of human beings. She gives a broad picture of several of the psychic terms, emphasising the fusion of what we would call "physical" and "psychological" aspects (44–8). Padel does not focus in particular on Euripides but refers to many passages from different plays of all three tragedians. Her specific interpretations are often of great interest.

This description of the scholarship available on psychological terminology in Euripides suggests that a new detailed study of his usage may be of interest. The present work aims to show how his usage either resembled that of earlier poets or differed from it. It aims to show also how Euripides uses psychic terms in ways similar to or different from those of Aeschylus and Sophocles.

STRUCTURE OF THIS BOOK

The book will describe all instances of the seven psychic terms that occur in Euripides. Background on how psychic terms were used in earlier and contemporary poets has been presented in my recent studies on Aeschylus and Sophocles and will not be repeated here. With regard to traditional and contemporary uses, Euripides' usage to a large extent resembles the ways in which Aeschylus and Sophocles referred to these terms. In instances where this is so, comparative material from earlier and contemporary poets has been presented in my studies of these two dramatists and will not be repeated here. Instead, for such passages, parallels from Aeschylus and Sophocles will be chiefly noted.

To a large extent the material in this study will be descriptive. The specific nature of the subject of this study excludes the treatment of many aspects of Euripidean drama. These include problems of authenticity, interpretation of various passages, dramatic techniques, and the relationship of Euripidean thought to that of the fifth century.

Each chapter treating the psychic terms as separate topics includes discussion of:

Traditional and Contemporary Uses (with Euripidean Features).   An examination of passages where Euripides uses psychic terms in traditional and contemporary ways. In some cases he will add new features, in others, not.

Euripidean Uses.   An examination of passages where Euripides introduces new uses of the psychic terms.

Euripidean Images.   A discussion of passages where Euripides presents different images of the various psychic terms. Although many of the images that will be discussed can validly be termed "metaphors," the nature of "metaphor" in Greek literature is a major problem. It is the principal intent of this work to show what images of psychic entities Euripides used. The discussion will therefore focus on the various images that occur.

Relationship of Person and Psychic Entity.   An overview of how people related to their psychic entities (with detailed information provided in Appendix One).

An Overview of the Psychic Entity.   A summary of how Euripides uses each psychic entity. Here his usage will be compared to that of Aeschylus[8] and Sophocles.

The book will conclude with a discussion of Euripides' use of psychological terminology in general. We shall summarize which terms he uses, how often and in what manner he mentions them, and, in particular, how traditional or new his references to them may be.

2 *Phrēn* in the Tragedies: Part One

Of the psychic terms, *phrēn* appears most often in Euripides, as it does in Aeschylus[1] and Sophocles.[2] In the seventeen tragedies and fragments we encounter *phrēn* 160 times, *nous* 43, *prapides* 5, *thumos* 30, *kardia* 35, *kear* 3, and *psychē* 117. *Phrēn* and *phrenes* appear in all seventeen tragedies. Since there are so many instances of *phrēn*, they will be treated in two chapters. Our discussion will attempt to show why Euripides, like Aeschylus and Sophocles, used this particular psychic term so often.[3]

TRADITIONAL AND CONTEMPORARY USES (WITH EURIPIDEAN FEATURES)

Frequently Euripides uses *phrēn* in ways that resemble those of earlier and contemporary poets and of both Aeschylus and Sophocles. Categories will be introduced in the discussion to follow as a way of organizing the passages and illustrating prominent features of *phrēn*. But it may happen in many cases that a passage could fit more than one category; our classification remains, therefore, necessarily subjective in nature.

AGE

Hipp. 969, Fr. *619* (*Peleus*). Twice Euripides refers to *phrenes* in the young. At *Hipp.* 969 Theseus says: "I know of young men being in no way more stable than women when Cypris distresses (ταράσσω) their young (ἡβῶσα) *phrēn*." The "young" *phrēn* proves to be vulnerable to the influence of love,[4] which "distresses" it.[5] Fr. 619 reads: "my son, old age is wiser than younger (νεώτερος) *phrenes* and more firm and experience rules over inexperience." Both passages suggest that *phrenes* in an older person are superior to those in someone young.

Like Homer at *Il.* 3.108, Aeschylus likewise refers to the immature nature of *phrenes* in children (*Ag.* 277, *Choe.* 754). Sophocles has Oedipus remark that Antigone and Ismene are too young to have *phrenes* at all (*O.T.* 1151). At *O.C.* 805 Creon suggests that Oedipus never "grew" *phrenes*. *Phrenes* thus are thought to change with time and ideally to become better with age.[6]

PREDOMINANTLY INTELLECTUAL

In Euripides, as in earlier and contemporary poets, Aeschylus, and Sophocles, *phrenes* are associated most often with intellectual activity. This activity is often of a discursive and deliberative nature. Unlike *nous*, which can penetrate situations and circumstances and unerringly grasp reality – that is, what is true or appropriate – *phrenes* serve for the consideration of possibilities. Their range of activity is a broad one.

Several passages in Euripides suggest the role of *phrēn* as "mind." As noted in chapter 1, we do not find in relation to psychological terminology a distinction between "agent" and "function," the two being fused. For some passages, none the less, we may use those descriptions separately, bearing in mind that this fusion exists. Thus we shall use the categories of, for example, "mind," "intelligence," "planning," "purpose," and "memory."

Mind

And. 482.   The Chorus describe the difficulties that occur in a household where there are two wives. They then use a nautical image: "when swift breezes carry sailors, a double judgment (γνώμη) of *prapides* at the helm and a combined throng of wise men is weaker than an more paltry (φαυλότερος) *phrēn* that has full authority (αὐτοκρατής)." In these lines *prapides* and *phrēn* appear to be synonyms, *prapides* often resembling *phrēn* in function.[7] *Gnōmē*, "practical judgment," of *prapides* is judged of less value when found in two pilots than a single *phrēn*, which is of less high quality but possessing full command in one pilot. Theognis relates *gnōmē* to *phrenes*, saying that the person is blessed who has it in his *phrenes* (1173). Sophocles twice speaks of *gnōmē* present in *phrenes* (*Aj.* 447, *O.T.* 524). *Phrēn* and *prapides* in this passage of Euripides appear to be related to practical activity and desirable judgment.

Euripides uses two new adjectives with *phrēn*: φαυλότερος and αὐτοκρατής. In earlier poets we hear several times of "good (ἀγαθός, ἐσθλός) *phrenes*."[8] One fragment of Sophocles likewise mentions "good (καλός) *phrenes*" (108). In contrast, in Homer, Zeus rages with *phrenes* that are "not good" (ἀγαθός: *Il.* 8.360). Euripides suggests that a *phrēn* can be "rather trivial" or "paltry," less than what one could desire. Yet this *phrēn* too can be in charge: αὐτοκρατής. The management of a practical situation is here connected with *phrēn*.

Bacc. 944, 947, 1270.   Three times in the *Bacchae* we hear of *phrenes* undergoing change. At 944, while Dionysus dresses Pentheus as a bacchant, he remarks: "I praise you that you changed (μεθίστημι) your *phrenes*." He praises Pentheus yet again at 947: "the *phrenes* you had before were not healthy (ὑγιής); now you have the sort you should have." Euripides here uses a medical image of *phrenes*, introducing a new adjective of *phrenes*: ὑγιής. Aeschylus has a similar reference to *phrenes* when he speaks of "health (ὑγίεια) of *phrenes*" (*Eum.* 536). Dionysus in this passage claims that Pentheus' *phrenes* were not "healthy" before. Aeschylus too speaks of a lack of health in *phrenes* when he mentions a "disease (νόσος) of *phrenes*" (*Per.* 750).[9] Euripides describes the gradual loss of rationality in Pentheus. Ironically, his *phrenes* were more "healthy" before than they will be in his behaviour as a bacchant.[10]

At *Bacc.* 1270 we hear of an opposite change in *phrenes*, from madness to sanity. At 1268 Cadmus asks Agave whether "bewilderment" (τὸ πτοηθέν) is still present in her *psychē*.[11] She responds: "I do not understand this word but I am becoming somehow rational (ἔννους), changing (μεθίστημι) from my former *phrenes*." Agave's *phrenes* return, it appears, to their normal way of functioning. She then becomes able to perceive reality.

Hec. 746.   Hecuba ponders how Agamemnon is thinking. She asks: "do I reckon the *phrenes* of this man as tending to the hostile (πρὸς τὸ δυσμενές), he not being hostile?" Here *phrenes* function as the seat of Agamemnon's thoughts and feelings, perhaps of a positive, not negative, kind. In this passage we see a possible conflict between *phrenes* within and outer behaviour. Outer appearance does not always correspond to *phrenes* within.

Hcld. 540.   Iolaus, praising the daughter of Heracles for her willingness to die, says: "you were born of the seed of Heracles, of that divine (θεῖος) *phrēn*." Euripides introduces a new description of *phrēn*. Pindar has spoken of a "mortal (θνητός, βροτός) *phrēn*;[12] Euripides likewise refers to a "mortal (βροτός) *phrēn*" at *Hipp.* 936. Heracles' *phrēn* is "divine," reflecting his own origin.

Hipp. 612.   In a line well known and parodied in Aristophanes,[13] Hippolytus tells the Nurse about his promise to remain silent: "my tongue swore but my *phrēn* is unsworn (ἀνώμοτος)." Euripides introduces a new adjective with *phrēn*, an adjective itself very rare in Greek poetry. It is found only once elsewhere, at *Med.* 737.[14] We see in this passage a contrast between what one says and what one thinks. This occurs frequently in earlier and contemporary poets.[15] Achilles, for example, tells Odysseus that he particularly dislikes the person who "hides one thing in his *phrenes* but says another" (*Il.* 9.313). In *Hipp.* 612 *phrēn* is the seat of commitment in Hippolytus. This line is crucial in the play since Hippolytus does stay true to his word but has given the impression that he would not. In fact, he considers that his *phrēn* "has sworn": it was not ἀνώμοτος.

Hipp. 1337.   Artemis says of Phaedra to Theseus: "then, by dying, your wife removed the chance for testing her words, so that she persuaded your *phrēn*." Both Homer and Pindar speak of *phrēn* being persuaded.[16] Aeschylus likewise mentions Clytemnestra attempting to persuade Cassandra's *phrēn* (*Ag.* 1052).[17] Once "persuaded," Theseus' *phrēn* leads him to punish his son.

Med. 104.   The Nurse gives Medea's children a stern warning as she urges them to enter the house: "be on guard against her fierce character (ἄγριον ἦθος) and the hateful nature (φύσις) of her self-willed (αὐθάδης) *phrēn*."[18] Euripides introduces a new adjective with *phrēn*: it is one that is "stubborn" or "self-willed."[19] Medea's *phrēn* is of the sort to plan terrible deeds.

Med. 677.   Another aspect of Medea's *phrēn* appears when Aegeus agrees to describe to her the oracle he received, since there was need "of a wise (σοφός) *phrēn*" for its interpretation. For the first time σοφός appears with *phrēn*. Medea proves able to interpret the oracle to her own advantage, showing that her *phrēn* has the ability to be "wise" in this regard.

Tr. 6.   Poseidon proclaims his support for Troy: "never has goodwill (εὔνοια) departed from my *phrenes* for the city of the Trojans." In earlier and contemporary poets we do not hear of εὔνοια of *phrenes*. Aeschylus refers to it at *Supp.* 940, describing it as a necessary prerequisite on the part of the Danaids if the Aegyptiads are to marry them. Sophocles once refers to a *phrēn* that is "well-intentioned" (εὔνους) as Philoctetes denies he will have such toward Neoptolemus (*Ph.* 1281). Poseidon claims that his *phrenes* have always been favourably disposed to Troy; they act as the seat of his thoughts and feelings.

Frs. 781.56 (Phaethon), 964.5 (Incerta).   In these two fragments *phrēn* again functions as "mind." In the first, someone "holds *phrenes*" on sacrificing: *phrenes* are the seat of attention. In the second, someone "imagines" (δοξάζω) disasters of *phrēn*.[20] It acts as the seat of various possibilities.

Frs. 362.6 (Erechtheus), 831 (Phrixus).   In these two fragments we find once again Euripides introducing new types of *phrenes*. In the first, a son is to have "gentle (ἤπιος) *phrenes.*" Sophocles refers similarly to this feature of *phrēn* when he describes it a "gracious" (ἵλεως) at *Tr.* 763. In the second, "the *phrēn* of those who are not slaves" is called "more free" (ἐλευθερώτερος). In both passages *phrēn* serves as a seat of attitude or way of thinking.

Intelligence

And. 361, 365.   Andromache, speaking frankly to Menelaus, says: "I fear one feature of your *phrēn*. Because of a quarrel over a woman, you also destroyed the wretched city of the Trojans." The Chorus then remark: "You have spoken too much, as a woman to a man, and the good sense (τὸ σῶφρον) of your *phrēn* has shot forth all its arrows" (ἐκτοξεύω). Andromache worries about the way in which Menelaus can think: in the past he could choose the course of destruction. But the Chorus think that she has been too frank in her comments.

In the response to the Chorus we find the image of archery. Pindar likewise uses this type of imagery when he speaks of sending "arrows of fame from a gentle *phrēn*" (*Ol.* 2.90). In this passage of Euripides it is "good sense" or "modesty (τὸ σῶφρον) that has been totally sent forth from Andromache's *phrēn.*[21] This being absent, she speaks in a way that the Chorus consider inappropriate.[22]

Bacc. [203], 427.   In the first passage, bracketed by Diggle but accepted by Dodds, Teiresias praises "inherited tradition": no reasoning (λόγος) will cast them down, not even if wisdom (τὸ σῶφρον) is found through the highest (ἄκρος) *phrenes.*"Euripides here uses ἄκρος for the first time with *phrenes*: even the most sublime thinking leading to the discovery of wisdom will never overthrow sound traditions. Aeschylus refers negatively to the "top of *phrenes.*" The Chorus show devotion not from there (*Ag.* 805). As in *Med.* 677, where we heard of a "wise" *phrēn*, *phrenes* here are associated with the discovery of wisdom.

At 427 the Chorus say that Dionysus hates the person for whom certain things are not a "care," namely "to live a happy life … and to keep a wise (σοφός) *prapis* and *phrēn* from excessive mortals."[23] Once again, as in *And.* 482, treated above, *prapis* and *phrēn* appear together, probably close in meaning.[24] As in *Med.* 677, *phrēn* here too is called "wise." Dionysus approves of people who keep their mind and understanding away from attachment to people who urge excess. The Chorus proceed to praise what "the common crowd thinks and uses" (430–1).[25]

Hel. 160.   In an amusing remark Teucer tells Helen: "having a body similar to Helen, you do not have similar (ὅμοιος) *phrenes*, but entirely different (διάφορος) ones." The real Helen is judged to have had *phrenes* of a negative type since her choices led to the death of so many.

Hipp. 701.   The Nurse, defending herself to Phaedra after her failure with Hippolytus, says that, if she had succeeded, she would have been numbered among the "wise" (σοφοί): "for, in light of our fortunes, we possess [a reputation] for *phrenes*." Here *phrenes* function as a seat of intelligence for which, as the Nurse claims, success is the criterion of their presence.[26]

IA 67.   Agamemnon describes how Tyndareus contrived to get the suitors of Helen to swear to defend her: "well, somehow, old Tyndareus outwitted (ὑπέρχομαι) them with a cunning (πυκινός) *phrēn*." Euripides here uses a traditional adjective with *phrēn*. We hear of Zeus' "cunning" *phrenes* (*Il.* 14.294, *H. Ven.* 38). Alcaeus, Stesichorus, Theognis, and Bacchylides likewise use this adjective of *phrēn*.[27] The passage suggests *phrēn* as a seat of deliberation and contriving.[28]

IT 815, 1322.   As Orestes recalls childhood memories in order to convince Iphigenia of his identity, she says to him: "o dearest, you come near (χρίμπτω) my *phrenes*."[29] What Orestes describes matches the memories that Iphigenia has.[30] At 1322 the Messenger tells Thoas not to "turn" (τρέπω) his *phrēn* to how Iphigenia, Orestes, and Pylades have fled but to listen to him. Here thinking is described as moving in a particular direction and being urged to stop. Aeschylus too speaks of the "turning" of *phrēn* at *Ag.* 219, and earlier poets likewise refer to this movement of *phrēn*.[31]

Or. 1204.   Orestes responds to Electra's suggestion of his killing Hermionē *by saying:* "*o you who possess the phrenes* of a man (ἄρσην) but your body appearing manifestly among women, how unworthy you are by nature to live rather than to die." Euripides here introduces the adjective "male" with *phrenes.* Sophocles at Fr. 943 speaks of "a male-minded woman" (ἀνδρόφρων γυνή). Aeschylus, in contrast, speaks of Aegisthus' *phrēn* as "womanly" (θῆλυς: *Choe.* 305). Electra's *phrenes* are "manly" in their capacity to make bold decisions. We see the association of *phrenes* with practical action.

Tr. 682.   Andromache, as she ends her speech describing her situation, says: "To me there is not even what remains to all mortals, hope, nor am I deceived (κλέπτομαι) in *phrenes* that I will do anything noble. But even to think of this is sweet." In earlier poets we hear of *phrenes* being "deceived" but not with this verb.[32] Aeschylus, however, uses this verb at *Choe.* 854 to describe someone failing to "deceive" *phrēn*. Andromache claims to be absolutely realistic in her thinking and hopes for no great achievement on her part in the future.[33] Yet the thought of such is "sweet," this thought too probably associated with *phrenes*.

Tr. 1158.   Hecuba, as she receives the body of Astyanax, says: "o having a greater weight (ὄγκος) of spear than of *phrenes*." Here *phrenes* signify "intelligence." Hecuba supposes that a "weight of spear" impelled the Greeks to murder the child. Better would have been the presence of a "weight of *phrenes*" as a compelling force.[34]

Planning

Med. 316.   Creon responds to Medea's entreaties: "you speak soft words to hear but I am terrified that in your *phrenes* you are planning (βουλεύω) some evil." The association of "planning" with *phrenes* is an early one and continues in the lyric poets.[35] Aeschylus relates "plans" to *phrēn* at *Sept.* 593 and *Choe.* 626. In this case *phrenes* are associated with the devising of evil.[36]

Pho. 746.   Eteocles asks Creon on what grounds he is to choose the seven captains: "choosing out for valour or for good counsel (εὐβουλία) of *phrenes*?" Creon responds that he is to choose on the basis of both: "each is nothing without the other" (747). Euripides here first mentions εὐβουλία with *phrenes*.[37] "Good counsel" is judged a necessary possession of the courageous soldier and is located in *phrenes*.

Purpose

Hipp. 685.   Phaedra in indignation exclaims to the Nurse after her failure to win over Hippolytus: "did I not warn you – did I not perceive your *phrēn* beforehand (προνοοῦμαι) – to be silent in the matters in which I am now suffering disgrace?" In this passage *phrēn* signifies "purpose." Phaedra had detected already what was in the Nurse's mind and had consequently requested silence. We see *phrēn* here as the seat of intent, one that can be apparent to others.

IA 1359.   When Achilles makes clear that he will try to save Iphigenia, Clytemnestra says: "may you be blessed (ὀνίνημα) in your *phrenes*." Once again *phrenes* indicate the purpose or intent of Achilles.

Pho. 1300.   The Chorus say of Polyneices and Eteocles: "wretched that they ever came to a single-combat (μονομάχος) *phrēn*." Euripides introduces a new adjective with *phrēn*. Polyneices and Eteocles have a single purpose: to fight each other. Their whole *phrēn* can be characterized in one way: "single-combat." The two brothers each share the same *phrēn*. Just as their *phrēn* is one, so will their destiny in death be the same.

Absence / Loss

A common idea in earlier and contemporary poets is that of the absence or loss of *phrenes*.[38] With their removal foolish behaviour results. Aeschylus refers to this feature of *phrenes* when he says that the *daimōn* "cheated" (ψεύδω) the Persians of their *phrenes* (*Per.* 472). Sophocles has the Tutor describe Orestes and Electra as "deprived" (τητάομαι) of their *phrenes*. At *Ant.* 492 Creon says that Ismene is "not in possession (ἐπήβολος) of her *phrenes.*" Creon warns Haemon not to "cast out" (ἐκβάλλω) his *phrenes* (*Ant.* 648) and later (754) says that his son is "empty" (κενός) of them.

Tr. 417.   Talthybius, speaking of Cassandra, says at 408 that she "raves" in her *phrenes.*[39] At 417 he says that he will ignore her words: "for you do not have ready (ἄρτιος) *phrenes.*" Euripides uses a new adjective with *phrenes*: "ready," "complete," or "proper."[40] Talthybius assumes that there is a deficiency in Cassandra's *phrenes*, that they are somehow lacking. They are in contrast to the persons described by Euripides as "ready-in-mind" (ἀρτίφρων) at *IA* 877 and *Med.* 294.

Alc. 327.   The Chorus reassure Alcestis the Admetus will keep her request about not remarrying: "he will do these things, if he does not lack in (ἁμαρτάνω) *phrenes.*" Once again the presence of *phrenes* is assumed to lead to acceptable behaviour; their absence, to the opposite.[41]

Or. 216.   Orestes, confused as he awakes during his illness after killing Clytemnestra, asks Electra: "From where have I come here? How did I come? For I forget, deprived (ἀπολείπω) of my former *phrenes.*"[42] Orestes cannot recall the thoughts he had before he fell asleep: that state of mind is now lost.

Distance

In certain passages a person can be somehow apart from *phrenes* – that is, be "distant" from them. Sophocles describes such a situation when Neoptolemus tells the Chorus not to "stand apart" (ἀφίστημι) from their *phrenes*. They are to speak in a more cautious way. Euripides likewise refers to *phrenes* in this way in several passages.

Bacc. 359.   Teiresias says to Pentheus, who has just ordered the arrest of Dionysus: "you are mad (μέμηνας) by now; even before you stood apart (ἐξίστημι) from *phrenes.*" Teiresias suggests that Pentheus is now fully mad and that even earlier he had not engaged in admissible or normal thinking.[43]

Bacc. 850.   Dionysus is requested concerning Pentheus: "set him (ἐξίστημι) outside of *phrenes*, placing into him light-minded madness (ἐλαφρὰ λύσσα); for thinking well (φρονέω εὖ), he would never be willing to put on female dress, but driving him outside of thinking (φρονέω), he will put it on." Pentheus must be set apart from his *phrenes* and their usual functioning (φρονέω). Only when these are replaced by "light-minded madness" will he change his behaviour.[44] As in 359 we find the image with the verb ἐξίστημι of one "set apart" from *phrenes*.

Hcld. 709.   Alcmene upbraids Iolaus as he prepares to fight the Argives: "what thing are you planning, not being within (ἔνδον) your *phrenes*, to leave me bereft with my grandchildren?" Like Hecuba who asks Priam where his *phrenes* "have gone" when he plans to rescue Hector's body (*Il.* 24.201), Alcmene assumes that Iolaus is acting foolishly. He is "at a distance" from his *phrenes* and therefore does not think well.

HF 776.   As Lycus is slain in the palace, the Chorus remark: "gold and good fortune draw (ἐξάγω) mortals away from *phrenes*, as they drag in their too unjust power." *Phrenes* are seen as the location of wise thought. From this appropriate way of thinking, money and power draw people away.

Hipp. 390.   Phaedra says that after considering her situation, her resolve to die would not be shaken: "it is not possible that I was about to be corrupted (διαφθείρω) by any drug (φάρμακον)[45] so that I once again departed (πίπτω) from my *phrenes*." Phaedra says that her *phrenes* functioned in a particular way which seems to her correct. She is determined not to be "distant" from these thoughts. This statement is very similar to the Danaids' resolve not to leave the "former track of their *phrēn*" (*Supp.* 1017).

Hipp. 1012.   In this passage two ideas about *phrenes* occur: "distance" and "damage."[46] In his response to Theseus, Hippolytus ironically refers to his attraction for Phaedra. Then he says: "I was foolish (μάταιος), no rather, nowhere (οὐδαμοῦ) in *phrenes*. But how is it sweet to be king? Is it such to the moderate (σώφρονες)? Least of all, since monarchy has corrupted (διαφθείρω) the *phrenes* of mortals whom it pleases."[47] Hippolytus says that, if he had been attracted to Phaedra, he would have been "foolish" or rather, not thinking at all. He would have been quite apart from his *phrenes*. Nor would "monarchy" have been pleasing to him since it is such to "destroy" the *phrenes* of those whom it does not please.[48] Hippolytus rejects the accusations made against him on the grounds that his *phrenes* were still working well and had not been damaged by any desire for kingship. Nor had he ceased to think, that is, to be "nowhere in *phrenes*" so that he would yield to any attraction for Phaedra.

Or. 1021.   Once again we find the verb ἐξίστημι with *phrenes* (as at *Bacc.* 359 and 850, above). Electra says to Orestes: "as I see you for this last look with my eyes, I stand apart (ἐξίστημι) from my *phrenes*." Electra says that she loses her capacity for rational thought as she "moves away from" her *phrenes*. In her grief she has lost the power to think.[49]

Damage

In earlier and contemporary poets we find several references to *phrenes* being damaged.[50] In Aeschylus we encounter "wandering" (φοῖτος) of *phrenes* (*Sept.* 661). One can be "stricken" (κόπτω) in *phrenes* (*Ag.* 479). "Confusion" (ταραγμός) can fall upon them (*Choe.* 1056). Sophocles likewise refers to "damaged" *phrenes*. Ajax (447) calls his *phrenes* "distorted" (διάστροφος).

Hipp. 238.   In the early part of their exchange the Nurse tells Phaedra that interpretation is needed to learn this: "who of the gods reins you back (ἀνασειράζω) and strikes (παρακόπτω) your *phrenes*?" Just as Aeschylus speaks of one "stricken" (κόπτω) in *phrenes* (*Ag.* 479), the Nurse describes Phaedra as "struck" there. Clearly her mind is not working coherently: some damage has occurred.

Hipp. 283.   The Chorus ask the Nurse about her questioning of Phaedra: "are you not applying force, trying to learn the disease (νόσος) of this woman and the wandering (πλάνον) of her *phrenes*?" Like Aeschylus, who speaks of "wandering" (φοῖτος) of *phrenes* (*Sept.* 661), Euripides describes the way in which Phaedra's thoughts are moving as "wandering." Phaedra herself had asked at 240: "where have I wandered (παραπλάζω) from good judgment (γνώμη)?" *Phrenes* here appear to be in a damaged condition.

Hipp. 511.   The Nurse tells Phaedra that she has "soothing charms of love (φίλτρα θελκτήρια)." "These," she says, "will stop you from this disease (νόσος), neither in shameful acts nor with harm (βλάβη) to your *phrenes*, provided you are not cowardly (κακή)."[51] Here the possibility of "harm" to *phrenes* is mentioned.

Or. 297.   Orestes asks Electra: "when you see my affairs full of despair, strengthen and comfort the horror (τὸ δεινόν) and the destruction (διαφθαρέν) of my *phrenes*." Once again, as at *Hipp.* 1014,[52] we find the verb διαφθείρω. In his illness Orestes feels that his *phrenes* are being destroyed. Added to this is the experience of τὸ δεινόν suggesting "dread" or "horror." In early authors we hear of the gods destroying *phrenes* (*Il.* 7.360, 12.234). Aeschylus speaks of their "destruction" (καταφθορά: *Choe.* 211). Sophocles too mentions their being "vanquished" (ἁλίσκομαι) at *Aj.* 649. Orestes suggests that his power of thought will be overcome.

Speech

Phrenes are often associated with speech in earlier and contemporary poets.[53] They serve frequently as a source of words.[54] Aeschylus describes Xerxes as speaking "with a cheerful *phrēn*" (*Per.* 372) and the Chorus of the *Agamemnon*, from a "loving *phrēn*" (1491). In Sophocles the Chorus tell Ajax that he "has spoken" from his own *phrēn* (482). Teiresias mentions "uttering secrets" of his *phrenes* (*Ant.* 1060). Heracles "prays with a cheerful *phrēn* (*Tr.* 763). Philoctetes describes the effects of words from a "deceitful *phrēn*" (1112).

Phrenes too can be receivers of words.[55] In Aeschylus *phrēn* is "delighted" by speech (*Supp.* 515) and "persuaded" by it (*Ag.* 1052). Words can enter *phrēn* (*Choe.* 452, 847) or "blind" *phrenes* (*Eum.* 332). In Sophocles words are "placed" in *phrēn* (*Aj.* 16, Frs. 597, 636). Euripides describes *phrenes* as both a source and receiver of words.

Alc. 346.   Admetus says that, after Alcestis' death, he will end celebrations in his home. "Not ever again would I touch the lyre nor lift up (ἐξαίρομαι) my *phrēn* to sing to the Libyan pipe." *Phrēn* could be the source of joyous song but will no longer be such for Admetus.

Bacc. 269.   Teiresias criticizes Pentheus: "like one who is intelligent (φρονῶν), you have an eloquent tongue but *phrenes* are not (ἔνειμι) in your words." *Phrenes*, if present in speech, endow it with "good sense" or "understanding."[56] If *phrenes* are absent, speech appears to be foolish.[57]

Hipp. 935.   Hippolytus reacts in amazement to Theseus' suggestion that he is being deceptive: "your words, going aside from the mark, outside (ἔξεδροι) of *phrenes*, astonish me." Words, it appears, are ideally drawn from "inside" of *phrenes*. These ones, being "outside," appear foolish and absurd to Hippolytus.[58]

Med. 143, 1052.   Twice we hear of *phrēn* as a receiver of words in the *Medea*. At 143 the Chorus describe Medea as wasting away: "soothed (παραθάλπω) in no way in her *phrēn* by the words of any of her friends." At 1052 Medea, as she resolves to kill her children, says: "these things must be dared; but it is a sign of my cowardice even to admit (πρόσιημι) soft words to my *phrēn*." In both instances *phrenes* are able to receive words that would alter their nature. Medea's anguish could lessen; her thoughts of revenge could be dispelled. In each case the words remain without effect.

PREDOMINANTLY EMOTIONAL

Euripides mentions a wide range of emotions in relation to *phrēn*.

Anger

Several times in Homer and Hesiod we encounter anger in *phrenes*. Zeus is "angry" (χώομαι, χολόω) there in *Il.* 19.127, Hes. *Theog.* 554, and

W. & D. 47.[59] Achilles can be "angry" (χολόω) in *phrenes*, as can Nausicaa (*Il.* 16.61, *Od.* 6.147).[60] The lyric and elegiac poets, Pindar and Bacchylides do not relate *phrenes* and anger. Neither do Aeschylus and Sophocles. Euripides does so a few times.

Alc. 674, Hec. 300.   In the first passage, the Chorus urge Admetus: "do not provoke (παροξύνω) the *phrenes* of your father."[61] Admetus should not make his father angry. In the second passage, Odysseus tells Hecuba: "do not in your anger (θυμουμένῳ) make one who is speaking well an enemy in your *phrēn* (φρενί)."[62] Anger here is related to *phrēn* which becomes filled with hostile thoughts.

Hipp. 689.   Phaedra describes Hippolytus as "sharpened (θήγω) in his *phrenes* with anger (ὀργή)" after he has learned of her passion for him. Euripides introduces a new image here with *phrenes*: "sharpness." Somehow Hippolytus' thoughts are to be made "sharp" by anger as a knife or weapon is sharpened.[63]

Hipp. 983.   Hippolytus tells Theseus who has just sent him into exile: "father, the rage (μένος) and tension (ξυνατασίς) of your *phrenes* are terrible (δεινός)." Euripides uses two new nouns with *phrenes*. These *phrenes* are filled with anger (μένος) and are drawn together tightly (ξυντασίς) in a frightening way. The second noun is related to the verb συντείνω, "to stretch together" or "to strain tightly." Euripides has vividly depicted the tension in his thinking that Theseus is demonstrating.

[Med. 38].   At the beginning of the play the Nurse says of Medea: "I fear that she may be planning (βουλεύω) something new. For her *phrēn* is heavy (βαρύς) and she will not endure being treated badly." Here Medea's *phrēn* is related to planning.[64] Its condition at the moment is "heavy" or "grievous," weighed down by rage. Euripides here uses a new adjective with *phrēn*. It suggests that *phrēn* is a "heavy" weight within Medea drawing her to action. Lines 38 to 43 are bracketed by Diggle in the *OCT* and also by Page; Kovacs in the new Loeb brackets only line 41.[65] If line 38 is authentic, it presents a clear picture of the condition of Medea's *phrēn*.

Med. 177.   The Chorus wish that Medea would come out to hear their words, "if somehow she might give up her indignant anger (βαρύθυμος ὀργή) and spirit (λῆμα) of *phrenes*." Here Euripides uses two new nouns with *phrenes*. Medea's "anger" is "heavy in *thumos*": in the line we hear an echo of the "heavy *phrēn*" in line 38 (if that line is authentic). The noun λῆμα can mean "spirit," "resolve," or "purpose." Medea's *phrenes* are angry and incensed.

Med. 1265.   As Medea kills her children, the Chorus ask her: "what heavy anger (βαρὺς χόλος) falls to you in your *phrenes*?" Here I follow an alternate reading to that presented in the *OCT*, where φρενοβαρής replaces φρενῶν βαρύς.[66] Medea's *phrenes* are filled with "heavy" or "grievous anger." The reference to "heavy" (βαρύς) echoes the description of Medea's *phrēn* itself in line 38 and her "anger" in line 177.

Supp. 581. Theseus answers the Argive herald as he utters his threats: "you will not arouse me so that I become angry (θυμιάομαι) in my *phrenes* over your boasting." We encountered the verb θυμιάομαι above in relation to *phrēn* when Hecuba was angry (*Hec.* 300). Here Theseus specifically mentions "becoming angry" in *phrenes*, the first time the verb appears in this context.

Calm

The association of "calm" and *phrenes* appears only a few times in earlier and contemporary poets. We hear of an "easier word" being placed in *phrenes* (*Od.* 11.146, *H.Ap.* 257). Pindar describes "shafts of song soothing (θέλγω) even the *phrenes* of the gods" (*Pyth.* 1.12). Bacchylides tells Hieron to make his *phrēn* "quietly cease from cares" (5.6). Aeschylus and Sophocles do not mention this feature of *phrēn*. Euripides does so in two passages.

Med. 143. As we heard above under "Speech," the Chorus describe Medea as "soothed (παραθάλπω) in no way in her *phrēn* by the words of any of her friends." Medea's *phrēn* is filled with distress: no speech of others brings relief.

Fr. 1079 (Incerta). This fragment suggests that drinking is not a remedy for grief (λύπη): "Whatever man, being in this disease, confuses (ταράσσω) and calms (γαληνίζω) *phrēn* with strong drink, is instantly delighted but grieves double later." The verb γαληνίζω is new with *phrēn*. It suggests the removal of grief-filled thoughts by some calming influence. Sadly this cannot last.

Courage

Homer and Hesiod relate *phrenes* with courage quite frequently,[67] and with θάρσος specifically several times.[68] Aeschylus three times connects *phrēn* with courage, calling it at *Sept.* 671 "bold" (εὔτολμος).[69] In Sophocles Odysseus asks "what boldness (θράσος) of *phrenes*" Ajax had (46). Euripides once refers to "courage" (θράσος) of *phrēn*.

Med. 856. With regard to killing her children, the Chorus ask Medea: "from where will you take courage of *phrēn* or courage of hand and *kardia* to dare this terrible deed?"[70] There is a problem in the reading of the text but the reference to "θράσος φρενός" seems to be clear. *Phrēn* is seen as the seat of the "boldness" Medea will need to perform her act of murder.

Desire

In Homer we find several mentions of *phrenes* with desire, these occurring with the verb μενοινάω. Thus Nausicaa at *Od.* 6.180 "desires in *phrenes.*"[71] Pindar likewise associates desire with *phrenes*, speaking at *Pyth.* 10.60 of "different desires (ἔρωτες) chafing *phrenes.*"[72] Aeschylus and Sophocles do not associate *phrēn* with desire but Euripides does so in one passage.

IT 655.   The Chorus is uncertain whether to grieve first over Orestes or Pylades: "which of you is more wretched? For still my *phrēn* desires (μέμονα) two doubtful things, whether I should grieve over you or you first." *Phrēn* here is uncertain, filled with a double desire for grief.

Distress

Several times in earlier and contemporary poets *phrēn* is connected with distress.[73] Aeschylus speaks of "care" (μέριμνα) and "pains" (ἄλγεα) affecting *phrēn* (*Per.* 165, *Choe.* 746). He also mentions someone "stricken" (κόπτω) in *phrenes* (*Ag.* 479). Sophocles speaks of a "disturbance" (ἀνακίνησις) of *phrenes* (*O.T.* 727). Creon at *Ant.* 1095 describes himself as "agitated" (ταράσσομαι) in *phrenes*. Euripides too tells of *phrenes* that are distressed.

El. 334.   Electra explains how longed for Orestes is: "many are summoning him and I am their mouthpiece (ἑρμνεύς), these hands, tongue, suffering (ταλαίπωρος) *phrēn*, my shorn head and the father who begot him." Euripides introduces a new adjective with *phrēn*, "wretched" or "suffering." It is in *phrēn* that Electra locates her reaction to her present situation.

Hipp. 1120.   At 1104 the Chorus react to the exile imposed on Hippolytus by saying that the "thoughts about the gods" relieve their *phrenes* from sorrow (see below, "Grief"). Later in this speech they also say: "for no longer do I have an untroubled (καθαρός) *phrēn* and beyond expectation are what I behold." Euripides uses the adjective καθαρός here in the sense of "calm" or "undisturbed," a new use of this adjective with *phrēn*.[74] The Chorus cannot think in a serene way after what has happened between Theseus and Hippolytus.

Ion 1538.   Ion is disturbed about the falsehood Apollo has told in describing him as Xuthus' son: "the god, does he prophesy true or in vain? It distresses (ταράσσω) my *phrēn*, mother, reasonably enough." Here, as in Soph., *Ant.* 1095, we find the verb ταράσσω with *phrēn*. Ion is troubled in his thinking about the trustworthiness of Apollo.[75]

Fear

Frequently are *phrenes* associated with fear in earlier and contemporary poetry.[76] Aeschylus refers several times to fear and *phrenes*. At *Eum.* 518 "fear (δεῖμα) sitting as a guardian of *phrenes*" leads to reverence for justice. Fear (φόβος) negatively influences the *phrenes* of the Danaids, Orestes, and the Chorus of the *Persae* (*Supp.* 379, 513; *Eum.* 88; *Per.* 115). "Evils terrify" (ἐκφοβέω) the *phrenes* of Atossa (*Per.* 606); "fear (δέος) hampers" the Chorus in their *phrenes* (*Per.* 703). Sophocles once describes the Chorus as "stretched out in a fearful (φοβερός) *phrēn*, shaking with fear (δεῖμα)" in *O.T.* 153.

Hcld. 356.   The Chorus address Iolaus, who has been praising the strength of the Athenian gods: "you will not alarm (φοβέω) my *phrenes* with your loud boasts." Like Aeschylus at *Per.* 606, Euripides uses the verb φοβέω to mean "to strike terror in" or "to make afraid." The Chorus' *phrenes* here prove resistant to fear.

Hipp. 574.   The Chorus ask Phaedra what alarms her as she hears Hippolytus revile the Nurse: "tell, what report (φήμα) frightens (φοβέω) you as it rushes in (ἐπίσσυτος) upon *phrenes*?" Euripides uses a new image with ἐπισσυτος: "rushing in on" or "sweeping into."[77] *Phrenes* are pictured as being suddenly filled with terror.

Or. 297.   As we discussed above under "Damage," Orestes in this passage asks Electra "to strengthen and comfort the horror (τὸ δεινόν) and destruction (διαφθαρέν)" of his *phrenes*. The madness that descends upon Orestes after he has killed his mother brings terrible dread (τὸ δεινόν) into his *phrenes*.

Pho. 1285.   The Chorus as they fear the fate of Polyneices and Eteocles say: "alas, alas, I have a trembling (τρόμερος) *phrēn*, trembling with shuddering (φρίκα)." Euripides has emphasized the state of fear by presenting a visual image of "shuddering" (φρίκα) and by repeating the adjective τρόμερος.[78] This is a new adjective with *phrēn*: fear makes it "tremble" within.

Grief

In Homer *phrenes* are associated with grief in several passages. "Sorrow" (πένθος) in particular affects them.[79] At *Il.* 6.285 *phrēn* in Hector forgets "grief" (ὀϊζύς).[80] We do not find *phrenes* connected with grief in Hesiod, the lyric and elegiac poets, Pindar and Bacchylides. Nor is it related to such in Aeschylus and Sophocles. In Euripides, however, it is frequently thus associated.

Alc. 108, 878.   Twice *phrenes* appear in a context of grief. At 108 the Chorus, on hearing that Alcestis must die, say: "you touched (θιγγάνω) my *psychē*; you touched my *phrenes*." Euripides here uses an image of "touching" to describe the inner sorrow of the Chorus.[81] This sorrow is felt both in *psychē* and in *phrenes*.[82] At 878 Admetus responds to the Chorus' remark that he will no longer see Alcestis: "you remind me of what has wounded (ἑλκόω) my *phrenes*." Euripides introduces a medical image in the verb ἑλκόω, appearing for the first time with *phrenes*. It is *phrenes* in Admetus that suffer the pangs of grief.

Hec. 590, Hel. 1192.   In the first passage, Hecuba addresses Polyxena, who has died: "I could not wipe out your suffering (πάθος) from my *phrēn* so as not to grieve (στένω)." In the second passage, Theoclymenus asks Helen why she weeps: "hearing some report from home, do you destroy (διαφθείρω) your *phrenes* with grief (λύπη)?" As in several other passages,[83] Euripides uses the verb διαφθείρω with *phrenes*, in this case to indicate the effect of grief. In both these passages *phrenes* are the seat of sorrow.

Hipp. 188, 1104.   As in *Hel.* 1192, with its reference to "grief" (λύπη), twice this same noun is found in the *Hippolytus*.[84] At 188 the Nurse says that it is better to be sick than to tend them, "for the one is a single activity; to the second, grief (λύπη) of *phrenes* and labour of hands is added." At 1104, as mentioned above with 1120 (see "Calm"), the Chorus say: "how greatly do thoughts (μελεδήματα) of the gods, when they enter my *phrenes*, relieve my griefs (λύπαι)." The gods think of human beings and show care for them: this consideration relieves grief. Again we see *phrenes* much involved in sorrow.

[Or. 545.]   This line is bracketed by Diggle in the *OCT* but accepted by West and Willink. Orestes tells Tyndareus: "old man, I fear to speak before you in what I cannot but grieve (λυπέω) you and your *phrēn*." Orestes knows what sorrow his speaking of the murder of Clytemnestra will cause her father. *Phrēn* is where Tyndareus will experience his grief.

Tr. 1216, Fr. 370K.60 (Erechtheus).   In these two passages we find once more the idea of grief "touching" *phrenes*.[85] The Chorus respond to Hecuba's speech over the dead Astyanax: "you have touched (θιγγάνω) my *phrenes*." In Fr. 370K.60, Athena asks Poseidon: "have you not touched (ἅπτω) my *phrēn* in concealing Erechtheus beneath the earth?"[86] Both passages suggest the involvement of *phrenes* in grief.[87]

Joy / Pleasure

A frequent association *phrēn* has in earlier and contemporary poets is that of joy or rejoicing.[88] Aeschylus relates *phrēn* to joy several times. At *Choe.* 233 it is a seat of joy (χαρά); at *Choe.* 1004 it can be "warmed" with happiness.

Phrēn can be "cheerful," "glad," "rejoicing" (*Per.* 372, *Choe.* 565, 772). Sophocles too relates *phrēn* to joy. Theseus is to give "joy" (χάρις) to his *phrēn* (*O.C.* 1182). Deianira mentions "rejoicing" (χαίρω) in *phrēn* (*Tr.* 294). Frs. 314.357, 677, and 910 all relate "delight" (τέρπω) with *phrēn*. Euripides connects *phrēn* with joy in several passages.

Alc. 346.   As discussed above under "Speech," in this passage Admetus says that he will not "lift up" (ἐξαίρομαι) his *phrēn* to sing in celebration. Here *phrēn* takes delight in festive occasions.

Hcld. 663.   Alcmene asks Iolaus why Hyllus, her grandson, has not yet come: "what misfortune prevents him, appearing here with you, from delighting (τέρπω) my *phrēn*?" Euripides uses the verb τέρπω, found so frequently in other authors, to describe the delight that *phrēn* feels.[89]

Hipp. 1262.   After the accident of Hippolytus, the Messenger asks Theseus: "what shall we do to please (χαρίζομαι) your *phrēn*?" Here *phrēn* acts as the seat of desire and pleasure in Theseus. Euripides once again uses a verb found often in earlier poets with *phrenes*.

IA 359.   Menelaus suggests that Agamemnon was pleased with his decision to sacrifice Iphigenia: "having taken delight (ἥδομαι) in your *phrenes*, you gladly (ἄσμενος) promised to sacrifice your child." The prospect of winning Troy so delights Agamemnon that any cost seems acceptable. Euripides uses a new verb to express this joy: ἥδομαι.

IT 1181.   Iphigenia tells Thoas that Orestes and Pylades tried to entice her with news of Orestes: "they cast a sweet bait (δέλεαρ ἡδύ) for my *phrenes*." Euripides uses here an image of a "bait." *Phrenes* are to be swept up in joy at the news of Orestes.[90]

Or. 1176.   Referring to his wish to take vengeance on Menelaus but not to die himself, Orestes says: "for as to what I wish, it is sweet (ἥδυ) also in my mouth, even verbally to delight (τέρπω) *phrēn* with winged words and without expense." Orestes can feel joy in his *phrēn* by imagining what he desires.[91]

Love

In earlier and contemporary poets we find *phrēn* connected with love quite often.[92] In Aeschylus we fear of the "loving" attitude of the Chorus (*Ag.* 805, 1491). Sophocles describes the *phrēn* of Deianira as "longing" (ποθέω) for Heracles (*Tr.* 103). He also describes the blood of Nessus as a "charm" (κηλητήριον) for the *phrēn* of Heracles (*Tr.* 575). The Chorus in *Ant.* 792

speak of love's irresistible power that affects *phrenes*. Euripides refers to love's effects upon *phrenes* in several passages.

Hipp. 256.   The Nurse, as she reacts to Phaedra's illness, says: "for it is necessary for mortals to mix moderate loves (μετρίας φιλίας) to one another and not to the deep marrow of *psychē*, but loves (στέργηθρα) of *phrenes* should be easily loosed (εὔλυτα), both to be driven away (ὠθέω) and to be tightened (ξυντείνω). For one *psychē* to feel pain over two is a difficult weight, as I suffer over this one." In this passage *psychē* and *phrenes* are mentioned together, both involved in love.[93] Euripides uses only here the noun στέργηθρα, meaning "love" or "affection." Ideally "loves" in *phrenes* should be flexible items, able to be removed or to be made more firm. Clearly they can be different, acting as a dominating power over *phrenes*.

Hipp. 511.   As discussed above under "Damage," the Nurse in this passage tells Phaedra that she has "soothing charms of love" (φίλτρα θελκτήρια ἔρωτος) which will rescue her mistress from her "disease," without "harm" (bl£bh) to her phrenes. Somehow these love-charms will act on Phaedra, affecting her phrenes that are much involved in love without hurting them.[94]

Hipp. 765, 775.   The Chorus describe the state of Phaedra: "Therefore, Aphrodite has broken (κατακλάω) her *phrenes* with the terrible disease of unholy loves (οὐκ ὁσίων ἐρωτῶν δεινᾷ νόσῳ)." At 775 they say also of Phaedra: "feeling shame at her hateful fate, choosing instead the glory of a good reputation and casting forth (ἀπαλλάσσω) painful love (ἀλγεινὸν ἔρωτα) from her *phrenes*." "Unholy loves" have invaded Phaedra's *phrenes* like a disease. Her choice has been to cast out this "painful love" from her *phrenes*. Euripides here uses a medical image to describe the state of Phaedra's *phrenes*. Love has made *phrenes* sick.

Hipp. 1268.   The Chorus describe Cypris: "you take captive (ἄγω) the unbending (ἄκαμπτος) *phrēn* of gods and mortals." Even though the *phrēn* of a god or mortal may be "unbending," that is, even though it may put forth resistance, love can take control. *Phrēn* cannot resist Cypris.[95]

Med. 661.   After the exchange between Medea and Jason, the Chorus speak of the horror of exile. They say: "may he die thankless to whom it is not possible to honour friends, opening (ἀνοίγω) the bolt (κλής) of pure (καθαρός) *phrenes*." Here we have an image of *phrenes* being "locked" but able to be "opened" to others. Euripides introduces the adjective καθαρός with *phrenes* in this passage as he did also at *Hipp.* 1120. There, as we saw under "Distress" above, it meant "untroubled." In this passage of the *Medea* it is used in a more familiar sense of "holy" or "pure."[96] It suggests that the feelings of *phrenes* are authentic and unsullied. We find a similar image of *phrēn* being "opened" in Scol. 889.[97] A friend is to welcome others with genuine feelings of *phrenes*.

Tr. 52.   At the opening of the *Trojan Women* Poseidon responds to Athena's request to speak to him: "for associations of kindred (συγγενεῖς ὁμιλίαι) are no small charm (φίλτρον) of *phrenes*." At *Hipp.* 511 we heard of "charms of love" affecting *phrenes*. Here family associations serve to win over *phrenes*.[98]

Tr. 662.   Andromache tells Hecuba: "and if, pushing aside dear Hector, I will open (ἀναπτύσσω) my *phrēn* to my current husband, I will appear as a traitor to the dead person." As in *Med.* 661, we find here the image of "opening" of *phrēn*.[99] Once again *phrēn* appears to be the seat of affection and love. Andromache's *phrēn* is filled with love for Hector; it is not to be "opened" and thus filled with affection for another.

Tr. 992.   Hecuba, upbraiding Helen, says of her reaction to Paris: "seeing his foreign dress, shining with gold, you were impassioned (ἐκμαργόομαι) in *phrenes*." Euripides introduces a new verb with *phrenes*. It suggests that Helen was "mad" with love for Paris.

Fr. 1054 (Incerta).   In this fragment we read: "for love (ἔρως) is untrustworthy and generally lives (οἰκεῖν φιλεῖ) in the most evil (κάκιστος) of *phrenes*." Once again, as in the passage from the *Hippolytus* discussed above, we see a negative picture of love. It chooses as its dwelling *phrenes* that are "most evil."

Madness

In earlier and contemporary poets *phrēn* and madness are related in a few passages.[100] Aeschylus makes this association several times. Cassandra is "mad in *phrenes*" (φρενομανής) at *Ag.* 1140. At *Sept.* 484 and 967 *phrēn* appears with the verb μαίνομαι and at *Ag.* 1428, with ἐπιμαίνομαι. Orestes had *phrenes* "hard to govern" (δύσαρκτος) at *Choe.* 1024, and the Chorus say at 1056 that "confusion" (ταραγμός) has fallen on his *phrenes*. Sophocles likewise connects *phrēn* and madness. He speaks of an "Erinys of *phrenes*" in Antigone (603). Creon describes Ismene "raging and not in possession of her *phrenes*" (492). Fr. 846 mentions "raging madness" (μαργότης) of *phrenes*. Euripides refers to *phrēn* and madness several times.

Bacc. 33.   Dionysus describes how he drove out the women of Thebes in "fits of madness" (μανίαι): "they dwell in the hills, frantic (παράκοποι) in *phrenes*." Euripides introduces a new description of *phrenes*. Aeschylus at *Ag.* 479 speaks of one "stricken (κόπτω) in *phrenes*." Euripides uses a similar image to describe the maddened state of *phrenes* in these women.[101]

HF 836.   Iris calls on the "child of Night" to make Heracles mad: "move, drive fits of madness (μανίαι) on this man and child-killing turmoils (παιδοκτόνος ταραγμός) of *phrenes* and boundings of feet." Like Aeschylus at *Choe.* 1056, Euripides uses ταραγμός to describe the mad state into which Heracles will fall. *Phrenes* will be distorted and lead him to kill his children.[102]

HF 1091, 1122.   As he recovers from his maddened state, Heracles says: "I have fallen (πίπτω) into the wave (κλύδων) and terrible distress (δεινὸν τάραγμα) of *phrenes*."[103] Euripides here uses a word similar to ταραγμός at 836: τάραγμα. He also uses a nautical image with κλύδων. *Phrenes* are like a sea filled with storm and fury. On to their disturbed state Heracles has plunged. At 1122 Heracles tells Amphitryon: "not in any way do I recall having been frenzied (βακχεύω) in *phrenes*." Euripides describes their raving and frantic state.[104]

Tr. 408.   Talthybius says of Cassandra: "if Apollo had not made you rave (ἐκβακχεύω) in your *phrenes*." Here, as in *HF* 1122, Euripides uses the verb βακχεύω, this time in the compound ἐκβακχεύω. At 417 Talthybius will also suggest that Cassandra's phrenes are not "ready" (ἄρτιος).[105] Aeschylus calls Cassandra φρενομανής (*Ag.* 1140). Euripides similarly locates her madness in *phrenes*.[106]

Pain

We saw above under "Distress" that Euripides pictures *phrenes* as agitated or disturbed. He also speaks of pain in them. In earlier and contemporary poets pain is associated with *phrenes* in several passages.[107] Aeschylus at *Choe.* 746 describes the Nurse as "pained" (ἀλγύνω) in her *phrēn*. Sophocles speaks of someone "paining" (ἀνιάω) Creon in his *phrenes* (*Ant.* 319). Fr. 910 says that both "delight" (τὸ τέρπον) and "pain" (τὸ πημαῖον) occur in *phrenes*. Fr. 952 describes one "suffering pain" (δυσάλγητος) in *phrenes*. Euripides speaks of *phrēn* in this context as follows.

Hcld. 483.   The Maiden asks Iolaus, as she wonders about her brothers: "I wish to learn whether ... some additional pain (πῆμα) is vexing (δάκνω) your *phrēn*." Euripides uses a new noun with *phrēn* here, similar to τὸ πημαῖον in Soph., Fr. 910. This "pain" is able to "bite" *phrēn*.[108]

Ion 927.   The Old Servant, sympathizing with Creusa, says: "for a wave of evils (κακῶν κῦμα) just now, exhausts (ὑπεξαντλέω) my *phrēn* while another from your words lifts me from the stern." He then goes on to say that "evil tracks of other pains" (πήματα) appear. Euripides here uses a nautical image with *phrēn*: evils are like a wave overwhelming the ship of *phrēn*. One wave had just "exhausted" *phrēn* and another comes hard upon it.[109] *Phrēn* once again is the location of this suffering.

Or. 608.   Tyndareus reproves Orestes: "since ... you answer in such a way as to pain (ἀλγέω) me in my *phrēn*." The words Orestes utters are able to strike *phrēn* and fill it with suffering.[110]

Pho. 383.   Jocasta asks Polyneices: "but how may I ask what I desire in order that I not pain (δάκνω) your *phrēn*?" Once again speech is thought capable of hurting someone in *phrēn*.[111]

Fr. 573 (Oinomaus).   This fragment reads: "even in evil circumstances there is pleasure (ἡδονή) for mortals, namely complaints and downpourings of tears. These lighten (κουφίζω) the pains (ἀλγηδών) of *phrenes* and release the too great sufferings (πόνος) of *kardia*." Here *phrenes* and *kardia* are seen as the seats of suffering in human beings.[112] The "pains" of *phrenes* can be lightened if people can speak and cry.

In this chapter we have examined many intellectual and emotional uses of *phrēn*. In the next chapter, the remaining instances of this psychic term will be considered.

3 *Phrēn* in the Tragedies: Part Two

In this chapter we shall examine the remaining instances of *phrēn*. Some of these are traditional and contemporary; some are new. We shall look too at the various images of *phrēn* and *phrenes* that Euripides introduces.

*TRADITIONAL AND CONTEMPORARY USES
(WITH EURIPIDEAN FEATURES)*

PREDOMINANTLY MORAL

In earlier and contemporary poets *phrēn* is associated with moral activity in several ways. People can behave well and admirably in *phrenes*.[1] People can also display negative moral behaviour in *phrenes*.[2] Pindar and Bacchylides in particular connect *phrenes* with moral activity. They relate *phrenes* to holiness,[3] justice,[4] and attitudes towards wealth (prosperity).[5]

Aeschylus likewise relates *phrenes* to different categories of moral behaviour. First, holiness. At *Choe.* 56 we hear of "reverence (σέβας) penetrating *phrēn*" that is passing away. At *Choe.* 704 Orestes speaks of a deed that would be "impiety (δυσσεβεία) in *phrenes*." The Aegyptiads at *Supp.* 751 are said to have "unholy (δύσαγνοι) *phrenes*." Second, justice. At *Ag.* 996 *phrenes* are called "just" (ἔνδικος). At *Choe.* 572 Electra and Orestes are "rightly decided (κατορθόω) in *phrēn* to act." At *Eum.* 489 the jurors are not to have "unjust" (ἔκδικος) *phrenes*. Both Polyneices (*Sept.* 663) and the Herald (*Supp.* 915) are thought to have *phrenes* of this sort.

Third, pride. At *Per.* 750 Aeschylus describes the *hybris* of Xerxes as a "sickness of *phrenes*." At *Ag.* 502 he speaks of the "fault (ἁμαρτία) of *phrenes*." The Aegyptiads have "stubborn *phrenes*" (*Supp.* 107). Fourth, prosperity. At *Eum.* 536 "prosperity" (ὄλβος) is said to come from "health (ὑγίεια) of *phrenes*." Blessings abide if *phrenes* function appropriately, honouring the gods and not attached to "profit" (κέρδος: 541).

Sophocles also connects *phrenes* with moral behaviour. First, he relates them to *atē*. At *Tr.* 264 he describes the *phrenes* of Eurytus as "baneful" (ἀτηρός).[6] At *Ant.* 623 the Chorus say: "the evil seems somehow to be good for the one whose *phrenes* the god is driving to ruin (*atē*)." Second, evil. At *Aj.* 445 Odysseus is called "completely unscrupulous (πανταουργός) in *phrenes*." The *phrēn* of Polyneices and Eteocles is called "sinful" (ἀλειτηρός: *O.C.* 371). At *Ant.* 298 Creon says that money corrupts "excellent" (χρηστός) *phrenes*. At *Ant.* 1261 he refers to "errors (ἁμαρτήματα) of *phrenes* functioning badly (δύσφρων)."

Third, Sophocles speaks of "good" *phrenes*. We encounter "excellent" (χρηστός), "better" (λῷων), and "good" (καλός) *phrenes*.[7] Fourth, justice. At *Ant.* 792 Eros can make *phrenes* "unjust" (ἄδικος). At *Tr.* 294 Deianira describes her *phrēn* as "all-just" (πάνδικος). Euripides connects *phrēn* with moral behaviour in several ways.

Evil

Hec. 359.   Polyxena says that one reason that she is not reluctant to die is that she might "receive masters cruel (ὠμός) in *phrenes*." The ways in which these individuals would think would bring her harm.[8]

Hipp. 474.   The Nurse urges Phaedra to give up her thoughts of suicide: "cease from evil (κακός) *phrenes*; cease acting in pride." We find the adjective κακός first in Aesch., *Ag.* 1064, describing the *phrenes* of Cassandra, and next in Soph., *El.* 992, describing those of Electra. The Nurse finds fault with Phaedra's way of thinking, suggesting that her "thoughts," *phrenes*, are "evil."[9]

Hipp. 936.   At 935, as we heard in chapter 2 under "Loss," Hippolytus has expressed astonishment at Theseus' words; he calls them "outside of *phrenes*." Theseus then responds: "alas for the mortal (βροτός) *phrēn*! How far will it go (προβαίνω)? What end of audacity (τόλμη) or brashness (θράσος) will there be?" He proceeds to say that, if *phrēn* "swells" (ἐξογκόω) and people become more "wicked" (πανοῦργος), the gods will have to provide another land for the "unjust" (μὴ δίκαιος) and "evil" (κακός). Euripides describes the "mortal" (βροτός) *phrēn*: this adjective occurs also in Pin., Frs. 61.4 and 222.[10] "Audacity" and "boldness" in *phrēn* lead to evil behaviour. Euripides pictures *phrēn* as "swelling," suggesting a medical image. With a "swollen" *phrēn*, someone will "dare any-

thing" (πανοῦργος). This person earns the adjectives "unjust" and "evil."
Phrēn in this passage is especially associated with negative moral action.

IA 327.   Agamemnon indignantly asks Menelaus about his theft of his letter: "where did you take it? O gods, for your shameless (ἀναίσχυντος)
phrēn!" Euripides introduces a new adjective here with *phrēn*: "shameless."
Phrēn has contrived this theft.[11]

Med. 266.   In her first speech Medea suggests that a woman is generally a
fearful being. "But whenever she has been wronged in love, there is no other
phrēn more murderous (μιαιφονώτερος)." Again Euripides introduces a new
adjective with *phrēn*: "murderous." *Phrēn* is seen as the location where the
wronged woman plots revenge.

Med. 316.   As we heard in chapter 2 under "Planning," Creon is suspicious
about Medea. "You speak soft things to hear but I am terrified that in your
phrenes you are planning (βουλεύω) some evil (κακόν)." Medea has become
a "wronged" woman and her *phrēn*, "murderous," plans evil.

Med. 1373.   Jason remembers about the *phrēn* of Medea: the gods "know
(ἀπόπτυστος) *phrēn.*" Here once more Euripides offers a new picture of
phrēn. Medea, murderess of her children, has a mind that is "worthy to be
spit forth"; it is "detestable."

Fr. 551 (Oedipus).   This fragment says: "envy (φθόνος), which corrupts
(διαφθείρω) the *phrēn* of many mortals, destroyed him and me along with
him."[12] *Phrēn* that envy affects becomes involved in evil behaviour and
brings about the destruction of the person in whom it is found and also others.

Good

El. 1061.   Clytemnestra has allowed Electra to speak freely. What Electra
begins her speech by saying is: "would that, mother, you had better
(βελτίων) *phrenes.*" In earlier and contemporary poets we find references to
"good" (ἀγαθός) and "noble" (ἐσθλός) *phrenes.*[13] Sophocles mentions
"excellent" (χρηστός) and "good" *phrenes (Ant.* 298, Fr. 108). In Sophocles
also, at *Tr.* 736, Hyllus wishes Deianira had "better" (λῴων) *phrenes* just as
Electra does in this passage. *Phrenes* functions as the seat of admirable
moral behaviour, thought to be missing in Clytemnestra.[14]

Hipp. 1390.   Artemis addresses Hippolytus as he dies: "your nobility
(εὐγενές) of *phrenes* destroyed you." Hippolytus proved himself totally
trustworthy in not betraying Phaedra's secret. He claimed at 612 that his

phrēn had "not sworn" to keep silence but in fact it had. This lofty moral behaviour Artemis locates here in *phrenes*.

Hipp. 1419, 1454. At 1419 Artemis says that Hippolytus will be revenged: "for the sake of your holiness (εὐσέβεια) and your good (ἀγαθός) *phrēn.*" At 1454 Theseus echoes these words: "alas for your holy (εὐσεβής) and good (ἀγαθός) *phrēn.*" Aeschylus at *Choe.* 56 speaks of "reverence (σέβας) penetrating ears and *phrēn.*" Hippolytus' *phrēn* is both "good" and "holy," functioning as the seat of his noble behaviour.

Pho. 1740. Antigone states that she will accompany her father into exile. Oedipus responds: "alas for the sense of duty (τὸ χρήσιμον) of your *phrenes.*" Euripides introduces this new noun with *phrenes.* τὸ χρήσιμον literally means "excellence;" in this case it is manifested as dutiful action.[15]

Frs. *212 (Antiope)* and *548 (Oedipus).* In both these fragments reference is made to the desirability of *nous;* then mention of *phrenes* is made. Fr. 212 reads: "if [*nous*] is not present, what need is there of a beautiful woman unless she has good (χρηστός) *phrenes*?" Fr. 548 reads: "It is necessary to watch *nous, nous.* What need is there of fair form when someone does not have good (καλός) *phrenes*?" In both fragments *nous* and *phrenes* are very close in meaning.[16] Intelligence joined with goodness is what is desirable.

Holiness

Hipp. 317. At 317 the Nurse tries to find out what is troubling Phaedra, who says: "my hands are clean (ἁγνός); my *phrēn* has some stain (μίασμα)."[17] *Phrēn* is the seat of moral wrong in Phaedra: it lacks holiness, being "stained." Euripides introduces here this new noun with *phrēn:* μίασμα. We can contrast Phaedra's *phrēn* with the "good" and "holy" one of Hippolytus, at 1419 and 1454, treated above.

Hipp. 1448. The reading in this line accepted by Diggle in the OCT and Kovacs in the recent Loeb is χέρα. An alternate reading, however, is φρένα, as follows.[18] Theseus asks Hippolytus as he dies: "and will you leave me with my *phrēn* unclean (ἄναγνος)?" If this were the correct reading, it would echo Phaedra's reference to a μίασμα on her *phrēn* at 317. Theseus' *phrēn* would be in contrast to the "unholy" *phrēn* of Hippolytus, the description that Theseus gives of it at 1454.

Or. 1604. Here we have a statement very similar to *Hipp.* 317 and 1448 (if *phrēn* is the correct reading). Menelaus states: "I am holy (ἁγνός) in hands."

Orestes replies: "but not in your *phrenes*." Once again holy behaviour is associated with *phrenes*. It is inward holiness that counts.

Justice

HF 212.   Amphitryon tells Lycus that it is he who should suffer, "if Zeus has just (δίκαιος) *phrenes* in regard to us." Like Bacchylides who mentions "just" (δίκαιος) *phrenes* (11.124, 14.11), Euripides uses this adjective for the *phrenes* of Zeus. As frequently in earlier and contemporary poets, Aeschylus and Sophocles, *phrenes* are connected with justice.[19]

Hipp. 1298.   Artemis tells Theseus: "I have come for this purpose, to show the just (δίκαιος) *phrēn* of your son, in order that he may die with a good name." The *phrēn* of Hippolytus is "good" (1419, 1454), "holy" (1454), and, as described here, "just." It is very much the source of his moral actions.

Pride

Supp. 217.   Theseus tells Adrastus that the gods have given manifold blessings to human beings who none the less are not content: "but our thinking (φρόνησις) seeks to be greater in strength than the god, and, having possessed haughtiness (τὸ γαῦρον) in our *phrenes*, we seem to be wiser than the gods."[20] Euripides introduces a new noun in *phrenes*: τὸ γαῦρον. By their "exalting" and "haughtiness," human beings fail to appreciate the good they do possess and form an erroneous picture of their intellect. *Phrenes* are the location of their mistaken thoughts.

Prosperity

HF 776.   The Chorus remark as Lycus is slain: "gold and good fortune draw (ἐξάγω) mortals away from *phrenes*, as they drag in their tow unjust power." Aeschylus at *Eum.* 536 says that "prosperity" (ὄλβος) comes from "health of *phrenes*." Euripides here suggests that mortals should stay "close to *phrenes*" but "wealth and good fortune" take them away. Distance from *phrenes* leads to foolish behaviour: wealth is thus potentially dangerous.

Med. 599.   Medea responds to Jason's claim that he married the princess to be a "bulwark for the house" (597): "may a prosperous life that is painful not be mine nor prosperity (ὄλβος) that torments (κνίζω) my *phrēn*." As in *HF* 776, "prosperity" is seen as something that can harm *phrēn*. It affects in a negative way how one thinks.

GODS

In Euripides we do not hear very often about the *phrēn* or *phrenes* of the gods. At *HF* 212 the Chorus mention the "just" (δίκαιος) *phrenes* of Zeus. At *Hipp.* 1268 Cypris "takes captive the unbending *phrēn* of gods and mortals." At *Tr.* 52 Poseidon tells Athena that "associations of kindred are no small charm of *phrenes*." Thus we see a moral connection of justice in *phrenes* with Zeus; we also see gods affected by love in *phrēn* and *phrenes*. We find no other references to divine *phrenes*.

EURIPIDEAN USES

Thus far we have studied the traditional and contemporary ways in which Euripides uses *phrēn*. We shall now look at new ways in which he refers to it. In terms of overall usage, these new uses are few in number.

KINDS OF *PHRĒN*

Euripides uses a wide range of adjectives with *phrēn*, 44 in all (see Appendix 3). Some of these are found in earlier and contemporary poets, namely ἀγαθός, βροτός, δίκαιος, ἐμός, θῆλυς, κακός, οἷος, πυκινός, σός, and τυφλός. Euripides introduces some new adjectives of *phrēn* while speaking of it in traditional and contemporary contexts. Table 3.1 summarizes these 33 adjectives with the context indicated.

These adjectives illustrate new ways that Euripides used to characterise *phrēn* while referring to it in contexts that would have been familiar to his audience. In one instance we find Euripides using a new adjective in a new context. At *Alc.* 775 Heracles says: "a servant should not be scowling at guests but receive them with a courteous (εὐπροσήγορος) *phrēn*." Here we have a new adjective with *phrēn*, which is to be involved in the affable reception of others.

INTELLECTUAL USES

Discernment

Hipp. 926.   As Theseus encounters Hippolytus after the death of Phaedra, he says: "alas there ought to be for mortals some reliable test (τεκμήριον) of their friends and discernment (διάγνωσις) of *phrenes*, who is a true friend and who is not." He also says that there should be in human beings two voices so that the one, which is just and thinking (φρονέω), can control the other, which may be otherwise. This passage resembles Scolion 889 in

Table 3.1
Phrēn: New Adjectives

Adjective or participle	Passage	Meaning	Context
ἀγύμναστος	Fr. 598 (*Pirithous*)	untrained	Speed
ἄκαμπτος	*Hipp.* 1268	unbending	Love
ἄκρος	*Bacc.* 203	highest	Intelligence
ἄλλος	*Med.* 266	other	"Evil"
ἄναγνος	*Hipp.* 1448	unholy	Holiness
ἀναίσχυντος	*IA* 327	shameless	"Evil"
ἀνώμοτος	*Hipp.* 612	unsworn	Mind
ἀπόπτυστος	*Med.* 1373	detestable	"Evil"
ἄρσην	*Or.* 1204	male	Intelligence
ἄρτιος	*Tr.* 417	ready, complete	Absence
αὐθάδης	*Med.* 104	self-willed, stubborn	Mind
αὐτοκρατής	*And.* 482	having full authority	Mind
βαρύς	[*Med.* 38]	heavy, grievous	Anger
βελτίων	*El.* 1061	better	"Good"
γυναικεῖος	Fr. 400 (*Thyestes*)	of women	Love
διάφορος	*Hel.* 161	different	Intelligence
ἐλευθερώτερος	Fr. 831 (*Phrixus*)	more free	Mind
εὐσεβής	*Hipp.* 1454	holy	"Good," Holiness
ἡβῶσα	*Hipp.* 969	young	Age, Love
ἤπιος	Fr. 362.6 (*Erechtheus*)	gentle	Mind
θεῖος	*Hcld.* 540	divine	Mind
καθαρός	*Hipp.* 1120	untroubled	Distress
	Med. 661	holy	Love
καλός	Fr. 548 (*Oedipus*)	good	"Good"
μιαιφονώτερος	*Med.* 266	more murderous	Age
μονομάχος	*Pho.* 1300	single-combat	Purpose
νεώτερος	Fr. 619 (*Peleus*)	younger	Age
ὅμοιος	*Hel.* 161	similar	Intelligence

Table 3.1 *(Continued)*
Phrēn: New Adjectives

Adjective or participle	Passage	Meaning	Context
σοφός	*Bacc.* 427 *Med.* 677	wise	Intelligence
ταλαίπωρος	*El.* 334	suffering	Distress
τρομερός	*Pho.* 1285	trembling	Fear
ὑγίης	*Bacc.* 947	healthy	Mind
φαυλότερος	*And.* 482	more paltry	Mind
χρηστός	Fr. 212 (*Antiope*)	good	"Good"

which the desire is expressed for the human chest to be opened, closed again, and then a person regarded as truly a friend with a "guileless (ἄδολος) *phrēn*." The lines resemble as well *Med.* 516–19, where Medea wonders why Zeus has given "clear tests (τεκμήρια) of gold" but failed to implant a "stamp" (χαρακτήρ) on people to tell whether they are good or bad.

Euripides introduces a new noun with *phrenes* in speaking of a "discernment" or "distinguishing" of them. Clearly *phrenes* are seen as the seat of a person's true thoughts or feelings. Theseus believes that he has been deceived about the *phrenes* of Hippolytus. Later in the play he will call his son's *phrēn* "holy and good" (1454).

IA 394. Agamemnon describes the suitors at 391–2 as "evil-minded and loving of marriage" (κακόφρονες φιλόγαμοι). He tells Menelaus to lead them: "for they are ready in the foolishness (μωρία) of their *phrenes*." Euripides introduces the noun μωρία with *phrenes*: the suitors are foolish in their way of thinking, specifically in their willingness to fight for Helen.

Fr. 776 (Phaethon). Here too Euripides relates foolishness to *phrenes* in a new way. He says: "it is ingrained in the rich to be foolish (σκαιός). What is the cause? Is it because blind prosperity helps them that they have blind (τυφλός) *phrenes*?"[21] Pindar at *Pae.* 7 b 18 refers likewise to "blind" (τυφλός) *phrenes*. When *phrenes* cannot "see," the result is foolishness.[22]

Swiftness

Bacc. 670. The Messenger, coming to describe the Bacchants, says to Pentheus: "O king, for I fear the swiftness (τάχος) of your *phrenes*, your quickness to anger (ὀξύθυμον) and your exceeding royal spirit (βασιλικόν)."[23]

Pentheus' *phrenes* are quick to react. His swift thoughts, accompanied by a tendency to anger and a haughty royal attitude, are to be feared by those over whom he can assert authority. Euripides introduces a new idea with *phrenes* in speaking of their swift movement.[24]

Fr. *1032* (Incerta).   This fragment reads: "this speed (ὠκύ) and the swiftness (λαιψηρόν) of *phrenes* have cast mortals into misfortune in many things." Once again we encounter this new idea of "swiftness" of *phrenes*. Here likewise it is described as a dangerous characteristic.

EMOTIONAL USES

Gloominess and Contraction

Alc. 797.   Heracles, trying to cheer up the servant, says: "I know clearly that the plash [of wine], falling from the cup, will unmoor (μεθορμίζω) you from the current gloominess (σκυθρωτόν) and contraction (ξυνεστός) of *phrenes*." Earlier Heracles had told the servant that he would welcome guests with a "courteous" (εὐπροσήγορος) *phrēn* (775).[25] Such a *phrēn* would be "open" and "affable." Instead, we find here the opposite picture. The servant's *phrenes* are "gloomy" and "sullen." They are "contracted," "drawn together" (συνίστημι), and "unexpansive." Euripides introduces there two new ways of referring to *phrenes*, presenting an apt picture of the effects of grief.

Jealousy and Hostility

And. 181.   The Chorus say, after Hermione has derided Andromache: "in some way jealousy (ἐπιφθονόν) is characteristic of a woman's (θῆλυς) *phrēn* and always hostility (δυσμενές), especially to rivals in marriage." Aeschylus once refers to a "woman's" (θῆλυς) *phrēn* when Orestes describes that of Aegisthus at *Choe.* 305; this is the first reference to this type of *phrēn*.[26] Euripides here generalizes about the *phrēn* of women: it is jealous and hostile to other women, especially if they happen to be rivals in love. *Phrēn* functions as the seat of envious and bitter thoughts. This is a new picture given of *phrēn*.

EURIPIDEAN IMAGES

In this section we shall survey the major images that Euripides uses with *phrēn*. All of these passages have already been discussed above in chapter 2 and in this chapter, but here the focus will be upon the images that appear in them.

ARCHERY

And. 365.   The Chorus tell Andromache that "the good sense" of her *phrēn* "has shot forth all its arrows." Pindar at *Ol.* 2.90 speaks of "arrows of fame from a gentler *phrēn.*" Euripides presents an image of a *phrēn* as a "bow" that has used up all its arrows. The Chorus believe that Andromache has gone beyond the bounds of appropriate speech.

MEDICAL

Alc. 878, Bacc. 947, Hcld. 483.   Like Aeschylus and Sophocles,[27] Euripides uses medical images of *phrēn* several times. At *Alc.* 878 Admetus speaks of grief "wounding" (ἑλκόω) his *phrenes.* Dionysus at *Bacc.* 947 tells Pentheus that the *phrenes* he had before were not "healthy" (ὑγιής). At *Hcld.* 483 the Maiden asks Iolaus whether a "new pain (πῆμα) is vexing" (δάκνω) his *phrēn.* In these three passages *phrēn* can be specifically injured or be in an unhealthy condition.

Hipp. 283, 765, 775, 936.   The image of the unhealthy *phrēn* appears in these four passages. At 283 the Chorus refer to the "disease" (νόσος) of Phaedra and the "wandering" (πλάνον) of her *phrenes.* At 765 the Chorus say that Aphrodite "has broken with the terrible disease (νόσος) of unholy loves" the *phrenes* of Phaedra. At 775 Phaedra "casts forth painful (ἀλγεινός) love from her *phrenes.*" Theseus at 936 speaks of *phrēn* "swelling" (ἑξογκόω) during someone's life, an image, perhaps, of infection.

Frs. 644 (Polyidos), 659 (Protesilaus).   The first fragment speaks of someone making *phrenes* "sick" (νοσέω). The second mentions "nothing healthy (ὑγιές) from *phrenes.*"

In all these passages *phrēn* or *phrenes* prove vulnerable to illness. When they are "sick" in thought or emotion, the person's behaviour becomes negative.

NAUTICAL

HF 1091, Ion 927.   Like Aeschylus,[28] Euripides uses an image of the sea with *phrēn.* At *HF* 1091 Heracles says that he had fallen into the "wave (κλύδων) and terrible distress of *phrenes.*" At *Ion* 927 the Servant speaks of a "wave (κῦμα) of evils exhausting" his *phrēn.* In the first passage *phrenes* are like the sea in a storm. In the second *phrēn* is a victim of a wave.

OPENNESS

Med. 661, Tr. 662.   The Chorus in the *Medea* criticize the person who cannot "honour friends, opening (ἀνοίγω) the bolt (κλής) of pure *phrenes.*"

Euripides uses here an image of "opening" *phrenes*, which are pictured as a door with a "bolt." *Phrenes* that cannot be opened are ones that conceal their feelings. At *Tr.* 662 Andromache mentions the possibility of "opening" (ἀναπτύσσω) her *phrēn* to a husband. Once again *phrēn* is considered a seat of feelings that can be expressed to others or not.

SHARPNESS

Alc. 674, Hipp. 689.   In the first passage, Admetus is urged not to "provoke" (παροξύνω) the *phrenes* of his father. There is a possible image of "sharpness" in this verb. In the second passage, Phaedra says that Hippolytus "is sharpened (θήγω) in his *phrenes* with anger (ὀργή)."[29] Euripides presents an image of the "thoughts" of Hippolytus becoming "sharp" or "piercing" and therefore potentially harmful.

SIGHT

Fr. 776 (Phaethon).   Like Aeschylus,[30] Euripides presents an image of sight with *phrenes*. This fragment mentions the rich having "blind" (τυφλός) *phrenes*. When *phrenes* fail to see, the thoughts of a person become foolish and his actions likewise.

TOUCH

Five times we find this image in Euripides, one that does not occur in Aeschylus or Sophocles.[31]

Alc. 108, Med. 55.   In the first passage, in a situation of grief, the Chorus say: "you touched (θιγγάνω) my *psychē*; you touched my *phrenes*." In the second passage, the Nurse says that the misfortunes of masters "touch" (ἀνθάπτω) the *phrenes* of slaves.

Supp. 1162, Tr. 1216.   In these two passages the context is also grief. At *Supp.* 1162 a word "touches" (θιγγάνω) *phrenes*. At *Tr.* 1216 Hecuba's words to the dead Astyanax "touch" (θιγγάνω) the *phrenes* of the Chorus.[32]

THE RELATIONSHIP OF PERSON AND PHRĒN

Euripides mentions *phrēn* 160 times. All these instances have been discussed in chapter 2 and above in this chapter. In earlier and contemporary authors and also in Aeschylus and Sophocles people appear to remain distinct from their *phrēn*. Is this the case also with Euripides?

Appendix One presents all the instances of *phrēn* analysed in terms of the relationship between this psychic entity and the person. Using this

Appendix as a guide, we shall present an overview of the instances of *phrēn*.

1 *Phrēn* or *phrenes* appear 43 times as either active or present in a person (Category A). Only 3 times are *phrenes* or *phrēn* active. *Phrēn* "shudders and fears" (*Hec.* 85); it "desires" (*IT* 685). In all other instances we find a description of *phrēn* or *phrenes*. Thus we hear, for example, of the "good sense of *phrēn*" or the "hateful nature of a self-willed *phrēn*" (*And.* 365, *Med.* 104). We encounter also "grief," "rage and tension," "courage," and "valour and good counsel" of *phrenes* (*Hipp.* 188, 983, *Med.* 856, *Pho.* 746). Several descriptions of *phrēn* or *phrenes* appear: "more paltry," "suffering," "unsworn," "shameless," and "pure" (*And.* 482, *El.* 334, *Hipp.* 612, *IA* 327, *Med.* 661).

2 *Phrēn* and *phrenes* appear only 9 times as a location or instrument that some-one acts in or with (Category B). These functions were most common for *phrēn* and *phrenes* in earlier and contemporary poets. They appear still quite frequently in this role in Aeschylus and Sophocles, but not in Euripides.

3 In 29 passages (Category C) someone has a direct relationship with *phrēn* or *phrenes*. Most frequently a person "has (ἔχω) *phrēn* or *phrenes*" (12 times). In these passages a person remains distinct from *phrēn* while acting upon it or relating to it.

4 In 19 instances (Category D) someone is described in relation to *phrēn* or *phrenes*. People can be "frantic," "cruel," "barbarous," or "maddened" in *phrenes* (*Bacc.* 33, *Hec.* 359, *Hel.* 501, *Hipp.* 1230). One can be "apart from" or "nowhere in" *phrenes* (*Bacc.* 359, *Hipp.* 1012). In these passages in particular the distinctness of person from *phrēn* or *phrenes* is evident.

5 In 59 passages (Categories E and F) outside objects or agents act upon *phrēn* or *phrenes*. These passages likewise suggest that *phrenes* are a sepa-rate entity within that can be affected from without. When this occurs, the behaviour of the person is affected in some way.

The detailed analysis of passages presented in Appendix One and briefly summarized here suggests that Euripides is quite traditional in the way he views the relationship of person and *phrēn*. Like earlier and contemporary po-ets and like Aeschylus and Sophocles, Euripides speaks of person and *phrenes* as distinct. His usage strongly resembles that of Homer in most respects.[33] When Homer speaks of *phrēn* or *phrenes* as present in a person, he rarely makes them an active agent; neither does Euripides. Homer quite often describes a person in relation to *phrenes*, as does Euripides. Homer frequently refers to outside objects and agents affecting *phrenes*; so does Euripides. In Homer, however, people rarely affect their own *phrenes*; Euripides speaks of this feature of *phrenes* quite often, as do the lyric and elegiac poets and also Sophocles.[34]

In Euripides, as in earlier and contemporary poets and in both Aeschylus and Sophocles, person and *phrenes* act in co-operation and harmony. *Phrenes* are a prominent seat of intellect within, which a person both respects and uses. If "lost" or "damaged," *phrenes* bring about foolish behaviour in the individual. *Phrenes* are open to outside influences. When they are affected positively or negatively, so are the actions of the person. *Phrēn* and *phrenes* are one of the psychic entities that people have within. People uses *phrenes*, act with them, but do not appear to identify with them.

OVERVIEW OF PHRĒN

As mentioned above, Euripides speaks of *phrēn* and *phrenes* 160 times. The specific and general features of this psychic entity are as follows.

SPECIFIC FEATURES OF *PHRĒN*

1 In the appearance of the singular or the plural metre is probably the decisive factor. There are 62 instances of the singular, 98 of the plural. There appears to be no difference in meaning in these usages.

2 Several factors may be present in each occurrence of the term: "intellectual," "emotional," "volitional," or "moral." Both Aeschylus and Sophocles make references to *phrēn* where the physical aspect is prominent.[35] Euripides does not. In Euripides, on a continuum of meaning from "physical" to "psychological," most instances of *phrēn* lie at the "psychological" end.

3 *Phrēn* and *phrenes* alter with age. They are less admirable in the young.

4 When *phrēn* or *phrenes* are predominantly "intellectual," they are connected with "mind," "intelligence," "planning," "purpose," and "speech." *Phrenes* can be absent or damaged. A person can lose them or stand at a distance from them.

5 In passages where *phrenes* are predominantly "emotional," they are associated with anger, calm, courage, desire, distress, and fear. They are also connected with grief, joy, love, madness, and pain.

6 In instances where the context is predominantly moral, *phrenes* can be "evil" or "good." They are related to holiness, justice, pride, and attitudes to prosperity.

7 We hear only three times of the *phrēn* or *phrenes* of gods. Zeus may have "just" *phrenes* (*HF* 212). "Love" and "family relationships" affect the *phrenes* of gods (*Hipp.* 1268, *Tr.* 52).

8 On a few occasions Euripides refers to *phrēn* or *phrenes* in new ways. He speaks of a "courteous" *phrēn* (*Alc.* 775). He refers to "discernment," "foolishness," and "swiftness" of *phrenes* (*Hipp.* 926, *IA* 394, Fr. 1032).

He mentions also "gloominess and contraction" and "jealousy" of *phrēn* or *phrenes* (*Alc.* 797, *And.* 181).

9 In traditional and contemporary contexts, Euripides introduces a large number of new adjectives with *phrēn* and *phrenes* (see Table 3.1).

10 Euripides uses several images with *phrēn* and *phrenes*. These include those of "archery," "medical," "nautical," "openness," "sharpness," "sight," and "touch."

11 With regard to the relationship of person and *phrenes*, Euripides appears to be quite traditional in his usage. People remain distinct from their *phrenes*. Person and psychic entity act in harmony and co-operation. A person acts frequently in a variety of psychological activities.

12 Outside objects and agents affect *phrēn* and *phrenes* in several ways. When they are affected within, a person's behaviour is strongly influenced.

GENERAL FEATURES OF *PHRĒN*

Euripides refers to *phrēn* and *phrenes* more often than to other psychic entities.[36] Although our evidence for all three tragedians is fragmentary, we can make some generalizations about numbers of occurrences of psychological terms. In mentioning *phrēn* 160 times, Euripides uses it significantly more frequently than other psychic terms. *Psychē* he uses next in frequency, 117 times. In mentioning *phrēn* so often, Euripides resembles both Aeschylus[37] and Sophocles.[38] Our examination of the instances of *phrēn* has shown that Euripides' usage is generally traditional and contemporary. The way in which he refers to the nature and range of meaning of *phrēn* resembles that of earlier and contemporary poets and of both Aeschylus and Sophocles.

Why does *phrēn* appear more often than other psychic entities in the tragedies of Euripides? As with Aeschylus and Sophocles, the answer seems to lie in the basic nature of *phrēn*. As a seat of intellectual activity, *phrēn* appears to have a wide range of activity. *Phrenes* are engaged in pondering, deliberating, thinking, reflecting, choosing. Possibilities they weigh; decisions concerning practical activity they engage in. Nor are they limited to intellectual involvement of a varying kind. A wide range of emotions are also connected to *phrenes*. In them people fear, grieve, rejoice, love, are angry, calm, or courageous. *Phrenes* too are associated with moral behaviour. They can be "good" or "evil." They can be affected with pride, unholiness, and injustice. *Nous*, in contrast to *phrēn*, seems capable of a single, although most valuable, function: it unerringly sees the truth of a situation and its needs. But *nous* does not always function. In times of crisis people often have only *phrenes* to use and use them they must.

Phrēn and *phrenes* are essentially versatile in nature. Their association with deliberative thought makes their frequent appearance in the three tragedians understandable. Euripides in particular shows us their wide range of activity within the human person.

4 *Nous* and *Prapides* in the Tragedies

In this chapter we shall look at the instances of *nous* and *prapides* in the plays and fragments of Euripides. We have several instances of *nous* but only five of *prapides*.

NOUS: TRADITIONAL AND CONTEMPORARY USES (WITH EURIPIDEAN FEATURES)

In the plays and fragments of Euripides that we have *nous* appears quite often.[1] It occurs 43 times, more than *thumos* (30) or *kardia* (35) but significantly fewer times than *phrēn* (160) or *psychē* (117). In the seven extant plays of Sophocles we find 38 references to *nous*, in those of Aeschylus, only 3. *Nous* appears in most plays of Euripides but not in the *Alc.*, *El.*, *Hcld.*, *HF*, *IT*, or *Supp.*[2]

As with *phrēn*, Euripides most often uses *nous* in ways similar to earlier and contemporary poets. His usage resembles also that of Sophocles in the range that both dramatists ascribe to *nous*.

AGE

In earlier and contemporary poets *nous* is mentioned several times in relation to age. These poets suggest that *nous* is inferior in young people, functions well in mature people, but then gradually declines with age.[3] Aeschylus at *Sept.* 622 praises Lasthenes for being "old in *nous*." Sophocles in six passages relates *nous* to age. *Nous* "grows" with age (*Ant.* 564). It can be present in an admirable way in the old (Frs. 260, 950) or can be absent in old age (*O.C.* 931, Fr. 949). In the young *nous* especially "feels pain" (*Ant.* 767). Euripides relates *nous* to age in two passages.

Bacc. 252.   Pentheus says to Cadmus as he appears in Bacchic dress: "father, I feel contempt, seeing your old age (γῆρας) not having (ἔχω) *nous*." In this passage and frequently in Euripides, we hear of *nous* as a psychic entity that someone has.[4] Pentheus suggests that Cadmus displays no intelligence in his behaviour.

Fr. 25.4 (Aiolos).   This fragment reads: "alas, alas, how well the old story holds: we old men are nothing except sound and form and we move as copies of dreams. *Nous* is not (ἔνειμι) in us but we imagine that we think well." In the old, *nous* is absent. Here, as quite often in other passages of Euripides, *nous* is described as "being in" or "failing to be in" (ἔνειμι) people.[5] In this fragment *nous* has been lost with age but the old men still imagine that they are "thinking well." As in earlier poets and in Sophocles, age brings loss of *nous*.

PREDOMINANTLY INTELLECTUAL

In Euripides, as in earlier and contemporary poets and also in Aeschylus and Sophocles, *nous* is associated most often with intellectual activity. In Sophocles in particular, 33 of the 36 passages, where *nous* is clear within the context, can be described in this way. In Euripides too we shall see that most occurrences fall into this category.

Mind: Positive

Hec. 603.   In this line Hecuba says: "these are comments my *nous* has shot (τοξεύω) in vain." Hecuba refers back to remarks that she has made. She uses here an image of archery, similar to the reference to "the good sense of *phrēn* shooting forth all of its arrows" at *And.* 365.[6] What does the line refer to? Diggle in the *OCT* and Kovacs in the recent Loeb both bracket lines 599–602. With these lines removed, Hecuba would in 603 be referring to lines 592–9, where she remarks that human beings remain consistent: the "base are base, the good, good."

We have here a picture of *nous* engaged in analysing a situation and offering its insights. Hecuba suggests that the "arrows" from *nous* will fail to hit their mark: they are sent forth in vain.

[Hel. 122.]   The *OCT* brackets lines 121–2, which read, as Helen speaks to Teucer:
Hel: "do you think that your fancy was sure?"
Teu: "yes, I myself saw with my eyes and *nous* sees (ὁρᾷ)."
Helen asks Teucer whether he was sure that he saw Helen herself. He affirms that this was so. He saw not merely with his eyes but inwardly his *nous* saw her.[7]

If these lines are genuine, we find a traditional association of *nous* with vision.[8] Sophocles uses the same image when he has Oedipus tell Teiresias: "you are blind (τυφλός) in your ears, your *nous*, and your eyes" (*O.T.* 371). At *Tr.* 988 Euripides describes Helen's *nous* too as "seeing" Paris (see below, "Love"). *Nous* can see inwardly, and what it sees can usually be trusted to be real and true.

[Hel. 731.]   This line also is bracketed in Diggle's *OCT* in the group of lines 728–33.[9] Lines 728–31 read: "On the one hand, even if I was born a hired servant, I would be numbered among the noble slaves, not having the name "free" but the *nous* (ἐλεύθερος)." Sophocles at Fr. 940 refers to a slave having a "free" (ἐλεύθερος) *nous*, using this adjective for the first time with *nous*.[10] Euripides, if these lines are genuine, is suggesting a contrast between the outer condition of a person and his inner nature, his *nous* or intelligence. The slave claims that he can think like a free person.

Ion 742.   The Old Servant tells Creusa: "the feature of the foot is slowness, that of *nous* is speed (ταχύ)." In Homer we find one reference to the "swiftness" of *nous*: he describes it as "leaping" (ἀΐσσω) in thought (*Il.* 15.80). Euripides here introduces τὸ ταχύ with *nous*.[11] One feature of *nous* is rapid movement.

[Or. 909.]   This line falls among lines 904–13 of the Messenger's speech bracketed in the *OCT*.[12] Lines 909–11 read: "whoever plans (βουλεύω) noble things with *nous*, even if not right away, eventually it will be profitable for the city."[13] Although the lines are suspect, we find in earlier and contemporary poets references to *nous* and "planning" (βουλεύω)[14] and to "counsel" (βουλή).[15] Sophocles at Fr. 260 says that "*nous* and planning (τὸ βουλεύειν) accompany old age." The picture is of *nous* devising advantages (χρηστά) for the city.

Tr. 652.   Andromache tells Hecuba how she worked to keep a fair reputation: "Inside my halls I did not bring in witty words of women but, having my *nous* as a good teacher (χρηστὸς διδάσκαλος) at home, I sufficed for myself." Euripides introduces a new picture of *nous* as a "good teacher" within the person. From her own thinking Andromache was able to work out what was the most admirable way to act.

Frs. 212, 548.   As we saw above in chapter 3, both these fragments mention the desirability of *nous* and "good" *phrenes*. The first reads: "if *nous* is present (ἔνειμι). If not, what need is there of a beautiful woman if she does not have noble (χρηστός) *phrenes*?" The second reads: "It is necessary to watch *nous*, *nous*. What need is there for fair form when someone does not have good (καλός) *phrenes*?" *Nous* and *phrenes* seem to be close in meaning in these fragments. A woman needs intelligence and thoughts that tend to goodness.

Fr. 964.2.   This fragment describes someone who makes a point of imagining disasters so that reality will be even less painful. The fragment mentions "imagining with *phrēn*" at line 5 (see above, chap. 2, "Mind"). It may mention *psychē* in line 6 (see below, chap. 8). In line 2 we hear: "I thrust misfortunes (συμφορά) into my thoughts (φροντίδες) and *nous*." Here *nous* and *phrontides* are the location of this person's imaginings about potential sufferings.

   In these 9 passages treated thus far we see *nous* presented in a positive light. It is a seat of thought and imagination. It can teach; it can see. It is related to positive moral behaviour.

Mind: Negative

And. 237.   Hermione, in her exchange with Andromache, says: "may your *nous* not dwell (ξυνοικέω) with me, woman!" She rejects Andromache's claim to be "modest" (σώφρων: 234–5). Here *nous* and its features are judged by Hermione to be of a negative nature.[16]

IA 334.   Menelaus, in speaking to Agamemnon, makes the general comment: "a *nous* which is not firm (βέβαιος) is an unjust possession (ἄδικον κτῆμα), one not reliable (σαφές) for its friends." Euripides introduces the idea of a "*nous* not firm."[17] This *nous* leads to unjust behaviour and remains ambiguous to its friends. Menelaus has discovered Agamemnon's plot to bring Iphigenia to Aulis under false pretences. He suggests that Agamemnon's *nous* is "not firm," that it is "unjust," and that it is proving to be "unreliable" for others.

Med. 529.   In his response to Medea Jason says: "you have a subtle (λεπτός) *nous*." Euripides uses a new adjective here with *nous*: "subtle," "clever," or "devising." Jason aptly describes Medea's capacity for thinking and planning. He sees her *nous* as negative. This is the only reference to *nous* in the *Medea*, unlike *phrēn*, which occurs 14 times. This description of Medea well sums up her character.

Mind: Attention

Above, at [*Hel.* 122] we had a reference to *nous* "seeing." This activity, on an inner level, characterizes a chief function of *nous*: the capacity to grasp the essence of a situation. In five passages we find *nous* associated with close observation or attention.

Ion 251, 1370.   Creusa explains to Ion why she weeps as she sees Delphi: "I, seeing these homes of Apollo, traversed again some old memory. I held (ἔχω) my *nous* there, being somehow here." We can compare here especially *Il.* 15.80–2: "as when the *noos* of a man leaps who, having travelled over much land, thinks in his wise *phrenes*, 'would that I were here or there' and expresses many desires." Creusa describes how her attention was fixed on a memory from of old. At 1370 Ion says that he weeps as he "directs (δίδωμι) his *nous*" to the thought that his mother sold him as a baby. Here *nous* indicates attention to an imagined scenario from the past.

Or. 1181.   Electra asks Orestes: "hear now and hold (ἔχω) your *nous* here." He is to pay attention to what she is about to say.

Pho. 360, 1418.   Polyneices says that all people of necessity love their native land. "whoever speaks otherwise sports with words but holds (ἔχω) his *nous* there." A person directs his attention to his homeland and places his affections there. At 1418 Eteocles, believing that he has slain Polyneices, "does not hold (ἔχω) his *nous*" towards him and thereby gives his brother a chance to slay him in turn. Eteocles instead was considering stripping Polyneices of his armour. Again *nous* indicates "attention," directed in this case to another purpose.

Intelligence

Most often, as also in Sophocles, *nous* functions as "intelligence" in the person. When its nature is positive, it is seen as a presence most desirable.

And. 231, 252.   Andromache warns Hermione not to be like her mother, Helen. "For it is necessary for children in whom there is (ἔνειμι) *nous* to avoid the ways of their evil mothers." Hermione is to use her intelligence to avoid her mother's evil behaviour. At 252 Andromache tells Hermione: "I say that you do not have (ἔχω) the *nous* you ought to have had."[18] Andromache believes that Hermione has not shown sufficient intelligence in handling the situation of having herself and her son as part of Neoptolemus' household.[19]

Bacc. 252, 271.   In the first passage, as we heard under "Age" above, Pentheus suggests that the "old age" of Cadmus does not have "(ἔχω) *nous*" since he is dressed in Bacchic apparel. At 269–71 Teiresias answers Pentheus' criticisms by telling him that "*phrenes* are absent" from his words.[20] He then says: the bold person, powerful and capable of speech, becomes a bad citizen, not having (ἔχω) *nous*." In this passage phrenes and nous appear to be close in meaning. Pentheus, bold and confident in speech, lacks two essentials: *phrenes* and *nous*. Without these, what he says will prove harmful to the state.

Hipp. 105, 920.   As Hippolytus insists that honouring only one of the gods is acceptable, the Servant replies: "may you be fortunate, having (ἔχω) the *nous* which you ought to have here." Hippolytus needs "intelligence" to see how to honour divinity appropriately. It is this *nous* that he fails to have.

Theseus, at 920, detects the same lack in Hippolytus in another context. When Hippolytus asks how Phaedra died, Theseus responds that human beings have devised many wondrous skills but have not sought or found this: "to teach those in whom *nous* is not present (ἔνειμι) to think (φρονέω)." Theseus imagines that Hippolytus is purposely hiding his guilt. At 925–6 he will speak further of the need of a test for "discernment of *phrenes*."[21] In Theseus' view Hippolytus' *phrenes* are deceptive. He does not have *nous* to think properly. If he did have this *nous*, his behaviour would have been different in the past and also in the present.

IA 374.   Menelaus, after discovering Agamemnon's plot concerning Iphigenia, speaks generally about a leader: "it is necessary for a leader of a city to have (ἔχω) *nous*. For every man is sufficient, if he happens to have understanding (ξύνεσις)." In *Bacc.* 671 we heard that a citizen without *nous* can harm the city. Here it is a leader who needs *nous*, "intelligence." What is present with *nous* is "understanding" (ξύνεσις). *Nous* allows the leader to perceive the needs of the city.

IA 1139.   Clytemnestra, as she confronts Agamemnon about his intentions concerning Iphigenia, hears him say: "whom have I wronged?" She replies: "you ask this of me? This *nous* itself does not have (ἔχω) *nous*." Clytemnestra is astonished and suggests that Agamemnon's "intelligence" shows itself to be no "intelligence" at all. Her remark makes Agamemnon fully aware that his secret has been discovered. Euripides offers a new expression here of "*nous* not having *nous*." It suggests that *nous* is considered the essence of intelligence or thought.

Frs. 149 (Andromache), 256 (Archelaus).   The first fragment reads: "youth amuses me and boldness (θράσος) more than *nous*." The second fragment reads: "blessed is he who, having (ἔχω) *nous*, honours God and makes this a great profit for himself." In both passages we find a positive picture of *nous* or "intelligence." In the first, *nous* is neglected in favour of "boldness." In the second, *nous* provides a course of action advantageous to the person.

Frs. 909.5, 6 (Incerta).   In this fragment a picture of a successful wife is given. Lines 4–6 read: "even if her husband is not handsome, it is necessary at any rate for the one possessing (κτάομαι) *nous* to think him so. For the eye is not to judge (κρίνω), but the *nous*." For the wife with "intelligence," the judgment of a husband will come, not from the eye, but from the "mind." Here we see *nous* associated with thought that leads to a harmonious marriage.

Frs. *25 (Aiolos)*, *265 (Augē)*.   In the first fragment, as we heard under "Age," old men admit that "*nous* is not present (ἔνειμι) in them." They lack the "intelligence" that they once had, even though they imagine that they still "think well." In the second fragment there is a different cause of the absence of *nous*: "wine set me apart (ἐξίστημι) from *nous*." As with *phrenes*,[22] wine negatively affects a person's ability to think clearly.[23]

Speech

In earlier and contemporary poets *nous* is frequently associated with speech.[24] Sophocles relates *nous* and speech several times. He speaks of the activities of *nous* and tongue at *Ant.* 1909, *O.C.* 936, and Fr. 351. He suggests that wine, making a man "empty" of *nous*, causes him also to speak foolishly (Fr. 929). Euripides mentions the connections of *nous* and speech in one passage.

Fr. *67.4 (Alcmeon)*.   This fragment says: "fear ... prevents (ἀπείργω) the *nous* from speaking (λέγω) what it wishes" when one has to speak before others. *Nous* is treated as the source of words but fear keeps the person from speaking freely.

PREDOMINANTLY EMOTIONAL

Nous is sometimes associated with primarily emotional activities in earlier and contemporary poetry. It is connected with anger (*Il.* 9.554), courage (*Il.* 3.63), joy,[25] love,[26] and pain (*H.Cer.* 37). Sophocles associates it with pain at *Ant.* 767 when the Chorus say that the *nous* of a young person "feels pain deeply." Euripides relates *nous* to two emotions.

Fear

Fr. *67.4 (Alcmeon)*.   As we heard above under "Speech," fear (φόβος) can keep a person from speaking "what *nous* wishes." Fear impedes *nous* and prevents its expression.

Love

Tr. 988.   Hecuba upbraids Helen about her response to Paris: "my son is outstanding in beauty and your *nous*, seeing (ἰδών) him, was made Kypris." As at [*Hel.* 122], we have here a reference to *nous* "seeing." As a result of what it sees, it is transformed into "Kypris." Hecuba goes on to explain what she means by this description: "for all foolish things (μῶρα) are Aphrodite for mortals, and the name rightly of foolishness (ἀφροσύνη) rules the goddess." When *nous* becomes Kypris, it becomes "foolishness." Helen's actions lacked all good sense as her *nous* was filled with love.

Tr. 1052.   Hecuba tries to keep Menelaus from taking Helen home. She warns him: "there is not a lover who does not always love." He answers: "that depends on how the *nous* of lovers (ἐρώμενοι) turns out (ἐκβαίνω)." Menelaus suggests that, if the *nous* of lovers has not been true, the love may not last.[27] *Nous* here acts as the seat of the true feelings of a person.

PREDOMINANTLY MORAL

In earlier and contemporary poets, but not in Aeschylus and Sophocles, *nous* is frequently associated with moral activity. It is related to admirable moral behaviour.[28] It itself can be "good" (ἀγαθός, ἐσθλός).[29] It is connected also with negative moral behaviour.[30] It is specifically associated with pride,[31] justice,[32] and injustice.[33] Euripides refers to this type of connection of *nous* in two passages.

Goodness

Tr. 652.   As discussed above under "Mind," Andromache says that she worked to keep a fair reputation: "having *nous* as a good (χρηστός) teacher at home, I sufficed for myself." Here *nous* contributes to admirable moral behaviour. It serves as a "good teacher," leading Andromache to act well.

Justice

IA 334.   As discussed also under "Mind," in this passage Menelaus tells Agamemnon: "a *nous* which is not firm (βέβαιος) is an unjust (ἄδικον) possession and not clear to its friends." Menelaus sees in a "weak" or "unstable" *nous* the seeds of injustice. Agamemnon himself is acting unjustly towards both Iphigenia and the Argives. Ideally, *nous* would be "firm" and a "just possession."

EURIPIDEAN USES

We have now seen how often Euripides uses *nous* in traditional and contemporary contexts. We shall now look at new ways in which he refers to this psychic entity.

KINDS OF *NOUS*

Euripides uses two adjectives found also in traditional and contemporary poetry, namely ἐμός (Fr. 144) and σός (*And.* 237). Within traditional and contemporary contexts, he introduces several new uses, as Table 4.1 shows.

Table 4.1
Nous: Traditional and Contemporary Contexts

Adjective or participle	Passage	Meaning	Context
βέβαιος	*IA* 334	firm, steady	Mind
ἰδών	*Tr.* 988	seeing	Love
λεπτός	*Med.* 529	subtle	Mind

Table 4.2
Nous in Wider Contexts

Adjective or participle	Passage	Meaning
ἐλεύθερος	[*Hel.* 731]	free
ἐμπεσών	*Hel.* 1015	falling

Twice Euripides places *nous* in a wider context than found before, as Table 4.2 shows. In the questionable passage, *Hel.* 731, a slave refers to his *nous* as "free." Sophocles likewise mentions a "free" *nous* (Fr. 940). With this adjective we find a new feature of *nous*. In *Hel.* 1015 we hear of a *nous* "falling into eternal aether" after death. This image of *nous* (to be discussed below) is likewise a new one.

DIVINE ASPECT

In three passages Euripides speaks of *nous* in an unusual way. It is possible that he reflects current philosophical discussions and, in particular, the ideas of Anaxagoras, for whom *nous* was the divine principle.[34]

Hel. 1014. Theonoë agrees to save Menelaus to protect her father's honour. She suggests that he would have reunited Helen and Menelaus. She then makes a general philosophical statement: "For there is recompense (τίσις) for these deeds to all people, both those below and those above. The *nous* of the dead (κατθανόντων) does not live (ζάω) but it has (ἔχω) immortal judgment (γνώμη), as it falls (ἐμπεσών) into eternal aether." *Nous* apparently loses the awareness it had of an early life but possesses an "immortal judgment" as it takes up its abode in "eternal aether."[35] To this *nous*, existing after death, deeds done on earth are somehow relevant.[36] Because there is some form of "recompense,"

Theonoë is determined to act justly. Euripides in this passage may describe the priestess as offering views that match her name. She is "Theonoë": "of divine *nous*." Her belief is that *nous* has an immortal existence after death.

Tr. 886.   When Menelaus announces his intention to take Helen home, Hecuba utters a prayer: "O support of earth and having your throne on earth, whoever you are, most difficult to discern, Zeus, whether necessity of nature or *nous* of mortals, I invoke you. For travelling through a soundless path, you guide all mortal affairs in justice." As in the views of Anaxagoras, where the *nous* of human beings is a share in the divine *nous* that guides the universe,[37] so here we find the suggestion that the human *nous* is a share of the divine. Thus Euripides presents an aspect of the divine *nous* as present in human beings.

Fr. 1018 (Incerta).   This fragment reads: "for our *nous* is (εἰμι) in each a god (θεός)." The idea presented here seems to be similar to that of *Tr.* 886. It resembles also what Pindar says at *Nem.* 6.5: "in some way we are similar either in great *noos* or nature to the gods." In this fragment of Euripides we find again the suggestion that the human *nous* has a divine aspect.

EURIPIDEAN IMAGES

Euripides uses two images with *nous*, as follows.

ARCHERY

Hec. 603.   With regard to *phrēn*, we encountered the image of its "good sense sending forth all its arrows" (*And.* 365). At 603 Hecuba mentions the comments that her *nous* "has shot forth (τοξεύω) in vain." We have the image of *nous* having "arrows" that it can discharge. In this case, in Hecuba's view, they have failed to hit their mark. The image of archery in both these passages suggests a strong similarity within them of *phrēn* and *nous*.

SIGHT

[Hel. 122, Tr. 988.]   In the first passage, the *nous* of Teucer "sees" (ὁράω) Helen at Troy. In the second passage, Helen's *nous* is described as "seeing" (ἰδών) Paris. In both cases *nous* is given a capacity of inner vision even though the Helen at Troy was only a wraith (*Hel.* 122).[38]

RELATIONSHIP OF PERSON AND NOUS

Nous appears in our extant evidence of Euripides 43 times. In earlier and contemporary poets, a person appears to remain distinct from *nous*.[39] What is the situation with Euripides?

Appendix One lists all the instances of *nous* analysed in terms of the relationship between this psychic entity and the individual. With this Appendix as a guide, we can say the following about *nous*.

1 *Nous* appears 20 times as either active or present in a person (Category A). In 5 passages it is active. It "sees" ([*Hel.* 122], *Tr.* 988), for example, or it "falls into eternal aether" (*Hel.* 1014). In 15 passages it is described in some way. For instance, it is often "present" (*And.* 231) or "absent" (*Hipp.* 920).[40] It can be "subtle" (529) or "not firm" (*IA* 334).
2 Only once do we hear of someone acting in *nous*, and this passage is suspect (Category B). At *Or.* 909 someone "plans" in *nous*.
3 In 18 passages a person has a direct relationship with *nous* (Category C). Of these, 15 describe someone "having" *nous*.[41]
4 We do not have any instances of a person described in relation to *nous*.
5 In 3 passages an outside object or agent affects *nous* (Categories E and F).

The detailed overview of passages given in Appendix One and briefly summarized here suggests that Euripides is traditional in his way of looking at the relationship of person and *nous*. Person and *nous* seem to be separate entities. *Nous* has a strong impact on how a person behaves. As with *phrēn*, Euripides' usage resembles most closely that of Homer. He too describes *nous* most often as either a psychic entity present and active in a person or as a psychic entity that someone affects. Both Homer and Euripides speak often of *nous* as a psychic entity that people "have." Neither refers to *nous* very frequently as a location or means.

In Euripides we see that *nous* is a distinct presence within the person. Its nature strongly influences what people do. *Nous* of a positive kind is greatly desired. If it is of a negative form or if it is absent, the person behaves foolishly or badly. Euripides suggests that *nous* may be a portion of the divine. As such, it is a most valuable possession within.

OVERVIEW OF NOUS

Our discussion of the occurrences of *nous* in Euripides allows us to make the following observations.

SPECIFIC FEATURES OF *NOUS*

1 Only the singular of *nous* is found, always in the form "*nous*."
2 On a continuum of "physical" to "psychological," *nous* appears to lie at the "psychological" end.
3 *Nous* changes over a lifetime. It may be "absent" in the old (*Bacc.* 252, Fr. 25).

4 *Nous* appears most often in intellectual contexts. As "mind," it can be positive in nature (*Hec.* 603, e.g., *Med.* 529).

5 Sometimes *nous* signifies "attention" (*Ion* 1370, e.g., *Pho.* 360).

6 Very often *nous* signifies "intelligence." It is something that people ought to "have" (*Hipp.* 105, e.g., *IA* 374).

7 *Nous* can be associated with speech.

8 *Nous* is connected with the emotions of fear (Fr. 67.4) and love (*Tr.* 988, 1052).

9 In moral contexts *nous* is associated with goodness (*Tr.* 652) and justice (*IA* 334).

10 We do not hear of the gods affecting the *nous* of human beings. Nor do we hear of the *nous* of the gods.

11 Euripides introduces new descriptions of *nous* in traditional and contemporary contexts (see Table 4.1). He offers new descriptions of *nous* (see Table 4.2) as "free" ([*Hel.* 731]) and "falling into eternal aether" (*Hel.* 1015).

12 Euripides introduces new references to *nous* related to divinity. Zeus may be the "*nous* of mortals" (*Tr.* 886). In each human being *nous* is a "god" (Fr. 1018). *Nous* has "immortal judgment, as it falls into eternal aether" (*Hel.* 1014).

13 With respect to relationships of person and *nous*, Euripides' use appears to be quite traditional. The two remain distinct.

GENERAL FEATURES OF *NOUS*

In his usage of *nous* Euripides appears on the whole to resemble that of earlier and contemporary poets. Apart from his references to possible divine aspects of *nous*, he refers to this psychic entity in traditional and contemporary ways. In his number of references to *nous*, Euripides is similar to Sophocles.[42] Both dramatists refer much more often to *phrēn*. Passages in Euripides show *nous* as a psychic entity of great value within the person. Ideally it is "present" or the person "has" it. People call for its attention. If it is of a negative kind, it can harm both the individual in whom it is found and the state. Unlike *phrēn*, it does not appear to engage in pondering or deliberation. Its function is related instead to inner vision and what it "sees" seems to be real or true. As such, it can significantly affect how characters within the dramas behave.

PRAPIDES

This psychic entity does not appear very often in early Greek poetry. We hear of *prapides* 11 times in Homer, 7 in Hesiod, and 9 in Pindar.[43] *Prapides* are not mentioned in the lyric and elegiac poets nor in Sophocles. Aeschylus refers to them only three times. In function they closely resemble *phrenes*. They are associated with intellectual activity and also with a range of emotions (grief, e.g., pain, joy). A person usually acts in harmony with *prapides*; they are often a location that people act in or an instrument they use. Euripides mentions *prapides* five times.

INTELLIGENCE

And. 480.   As the Chorus remark on the difficulties caused by two wives, they say: "when swift breezes carry sailors, a double judgment (γνώμα) of *prapides* at the helm (πηδάλιος) and a combined throng of wise men is weaker than a more paltry *phrēn* that has full authority." Here *prapides* are mentioned with *phrēn* in this nautical image. The two seem to be very close in meaning. Euripides refers to "*gnōmē* of *prapides*" – that is, their "practical judgment." Even if this is present twice over, it is of less value than a "more paltry" *phrēn* that is in command. *Prapides* and *phrēn* are connected here with decision on how to guide or direct. Euripides introduces a new adjective with *prapides*: "at the helm" (πηδάλιος). He presents them also in a nautical image. In this he resembles Aeschylus, who speaks of a "helm" (οἴαξ) of *phrenes* at *Ag.* 802.

Bacc. 427.   In this passage the Chorus say that Dionysus hates the individual for whom certain things are not a "care," namely "to live a happy life ... and to keep a wise (σοφός) *prapis* and *phrēn* from excessive mortals." As in *And.* 480, *prapis* and *phrēn* are mentioned together and seem to be close in meaning. The adjective σοφός probably goes with both nouns and is one found of *prapides* also in Pin., *Ol.* 11.10. Dionysus approves the person who, with intelligence, avoids people given to excess. *Prapis* acts as a location here of good judgment.

Fr. 27.2 (Aiolos).   This fragment reads: "surely the strength of a man is small. But with versatility (ποικιλία) of *prapides* he conquers the terrible tribes of the sea and the offspring of earth and air." Euripides introduces a new noun with *prapides*: "versatility" (ποικιλία). With their capacity for complicated thinking, *prapides* allow human beings to master other living creatures.

Fr. 901.1 (Incerta).   This fragment describes a "thought (φροντίς) coming (διέρχομαι)" to someone in *prapides* concerning whether chance governs human affairs. Here we see *prapides* as a seat of consideration.

MIND

Bacc. 999.   The Chorus remark as they see Pentheus leave to observe the Bacchants (997–1001): "who with unjust purpose (ἀδίκῳ γνώμᾳ) and lawless mood (παρανόμῳ ὀργᾷ) ... is sent with raging (μανεῖσα) *prapis* and frantic spirit (παράκοπος λῆμα), as about to conquer the invincible with force."[44]

Here *prapis* is called "raging," associated with madness sent by Dionysus. We heard also in the *Bacchae* of *phrēn* being "frantic" (παράκοπος), the adjective used here of λῆμα (33). Twice also "distance" from *phrenes* indicates a mad state (850, 1270). *Prapis*, like *phrenes*, appears to be distorted as madness descends. Euripides introduces a new participle with *prapis*: μανεῖσα. In this description of Pentheus he uses four nouns to suggest the intensity of his maddened state: *gnōmē*, *orgē*, *prapis*, and *lēma*. *Prapis*, in particular, suggests his disordered thinking.

In these five references to *prapides* (two singular, three plural), Euripides ascribes a broad range of function to this psychic entity. *Prapides* appear to be similar to *phrenes* as seat of intelligence. They can "guide;" they have "versatility;" they have "wisdom." They can be a seat of "thought." *Prapis*, however, can also become "maddened." Euripides' use of *prapides*, like that of *nous*, seems in large part to be traditional and contemporary. With both psychic terms he introduces new features, but, generally speaking, his use of them is a familiar one.

5 *Thumos* in the Tragedies

In this chapter we shall examine how Euripides refers to *thumos*. This psychic entity appears 30 times, similar in frequency to *nous* (43) and *kardia* (35) but far less than *phrēn* (160). It occurs in thirteen tragedies; it is not found in the *Hel.*, *Ion*, *IT*, or *Tr.* As before, we shall discuss in particular how traditional or new Euripides' usage is.

TRADITIONAL AND CONTEMPORARY USES (WITH EURIPIDEAN FEATURES)

Euripides shows us *thumos* as a psychic entity with a broad range of function.[1] In this usage Euripides resembles traditional and contemporary poets.

PREDOMINANTLY INTELLECTUAL

Seat of Mind

And. 1072. As the Messenger arrives to announce the death of Neoptolemus, Peleus says: "alas, my prophetic (πρόμαντις) *thumos*, how it expects (προσδοκάω) some [disaster]!" In earlier and contemporary poets we once hear Zeus "boding evils (ὄσσομαι) in his *thumos* for mortals" (Hes., *Theog.* 551). Aeschylus at *Per.* 10 has the Chorus say: "my *thumos*, prophesying evil (κακόμαντις), is greatly troubled within." In a similar way Euripides pictures *thumos* in distress, "expecting" evils. He uses a new adjective with *thumos*: "prophetic" (πρόμαντις). *Thumos* has forebodings of the bad news Peleus is to hear.

El. 578.   After the Old Man has given proofs of who Orestes truly is, Electra hastens to embrace her brother: "for I am persuaded (πείθω) by your signs (σύμβολον)." In Homer, *thumos* frequently appears with πείθω, as it does occasionally too in Hesiod and the lyric poets.[2] *Thumos* here functions as a seat of the mind, but clearly emotion is present as Electra realizes that Orestes has come home.

PREDOMINANTLY EMOTIONAL

Seat of Emotion

In three passages *thumos* appears to be generally regarded as a seat of emotion within the person. Aeschylus refers to *thumos* in this way when he speaks of "*phrenes* steering *thumos*" (*Per.* 767) and when he mentions the "implacable *thumos*" of Clytemnestra (*Choe.* 422).[3]

[Med. 1056, 1079].   These lines fall within the speech of Medea, just before she kills her children. Diggle in the *OCT* brackets lines 1056–80; Kovacs in the new Loeb, 1056–64. These lines have been much discussed, especially with regard to their being a possible criticism by Euripides of Socrates' idea that no one would knowingly choose to do evil.[4] Here we shall look at them as being possibly authentic, with a focus simply upon how *thumos* is pictured in them.

   In line 1056 Medea addresses *thumos* directly: "do not, *thumos*, do not do (ἐργάζω) these things." Here we find the vocative of *thumos*. This vocative does not appear in Homer or Hesiod but becomes quite common in the lyric and elegiac poets and in Pindar.[5] In Homer we do not find this form of direct address but we do hear quite often of someone "speaking to *thumos*."[6] Medea locates the motivating force of her intended actions in her *thumos*. Part of her does not wish for this *thumos* to have control, and she can urge it not to act.

   In 1079 Medea says: "I understand what evils (κακά) I am about to do but *thumos* is stronger (κρείσσων) than my plans (βουλεύματα), *thumos* which is responsible (αἴτιος) for the greatest evils (κακά) for mortals." Medea here separates her inner nature into two parts, namely *thumos* and "plans" (βουλεύματα), the latter suggesting some rational and considered activity. These "plans" appear to be different from those she mentions in 1044 and 1048, which she identifies with her intent to slay her children. Here she appears to indicate by "*bouleumata*" simply the capacity for rational thought. *Thumos*, which in Medea is filled with anger and desire for revenge on her enemies (1049–51), proves "stronger" than this rational capacity. She fully recognizes that what *thumos* is driving her to do is evil. She specifies this by describing her *thumos*, one that is filled with passion, as the cause of the "greatest evils for human beings."

These two passages, if they are authentic, present a powerful picture of the force of *thumos*. It is seen as a seat of emotion that drives Medea to act. It is described as being stronger than rational thinking. It victimizes the person and works only ill.[7] *Thumos* appears to be a psychic entity that is distinct from Medea. It is active within, driving her to make choices in opposition to her "plans" and leading to "evils." By this psychic entity Medea feels carried away.

[Or. 702].   Menelaus, as he advises Orestes how to win over the Argives, says: "in them is pity; in them is great (μέγας) *thumos*, a most valued possession to one anxiously waiting." Euripides here uses a traditional adjective with *thumos*: "great" (μέγας). We hear of this type of *thumos* in Homer (see, e.g., *Il.* 2.196), Archilochus (98.16 W), and Tyrtaeus (10.17 W). *Thumos* in this passage is a positive presence as a seat of emotion. There is a bountiful spirit within the Argives that Orestes can trust; it may suffice to bring him pardon for killing Clytemnestra.

Anger

Most frequently *thumos* in Euripides signifies "anger" or "rage." This emotion was probably present in the two instances of *thumos* at *Med.* 1056 and 1079 treated above. Aeschylus uses *thumos* to signify "anger" when he speaks of "bitter *thumos* blowing from *kardia*" (*Choe.* 393). In Sophocles *thumos* in 17 of 35 instances appear to be a seat of "anger." Creon, Heracles, and Oedipus in particular are filled with *thumos*, "rage" or "anger" (*Ant.* 718, *Tr.* 1118, *O.C.* 434).

Bacc. 620.   Dionysus describes the emotional state in which Pentheus tried to chain him up: "he would pen me ... breathing out (ἐκπνέω) *thumos*, dripping sweat from his body, gnawing his lips."[8] Here Euripides presents an image of "breath" with *thumos*.[9] Early usage of *thumos* may suggest that its basic meaning is associated with that of "breath" or "wind."[10] Aeschylus twice uses such an image. At *Sept.* 52 *thumos* "breathes" (ἐκπνέω); at *Choe.* 393, it "blows from the prow of *kardia*." Euripides pictures Pentheus as "breathing out" fury against Dionysus.

Hec. 1055.   Hecuba says that she will withdraw from the presence of Polymestor. "I will go out of the way and stand aside from his boiling (ζέων), Thracian (Θρᾷξ) *thumos*, most difficult to fight against (δυσμαχώτατος)." Sophocles describes Oedipus' *thumos* as "boiling" (ζέω) after he learns his identity (*O.C.* 434). So here Euripides presents the same image of Polymestor in his rage. Plato later describes *thumos* as having its name "from the storming (θύσις) and boiling (ζέσις) of the *psychē*" (*Crat.* 419 e). Once *thumos* gets into a "boiling" condition, it is most difficult to resist.

IA 125.   Agamemnon tells the Old Servant to write a letter asking for Iphigenia to come to be Achilles' bride. The Servant protests: "and how will Achilles, being greatly indignant (μέγα φυσῶν) over his lost bride, not raise (ἐπαίρω) *thumos* against you and your wife?" Here Euripides presents an image of *thumos* being "raised" or "lifted."[11] *Thumos* appears in this passage to be "anger" in Achilles, an emotion in that hero which all knew to fear.

Med. 879, 1152.   In the first passage, Medea, trying to conciliate Jason, asks: "shall I not be released (ἀπαλλάσσω) from *thumos*?" She suggests that she could be freed from the "anger" that consumes her. In the second passage, Jason urges his new wife, as she catches sight of his children: "cease (παύω) from your *thumos*." At *Ant.* 718 Sophocles has Haemon urge Creon: "yield (εἴκω) from your *thumos*." So here the princess is to stop being "angry" at her step-children.

Pho. 454.   Jocasta urges Eteocles not to react violently to the presence of Polyneices: "check your terrible look and breaths (πνοή) of *thumos*." Again, as in *Bacc.* 620 above, we find an image of the "breath" of *thumos*. Eteocles is making his anger evident, showing it in his very breathing.[12]

Supp. 556.   Theseus, giving advice on how human beings should act, says: "it is necessary, if we are treated unjustly, to endure moderately, not with *thumos*." Human beings may be tempted to show "anger" in unjust circumstances, but that behaviour is not positive. *Thumos* here is seen as an emotion that should be checked.

Courage

IA 919.   At *IA* 125 we heard the fear expressed that Achilles' *thumos*, "anger," might be "raised" if he lost his bride. At 919 Achilles himself refers to his own *thumos*, but in a positive way: "my lofty-spirited (ὑψηλόφρων) *thumos* is lifted (αἴρω) on high." Euripides introduces a new adjective with *thumos*: "lofty-spirited."[13] *Thumos* appears here to be a seat of courage. *Thumos* is frequently associated with this emotion in earlier and contemporary poets.[14] Aeschylus speaks of the Argives as having a "*thumos*, iron-minded, blazing with courage" (*Sept.* 52). In Sophocles, Teucer has a *thumos* that is "terrible" (δεινός) in its daring (*Aj.* 1124). Achilles describes his *thumos* as one that is eager to save the life of Iphigenia.

Med. 865. The Chorus ask Medea how she will be able to kill her children. They tell her: "you will not be able, as your children fall to pray, to stain your murderous hand with bold (τλήμων) *thumos*." Euripides here uses a traditional adjective with *thumos*: "bold" or "daring" (τλήμων).[15] *Thumos* is the seat of boldness in Medea. It will need to be of a "daring" nature for such a horrendous deed to be committed. As we heard above under "Seat of Emotion," Medea calls upon *thumos* to stop its activity (1056), but her *thumos* has been victorious (1079).

Desire

Four times *thumos* is connected with desire in Euripides. We find this association often in earlier and contemporary poets.[16] Aeschylus does not mention *thumos* with this meaning, but Sophocles does twice. Electra tells Orestes to speak as "his *thumos* is" to him (*El.* 1319). Oedipus at *O.C.* 778 describes a *thumos* "full" of what one "desires."

El. 177. When the Chorus tell Electra of a coming festival, she responds: "not for adornments, my friends, not for golden chains am I set aflutter (ἐκποτάομαι) in *thumos*."[17] Twice in the lyric and elegiac poets we find a similar picture of *thumos*. Alcaeus says that either Paris or Kypris "set aflutter" (πτοέω) the *thumos* of Helen (283.4). Theognis says that the *thumos* and *nous* of "those who are maddened flutter about (πέτομαι)" (1053).

Hipp. 1087, 1328. Hippolytus at 1087 tells Theseus to cast him from the land if "*thumos* is such" to him. At 1328 Artemis says that Kypris, "fulfilling (ἀπαντάω) her *thumos*," willed the events that took place to happen. In both these instances *thumos* is a seat of desire within the person.

Med. 310. Medea, as she speaks in a conciliating way to Creon, tells him: "you married your daughter to whom your *thumos* led (ἄγω) you." Once again *thumos* was the location of desire within Creon.

Hope

In one passage *thumos* is associated with hope. This is a connection found frequently in Homer but not in other early poets.[18] Aeschylus at *Ag.* 992 speaks of a *thumos* that does not have the "confidence of hope." Sophocles does not associate *thumos* with hope.

Supp. 480. The Herald tells Theseus: "hope (ἐλπίς) is an untrustworthy thing, which has engaged many cities in conflict, leading *thumos* into excesses (ὑπερβολή)." When people become too hopeful, their *thumos* expands and leads to excessive behaviour. Hope, however, may prove illusory.

Love

In earlier and contemporary poets we find frequent mentions of *thumos* and love.[19] Neither Aeschylus nor Sophocles relates *thumos* to love. Euripides here does so twice.

Med. 8.   The Nurse describes Medea before she came to Greece as "smitten (ἐκπλήσσω) in *thumos* with love (ἔρος) of Jason." As in Alcaeus 283.9, Theognis 1321, and Pindar, Frs. 123.1 and 127.4, œroj is here mentioned as afflicting Medea's *thumos*. The verb ἐκπλήσσω suggests the intensity of emotion in *thumos*.

Med. 640.   In their ode on love the Chorus say: "may terrible Kypris never cast contentious tempers (ὀργά) and insatiable quarrels, striking (ἐκπλήσσω) my *thumos* for other beds." Here Euripides once again uses the verb ἐκπλήσσω to describe the presence of strong emotion in *thumos*. The Chorus wish to feel no strong attraction outside their own marriages.

Pain

A frequent association of *thumos* in earlier and contemporary poetry is that of "distress" or "pain."[20] Aeschylus describes *thumos* as "greatly troubled" (ὀρσολοπέω) at *Per.* 10 and speaks of "things that are painful goads stirring up *thumos*" at *Supp.* 448. Euripides twice connects *thumos* with pain.

Hipp. 1114.   The Chorus, after Hippolytus has been sent into exile, pray: "would that to me, as I pray, fate might give these things from the gods, fortune with blessedness and a *thumos* unmixed (ἀκηρατός) with pains (ἄλγος)." Here *thumos* in a desired state is free from "pains" or "distress."

Fr. 1039 (Incerta).   This fragments reads: "the *thumos* in pain (ἀλγῶν) does not have stability (ἀσφάλεια)." Euripides introduces a new noun with *thumos*: "stability" or "secureness" (ἀσφάλεια). If *thumos* is not in pain, it can act as some form of steady strength. When it is in pain, it lacks any "sureness."

Passion

In some passages *thumos* may indicate chiefly "anger," as in those we have discussed above. In others it may have this meaning and also a wider one of "passion." This happens in certain passages of Sophocles, especially, for example, in *O.C.* 434 and 438. It is true of the following four passages of Euripides.

HF 1211.   After Heracles had murdered his children, Amphitryon urges him: "o son, check (κατέχω) the *thumos* of a fierce lion, by which you are setting out on a murderous, unholy course, wishing to bind evils to evils, my son." In earlier and contemporary poets we hear of the "*thumos* of a lion." Homer does not mention such but does call Heracles θυμολέων (*Il.* 5.639, *Od.* 11.267). Hesiod refers to a "lion that has a shameless *thumos*" (*Theog.* 833). Sappho, Tyrtaeus, Simonides, and Bacchylides mention the "*thumos* of a lion."[21] Aeschylus compares the *thumos* of the Argives ready for battle to that "of lions" (*Sept.* 52). In this passage of Euripides, passion is overwhelming Heracles as he considers suicide. Amphitryon urges him to restrain this onrush of emotion.

Med. 108.   In her speech to the children of Medea, the Nurse urges them: "go quickly inside. It is clear that a cloud of lamentation (οἰμωγή), arising from the beginning, will quickly flare up (ἀνάπτω) with greater (μείζων) *thumos*. Whatever will her *psychē*, high-spirited, most hard to check, do as it is bitten with evils?" At 104 the Nurse had warned the children against Medea's "fierce character and the hateful nature of her self-willed *phrēn*."[22] These current lines show that the Nurse also fears the *psychē* of Medea.[23] With regard to *thumos*, she uses an image of a storm. A "cloud of grief" is present but will soon blow up into a full storm, one accompanied by "greater" passion or anger.

Fr. 257 (Archelaus).   This fragment reads: "the great (μέγας) *thumos* has destroyed (ὄλλυμι) many mortals and want of understanding (ἀξυνεσία), for those using two evils." Two negative things are described here: "great passions" or "anger" and "lack of understanding." As at [*Or.* 702], *thumos* here is called "great" (μέγας). In that passage its connotation was positive; in this fragment it is negative. *Thumos*, in excess, linked with foolishness, brings about the destruction of many.

Fr. 718 (Telephus).   This fragment says: "it is time for you to have judgment (γνώμη) stronger than *thumos*."[24] Here we find a description of what may be the best situation for human beings: *gnōmē* should rule and be "stronger than *thumos*."[25] We can contrast this description with that of *Med.* 1079, when she says that her "*thumos* is stronger (κρείσσων) than her plans (βουλεύματα)."[26] In Fr. 718 *thumos* appears to be a seat of passion; it should be brought under the control of rational thinking.

PREDOMINANTLY MORAL

In earlier and contemporary poets *thumos* is associated quite often with negative moral behaviour.[27] This is the case also in Sophocles. At *Ant.* 493 Sophocles relates *thumos* to the activity of "those who plan nothing uprightly in the dark." At *Aj.* 655 he refers to one "who exults maliciously in his dark-faced *thumos.*" With respect specifically to injustice we find *thumos* thus related only once: Hesiod urges Perses to "restrain his flighty *thumos* from unjust deeds" (*W. & D.* 335). Euripides connects *thumos* with injustice in one passage.

Hcld. 925.   The Messenger says of Athena: "she checked the *hybris* of a man whose *thumos* was violent (βίαιος) at the cost of justice (δίκη)." Here Euripides introduces a new adjective with *thumos*: "violent" or "forceful" (βίαιος).[28] This type of *thumos* led Eurystheus to behave in an unjust fashion.

GODS

We hear only once of the *thumos* of a goddess in Euripides. At *Hipp.* 1328 Kypris "fulfils her *thumos*" (see above, "Desire").

EURIPIDEAN USES

Our analysis of the 30 passages where *thumos* appears in our extant Euripides has shown that his usage is primarily traditional and contemporary. We find new aspects of *thumos* introduced only with regard to kinds of *thumos*.

KINDS OF *THUMOS*

With regard to adjectives with *thumos*, Euripides uses four that are found in earlier and contemporary poets: κρείσσων, μέγας, μείζων, and τλήμων, as detailed in Appendix Three. He introduces some new adjectives with *thumos* in contexts that are traditional and contemporary, as Table 5.1 shows.

Three times Euripides places *thumos* in a wider context than found before, as Table 5.2 shows.[29] In *Med.* 1079 we find Medea's statement that *thumos* is "responsible" for the greatest evils for mortals.[30] The adjective suggests an expanded role of *thumos*: it can harm people. In *Hcld.* 925 the adjective βίαιος is new with *thumos*. It too suggests the power of *thumos* to do harm. Fr. 362.34 (*Erechtheus*) reads: "for a womanly minded *thumos* does not belong in a wise man." Euripides introduces a new adjective here

Table 5.1
Thumos: Traditional and Contemporary Contexts

Adjective or participle	Passage	Meaning	Context
ἀκήρατος	*Hipp.* 1114	unmixed	Pain
ἀλγῶν	Fr. 1039 Incerta	in pain	Pain
δυσμαχώτατος	*Hec.* 1055	most difficult to fight	Anger
ζέων	*Hec.* 1055	boiling	Anger
πρόμαντις	*And.* 1072	prophetic	Seat of Mind
ὑψηλόφρων	*IA* 919	lofty-minded	Courage

Table 5.2
Thumos in Wider Contexts

Adjective or participle	Passage	Meaning
αἴτιος	[*Med.* 1079]	responsible
βίαιος	*Hcld.* 925	violent
γυναικόφρων	Fr. 362.34 *Erechtheus*	womanly-minded

with *thumos*: "womanly-minded."[31] The context is one in which restraint in showing affection is praised. Clearly a woman's *thumos* is not slow to show emotion.

EURIPIDEAN IMAGES

From the passages discussed above we shall describe three major images that Euripides uses.

"BREATH"

Bacc. 620, Pho. 454.   In the first passage Pentheus "breathes out *thumos*." In the second Eteocles is to check his "breaths of *thumos*." As mentioned above, *thumos* has been associated in its original meaning with "breath" or "wind."[32] In both passages *thumos*, signifying "anger," is connected to strong breathing of some kind.[33]

"LION"

HF 1211.   Heracles is to restrain "the *thumos* of a fierce lion." Euripides adopts an image familiar in earlier poetry.[34] Heracles' passion is bursting forth and is in need of curbing.

"STORM"

Med. 108.   The Nurse warns about Medea: "it is clear that a cloud (νέφος) of lamentation, arising from the beginning, will quietly flare up (ἀνάπτω) with greater *thumos*." A storm of lamentation is gathering, and it will be accompanied by "greater" passion and anger, like strong blasts of wind.

RELATIONSHIP OF PERSON AND THUMOS

As with *phrēn* and *nous,* Euripides appears with *thumos* to present a traditional picture of the relationship of person and that psychic entity.[35] Person and *thumos* appear to be distinct. Appendix One presents a detailed picture of this relationship. We can summarize the occurrences of *thumos* as follows.

1 Thumos appears 14 times as either active or described in a person (Category A). Four times it is active. It "expects" disaster (*And.* 1072), "leads" (*Med.* 310), and "destroys" (Fr. 257). Once it is addressed in the vocative and urged not to "act" ([*Med.* 1056]). In 10 passages it is described in some way. Thus we learn, for example, of a "lofty-spirited *thumos* lifted on high" (*IA* 919), "breaths of *thumos*" (*Pho.* 454), and a "*thumos* in pain" without stability (Fr. 1039).
2 Three times a person acts with *thumos* (Category B). One can do so simply "with *thumos*" (*Supp.* 556) or with "greater" or "bold" *thumos* (*Med.* 108, 865).
3 In 5 passages an individual has a direct relationship with *thumos* (Category C). One can "breathe out" (*Bacc.* 620), "check" (*HF* 1211), "fulfil" (*Hipp.* 1328), "raise" (*IA* 125) and "cease from" (*Med.* 1152) *thumos*.
4 In 4 passages an individual is described in relation to *thumos* (Category D). Electra is not "set aflutter in *thumos*" but she is "persuaded" in it (*El.* 177, 578). Medea is "smitten with love" in *thumos* and is desirous of being "released" from it (*Med.* 8, 879).
5 In 4 passages an outside object or agent acts upon *thumos* (Categories E and F).

The detailed overview of passages given in Appendix One and briefly summarized here suggests that Euripides treats person and psychic entity as distinct. This seems to be particularly the case when Medea urges her *thumos* not to "act" ([*Med.* 1056]) and when she owns herself defeated by it ([*Med.* 1079]). Both these lines are bracketed in the OCT but, if they are genuine, they suggest that Medea has her *thumos* as forcefully active within her and something distinct from herself.

Thumos occupies a prominent place within a person. Mentions of *thumos* include for the early Greeks the fused aspects of what we term "agent" and "function."[36] We see this characteristic in particular with *thumos*: it is seat of emotion and emotion itself. Unlike *phrēn* and *nous*, whose presence is considered valuable, *thumos* can be a negative presence in a person.[37] Thus, of the 30 occurrences in Euripides, 5 appear in positive contexts,[38] 4 in neutral contexts,[39] and the remaining 21 in negative contexts.[40] A person must be very aware of the presence of *thumos* within and yield to or resist its activities.

OVERVIEW OF THUMOS

We can make the following observations based on our discussion of *thumos*.

SPECIFIC FEATURES OF THUMOS

1 Only the singular of *thumos* occurs.
2 On a continuum of "physical" to "psychological," *thumos* appears to lie chiefly at the psychological end. In references to a "boiling" *thumos* (*Hec.* 1055) and to "breaths" of *thumos* (*Bacc.* 620, *Pho.* 454) we may have "physical" aspects of *thumos* present.
3 Unlike *phrēn* and *nous*, we do not hear of *thumos* changing with age.
4 *Thumos* appears twice as a seat of the mind (*And.* 1072, *El.* 578).
5 Most often *thumos* is a seat of emotion or an emotion itself. We find a wide range of emotions associated with *thumos*. These include anger, courage, desire, hope, love, pain, and passion. Of these, anger is most prominent.
6 *Thumos* appears once in a passage with a "moral" connotation. It is related to injustice at *Hcld.* 925.
7 We hear once of a *thumos* of a goddess, that of Kypris (*Hipp.* 1328).
8 Euripides introduces new descriptions of *thumos* in traditional and contemporary contexts (see Table 5.1). He also speaks of *thumos* in wider contexts (see Table 5.2) when he calls it "responsible" for evils ([*Med.* 1079]), "violent" (*Hcld.* 925), and "womanly minded" (Fr. 362.34).
9 Euripides uses *thumos* in images of "breath," "lion," and "storm."
10 With respect to relationship of person and *thumos*, Euripides appears to treat them as distinct. In this, he appears to be quite traditional in his usage.

GENERAL FEATURES OF *THUMOS*

As noted above, Euripides refers to *thumos* 30 times, far fewer than he does to *phrēn* (160) but similar to his mentions of *nous* (43). Our analysis has shown that *thumos* is particularly associated with emotion. Its presence within can sometimes be positive but is more often negative. As a seat of anger, love, pain, and passion, the impulses of *thumos* are potentially harmful to the individual. It is described as "responsible for the greatest evils for human beings" ([*Med.* 1079]) and also "destroying" them (Fr. 257). *Thumos* is a psychic entity within that people need to observe closely and to resist on some occasions, if possible. Yet it can also be positive, as a seat of courage. Euripides refers to *thumos* in ways that are primarily traditional and contemporary. He treats *thumos*, as it was seen before, as a seat of vital energy within, one that impels the individual to a range of activities.

6 *Kardia* and *Kear* in the Tragedies

In this chapter we shall discuss two words for "heart" in Euripides: *kardia*[1] and *kear*.[2] In Euripides *ētor* is not found in the extant tragedies and fragments, just as it rarely occurs in other Greek tragedy.[3] Here we see quite a change from Homer and Hesiod, where *ētor* is more common than either *kardia* or *kear*.[4] *Kardia* becomes more common than *ētor* in the lyric and elegiac poets, but *ētor* still remains prominent.[5] With regard to *kardia* and *kear*, Aeschylus refers to *kardia* 30 times and *kear* 7 times. Sophocles mentions *kardia* 6 times and *kear* 5 times.

In Euripides we find *kardia* 35 times and *kear* 3 times. In frequency *kardia* resembles *nous* (43) and *thumos* (30) but, like these two, is far less frequent than *phrēn* (160). *Kardia* appears in most plays of Euripides but not in the *And.*, *Ion*, *Pho.*, *Supp.*, and *Tr. Kear* occurs only in the *Med.* and *HF*. Once again, as with other terms, we shall examine how traditional or new Euripides' references to these terms for "heart" are.

TRADITIONAL AND CONTEMPORARY USES (WITH EURIPIDEAN FEATURES)

PREDOMINANTLY PHYSICAL

In earlier and contemporary poets *kardia* is frequently spoken of as the physical "heart."[6] In Aeschylus we hear of a "saffron-dyed drop running to *kardia*" (*Ag.* 1121). A "wave of bile stands before the *kardia*" of Electra (*Choe.* 183). Orestes speaks of "pains acting as goads" to his *kardia* (*Eum.* 466). "Poison" comes from *kardia* in the Furies (*Eum.* 782 = 812). Sophocles in

Fr. 120 speaks of the *kardia* "being squeezed" (θλίβω). Euripides refers to *kardia* in a primarily "physical" way in three passages.

Alc. 1067.   Admetus at the sight of the veiled lady, whom Heracles has led in, says: "she makes my *kardia* beat (θολόω) and from my eyes tears stream forth." Euripides uses a new verb here with *kardia*: θολόω. Literally, this verb means: "to make turbid." Admetus feels his *kardia* beating in a distressed way within.

Bacc. 1288.   Agave, realizing that she is holding Pentheus' head, hears Cadmus mention "a wretched truth that is now present." She says: "speak, for my *kardia* beats (πήδημα ἔχω) in relation to what is coming." Euripides uses the noun πήδημα here for the first time with *kardia*. Agave feels her heart beat in anticipation of dreaded news.[7]

Hipp. 841.   Theseus, as he sees the body of Phaedra, says that he wishes to hear: "whence the deadly fate (τύχα), my poor wife, came (βαίνω) against your *kardia*?" Phaedra's "heart" has ceased to beat in death.

PREDOMINANTLY EMOTIONAL

As in earlier and contemporary poets, *kardia* is most often associated with a range of emotions in Euripides. This will be particularly true of the *Medea*, where 8 of the 35 references to *kardia* occur, and 2 of the 3 instances of *kear*. In several passages *kardia* functions in a broad way as a seat of emotion.

Seat of Emotion

Hec. 242.   Hecuba asks Odysseus if he recalls the time she saved his life. He replies: "I know of this time. For it touched (ψαύω) me, not at the surface (ἄρκος) of my *kardia*." The "surface of *kardia*" would suggest an insignificant response; "not at the surface" indicates deep feeling.[8] Euripides uses ἄρκος with *kardia* for the first time. The adjective suggests the range of response of which *kardia* is capable.

Hec. 1129.   Agamemnon urges the blinded Polymestor not to wish to kill Hecuba: "casting (ἐκβάλλω) from your *kardia* this barbarous impulse (τὸ βάρβαρον)." Polymestor's anger and desire for revenge are centred in *kardia*.

Hel. 960.   Menelaus asks Theonoë for help: "what we consider worthy of ourselves and just, and in particular what will touch (ἀνθάπτω) your *kardia*, I will speak." Euripides introduces a new image of "touching" *kardia*. Words are to affect Theonoë in her "heart."[9]

IA 475.   As he urges Agamemnon not to kill Iphigenia, Menelaus says: "I swear … to speak (ἐρέω) to you clearly the things from my *kardia*." Here *kardia* functions as a seat of sincerity.[10]

IA 1173.   Clytemnestra, likewise begging Agamemnon not to kill Iphigenia, asks: "what *kardia* do you think that I shall have (ἔχω) when I see all chairs empty of her, and empty her maiden-bower and in tears I sit alone, ever lamenting this one?" *Kardia* appears to be the seat of all the terrible emotions Clytemnestra will endure if her daughter is killed.

Med. 911 (kear).   Jason, believing in Medea's change of manner, says: "but your *kear* has changed (μεθίστημι) to the better (ἐς τὸ λῷον) and you recognize the superior plan, even though late in time." *Kear* here appears to be the seat of emotion in Medea. It "has changed into a better form." Perhaps, principally, it has been freed from "anger," an association *kear* has also in Homer and Sophocles.[11]

Med. 1360.   Medea's last remark to Jason after the death of her children is: "I have touched (ἀνθάπτω) your *kradia*, as was needed." The form *kradia* occurs here. As in *Hel*. 960, we find once again the image of "touching." Jason has seemed impervious to feeling, especially in regard to the way he wounded Medea. By killing their children Medea discovered a way in which to make him "feel." The location of this emotion is *kardia*.

Or. 466.   Orestes dreads the arrival of Tyndareus, the grandfather who had treated him well as a child. About his relatives he says: "o wretched (τάλας) *kardia* and my *psychē*, to them I have paid no noble return."[12] Like Sophocles at *Tr*. 651, Euripides uses a new adjective with *kardia* as he calls it "wretched." He addresses both *kardia* and *psychē* directly. This address of *kardia* is found once in Homer at *Od*. 20.18, when Odysseus speaks to his *kradiē*. Euripides will use it also at *Alc*. 837, *IT* 344, and *Med*. 1242 (to be treated below). Both *kardia* and *psychē* appear to be a seat of feeling in Orestes.

Anger

A frequent occurrence of *kardia* is as a seat of anger in early Greek poetry.[13] Aeschylus speaks of "bitter *thumos* blowing from the prow of *kradia*" (*Choe*. 392). *Thumos* probably signifies "anger" that is arising out of *kradia*. At *Choe*. 1024 Aeschylus also speaks of *kardia* "ready to dance with Anger (Κότος)." Sophocles describes Euripides' *kardia* as "angry" (θυμουμένη) at *Ant*. 1254. Twice Euripides relates *kardia* to anger.

Med. 99.   The Nurse describes Medea to her children: "your mother is stirring up (κινέω) her *kradia*, stirring up her anger (χόλος)."[14] The form *kradia* occurs here. Medea is filling her *kradia* with angry thoughts and feelings against Jason.

Med. 590.   Jason replies to Medea's suggestion that he should have got her support for the marriage with Creon's daughter: "well, I suppose, you would comply with this proposal, if I had mentioned marriage to you, who even now cannot bring yourself to set aside (μεθίστημι) the great anger (χόλος) of your *kardia*." In this passage "anger" is explicitly placed within *kardia*.

Courage

Several times in earlier and contemporary poetry we find *kardia* connected with courage.[15] Aeschylus twice related *kardia* and courage. At *Ag.* 1402 Clytemnestra has a "fearless" (ἄτρεστος) *kardia*. At *Choe.* 832 Orestes is urged to have "the *kardia* in *phrenes* of Perseus." Sophocles at *Ant.* 88 has Ismene say to Antigone: "you have a hot (θερμός) *kardia* for cold deeds." Euripides four times connects *kardia* and courage.

Alc. 837.   When Heracles is resolved to save Alcestis, he says: "o *kardia*, enduring (τλᾶσα) many things and my *psychē*,[16] now show (δείκνυμι) what sort of son Tirynthian Alcmene ... bore to Zeus!" The description of *kardia* as "enduring" is traditional, found also at *Od.* 20.23.
   As at *Or.* 466, we have a direct address to *kardia*. Heracles calls upon *kardia* to be courageous as he descends to Hades. Like Odysseus at *Od.* 20.18, who tells his *kradiē* to "endure" (τέτλαθι δή, κραδίη) and reminds it of what it suffered with Polyphemus, Heracles describes his *kardia* as "enduring many things." At *Od.* 20.23 Odysseus' *kardia* "abides enduring" (μένε τετληυῖα). Heracles' *kardia* is to do the same.

Med. 858.   The Chorus ask Medea about her intention to kill her children: "from where will you take courage (θράσος) of *phrēn* or courage of hand and *kardia* to dare this terrible deed?" Both *phrēn* and *kardia* are associated with "courage" or "boldness" (θράσος) in this passage. Medea's *kardia* will need this if she is to slay her children.

Med. 1042.   In this passage Medea, as she beholds her children, says to the Chorus: "for my *kardia* has gone (οἴχομαι), women, as I see the shining face of my children." The "boldness" of *kardia* that the Chorus thought to be necessarily present in Medea at 858 seems to be absent after all. Medea says that her "*kardia* is absent": she has no strength or courage to carry out her intention.

Med. 1242.   As she ends her speech in which she tries to build her resolve to kill her children, Medea says: "but come, arm (ὁπλίζω) yourself, o *kardia*! Why do we delay to do the terrible deeds that must be done?" At 1042 *kardia* is "gone." Here Medea urges her *kardia* to become armed for battle. As at *Alc.* 837 and *Or.* 466, she addresses it directly. *Kardia* will need to be strong for Medea to act.

Desire

In earlier Greek poetry *kardia* is rarely found in expressions of desire.[17] Aeschylus does not associate it with desire, but Sophocles does once at *Ant.* 1105. Creon says that he "stands aside" (ἐξίστημι) from his *kardia* in respect to action. What he most desires to do, he gives up. Euripides twice associates *kardia* with desire.

Hec. 1026.   As Polymestor goes inside where he will be punished, the Chorus say: "like someone having fallen into the flood without harbour, you will fall aslant (λέχριος ἐκπίπτω) from your dear (φίλος) *kardia* for your robbery of life."[18] Although *kear* (*kēr*) and *ētor* in Homer are frequently called "dear,"[19] *kardia* is not called "dear" either in Homer or in the lyric and elegiac poets, Pindar, and Bacchylides. In Aeschylus *kear* is twice called "dear" (*Supp.* 785, *Choe.* 410) but *kardia* is not. Sophocles likewise does not use this adjective of *kardia*. Euripides here uses an adjective traditionally associated with "heart" but not before applied to *kardia*. This adjective is found only here with *kardia* in our extant Euripides.

Polymestor will encounter a fate (being blinded) that will cast him away from ("aslant from") what he really desires as expressed by his *kardia*. He is pictured as one toppling into the sea. Being "aslant from *kardia*" indicates the future impossibility of having what *kardia* wishes.

[Hipp. 912].   Both Diggle in the *OCT* and Kovacs in the recent Loeb bracket the lines 912–13.[20] Hippolytus encounters a silent Theseus after he has asked him what happened to Phaedra. Hippolytus says (911): "are you silent? There is not place for silence in misfortunes." Lines 912–13 read: "for the *kardia*, longing to hear (ποθοῦσα κλύειν) all things, is caught (ἁλίσκομαι) being curious (λίχνος) even in misfortunes." Even though the lines are in question, we can see in them a picture of *kardia* as a seat of desire. Even in adverse circumstances, the *kardia* wants to learn what has happened. A new use of λίχνος, "curious," as an adjective with *kardia* appears here.

Distress / Pain

A frequent association that *kardia* has in earlier and contemporary poets is that of pain or distress.[21] Aeschylus several times relates *kardia* and distress. At *Supp.* 71 the Danaids have a *kardia* "inexperienced in tears." At 466 a speech "scourges" *kardia*; at 799 marriage "pierces" it. At *Ag.* 834 the "poison" of envy sits on *kardia* and "doubles" one's pain. At *Ag.* 1031 *kardia* is "filled with pain" (θυμαλγής). At *Per.* 161 worry "stings" (ἀμύσσω) *kardia*. At *Ant.* 1085 Sophocles uses the image of "arrows" sent to *kardia*, arrows that will cause distress. In Euripides we find five references to *kardia* and pain, one to *kear*.

Bacc. 1321.   Cadmus recalls how Pentheus, when young, used to ask him: "who, being offensive (λυτηρός), distresses (ταράσσω) your *kardia*?" It is in *kardia* that Cadmus is thought to feel the effect of insult.

Hec. 235.   Hecuba wishes to ask questions of Odysseus. She says: "if it is possible for slaves to inquire of free people things not grievous (λυπρός) nor paining (δηκτήρος) their *kardia*." Here *kardia* is described as being able to be "bitten" or "pained" by the words of another.

Med. 245.   In her speech on the life that women lead, Medea describes the advantage a man has: "When a man is annoyed with the company of those within, going outside, he stops (παύω) his *kardia* from distress (ἄση)." *Kardia* here is the seat of vexation. This can be healed by distancing the *kardia* from the scene.

Med. 398 (kear).   Medea, as she mentions ways in which she will destroy her enemies, affirms: "not any of them will pain (ἀλγύνω) my *kear* and enjoy it." Like *kardia*, *kear* is associated with pain in earlier and contemporary poets, but not so frequently.[22] Medea makes *kear* the location of the pain she has suffered, pain that she will endeavour to inflict in turn.

Fr. 573 (Oinomaus).   This fragment reads: "But there is, even in evil circumstances, pleasure for mortals, complaints and downpourings of tears. These lighten the pains of *phrenes* and release (λύω) too great sufferings (πόνος) from the *kardia*."[23] Both *phrenes* and *kardia* endure distress in evil times. *Kardia* is the seat of "sufferings" that could become "too great." Talking and weeping help to relieve *kardia* from these sufferings.

Fr. 1038 (Incerta).   This fragment says: "for terrible fits of rage befall human beings in misfortune, and wandering (πλάνος) stands near (προσίστημι) *kardia*." At *Hipp.* 283 we heard of "wanderings of *phrenes*" present in the disturbed and sick Phaedra.[24] In this fragment the "wandering" of *kardia* seems to refer to distress or pain of some kind.

Fear

In earlier and contemporary poets *kardia* is found in contexts of fear only a few times.[25] Aeschylus relates *kardia* and fear in five passages. At *Ag.* 977 "fear (δεῖμα) stands before a prophetic *kardia*." At *Choe.* 167 the Chorus say that their "*kardia* dances with fear (φόβος)." At *Choe.* 1024 "fear (φόβος) is ready to sing at *kardia*." The Chorus at *Eum.* 523 praises the effect of "fear" (δέος) in *kardia*. At *Sept.* 288 "cares, neighbours of *kardia*, kindle terror (τάρβος) into flame." Sophocles does not mention *kardia* in a context of fear, but Euripides does once.

Fr. *908.6* (Incerta).   Speaking of the ills of having children, a person says that in some circumstances, over them, "I melt (τήκω) my wretched (τάλας) *kardia* with terror (ὀρρωδία)." *Kardia* here is a seat of "fear" or "terror" over children.[26] The picture is probably that of worry over what will befall children from day to day. Like Sophocles at *Tr.* 651, Euripides uses a new adjective with *kardia* here: "wretched," as we saw also at *Or.* 466 above.[27] He also uses the noun ὀρρωδία for the first time with *kardia*.

Grief

In earlier and contemporary poets, *kardia* is connected quite often with grief.[28] Aeschylus once describes *kardia* "groaning (στένω) within" (*Sept.* 968). Sophocles describes Deianira, in her grief for Heracles, as "always perishing in her wretched *kardia*" (*Tr.* 651). Euripides associates *kardia* with grief three times.

Alc. 1100.   Admetus tells Heracles that, if he takes the veiled woman into his house, he will suffer: "and, doing so, I will be stung (δάκνω) in my *kardia* with grief (λύπη)." At *Hec.* 235 we heard of things "grieving" or "biting" (δηκτήριος) *kardia*. Here "grief" (λύπη) is able to "sting" or "bite" *kardia*.[29]

Hec. 433.   Polyxena asks Odysseus to lead her away: "for, before my being killed, I have melted (τήκω) my *kardia* with laments (θρῆνος) of my mother and I am melting her with my mournings." As at Fr. 908.6, we find there the verb "melt" (τήκω) with *kardia*. Grief is making the *kardia* of Polyxena "dissolve" or "melt." It may be losing the strength that Polyxena will need to face her death.

HF 833.   Iris addresses Madness, who will soon drive Heracles insane: "come, keeping (συλλαμβάνω) your *kardia* untouched (ἄτεγκτος)." Madness is not to allow any sorrow or grief for Heracles to prevent her from attacking him. Euripides introduces a new adjective with *kardia* here: "untouched." *Kardia* could be a seat of sympathy but must not be allowed to be such in these circumstances.

Joy

Kardia in earlier and contemporary poets is connected with joy several times.[30] Aeschylus puts *kardia* in this context when he describes someone as "fired" in his *kardia* (*Ag.* 481). Sophocles does not connect *kardia* with joy; Euripides does so twice.

El. 402.   As their hope for the future grows, the Chorus say: "now, more than before, we are warmed (θερμαίνω) with joy (χαρά) in our *kardia.*" Like Aeschylus and Sophocles, Euripides here uses an image of "heat" with *kardia.*³¹ *Kardia* "grows warm" with "gladness" as the heating factor.

Hcld. 583.   The Maiden generously prays for her brother: "may you be happy and may there be for you whatever my *kardia* beforehand will be foiled of (σφάλλω)." The Maiden, about to die, wishes her brother to have the joys her own *kardia* is going to lose. *Kardia* is pictured as the seat of joys and happiness that life can bring.

Love

In earlier and contemporary authors *kardia* and love are rarely associated. Archilochus speaks of love "twisting its way under *kardiē*" (191 W). Alcman says that Eros "delights *kardiē*" (59 a 2). Sappho describes a situation that makes her *kardiē* "beat" (31). Aeschylus and Sophocles do not connect *kardia* with love; Euripides does so four times.

Hipp. 27.   Aphrodite describes Phaedra's reaction to Hippolytus: she "was held (κατέχω) in her *kardia* with terrible love (ἔρος δεινόν) by my plans." *Kardia* is the location for the strong passion that Phaedra feels.

Hipp. 1274.   The Chorus say of Eros: "he charms (θέλγω) the one with maddened (μαινομένα) *kradia* whom he ... arouses." The form *kradia* occurs here. Aeschylus at *Sept.* 781 describes Oedipus as putting out his eyes with "maddened *kardia*." Euripides here introduces the participle "maddened" with *kardia* in a context of love. When Eros "charms" or "bewitches" (θέλγω) someone, the *kardia* becomes a seat of madness or frenzy.

Med. 432.   Euripides refers again to a "maddened" *kradia* with this form of the noun. The Chorus describe Medea: "you sailed (πλέω) from your father's halls with raging (μαινομένα) *kradia.*"³² Once again we find *kradia* as the seat of passion within Medea.³³

GODS

Euripides mentions the *kardia* of a goddess only in the case of Madness at *HF* 833. This goddess is to keep her *kardia* "untouched" by sympathy.

Table 6.1
Kardia: Traditional and Contemporary Contexts

Adjective or participle	Passage	Meaning	Context
ἄκρος	*Hec.* 242	top, surface	Seat of Emotion
ἄτεγκτος	*HF* 833	untouched	Grief
μαινομένα	*Hipp.* 1274 *Med.* 432	raging, maddened	Love Love
πθοῦσα κλύειν	[*Hipp.* 912]	desiring to hear	Desire

Table 6.2
Kardia in Wider Contexts

Adjective or participle	Passage	Meaning
ἀναμετρουμένη	*IT* 346	measuring out tears
γαληνός	*IT* 345	gentle
λίχνος	[*Hipp.* 912]	curious
τάλας	*IT* 344 *Or.* 466 Fr. 908.6 Incerta	wretched
φιλοικτίρμων	*IT* 345	showing pity

EURIPIDEAN USES

The analyses of the passages given above show that for the most part Euripides refers to *kardia* and *kear* in ways that are traditional and contemporary. The only manner in which he introduces new uses is with respect to kinds of *kardia*.

KINDS OF *KARDIA*

Euripides mentions five adjectives that are found with *kardia* in earlier and contemporary poets. These are: ἐμός, σός, τίς, τλᾶσα, and φίλος (see Appendix Three for details). With *kear*, he uses only two adjectives, both of which are traditional: ἐμός and σός. Within traditional and contemporary contexts, Euripides introduces a few new uses, as Table 6.1 shows. Six times we find Euripides using new adjectives with *kardia* that suggest a wider range of meaning, as Table 6.2 shows.

In the questionable passage, *Hipp.* 912, *kardia* is called "curious." It wishes to hear about evil events. This is a new picture of *kardia*. Three times

Euripides calls *kardia* "wretched." In doing so, he resembles Sophocles, who also calls *kardia* τάλας at *Tr.* 651, this being the first occurrence of this adjective with *kardia*.

IT 344–6. In this passage we encounter three new descriptions of *kardia*. Iphigenia, as she is ordered to kill the Greeks who have come, says: "o wretched (τάλας) *kardia*, before you were gentle (γαληνός) to strangers and always showing pity (φιλοικτίρμων), measuring out tears (ἀναμετρουμένη δάκρυ) for those of the same race, when you took (λαμβάνω) Greeks into your hands." Iphigenia claims that now that Orestes is reported to be dead, she will be "hostile" (δυσνοῦς) instead (350). Iphigenia here directly addresses *kardia*. We have seen a similar use of the vocative at *Alc.* 837, *Med.* 1242, and *Or.* 466. Iphigenia locates her feelings of gentleness, pity, and sorrow for the Greek victims in her *kardia*. All three adjectives introduced to describe these feelings are new. In the future, Iphigenia says, she will resist such feelings of *kardia*. Her attitude will be negative instead.

EURIPIDEAN IMAGES

We find three major images that Euripides uses with *kardia*, as follows.

ARMOUR

Med. 1242. Medea calls on her *kardia* to "arm" (ὁπλίζω) itself for the murder of her children. An "unarmed" *kardia* could not perform this act. This image is new with Euripides. In contrast, Sophocles has an image of *kardia* receiving "arrows" sent by another (*Ant.* 1085). Euripides presents the picture of a *kardia* armed with weapons for a battle.

HEAT

El. 402. The Chorus happily say to Electra: "now, more than before, we are warmed (θερμαίνω) with joy in our *kardia*." Aeschylus uses an image of "fire" with *kardia* at *Ag.* 481 when he speaks of someone "fired (πυρωθέντα) in *kardia*." A similar image may be present at *Sept.* 288 when "cares, neighbours of *kardia*, kindle (ζωπυρέω) terror." Sophocles likewise relates *kardia* with heat when he speaks of a "hot (θερμός) *kardia* for cold deeds" (*Ant.* 88). Euripides describes *kardia* being "warmed" with delight. In this case a "warm" *kardia* indicates a positive state.

TOUCH

Hel. 960, Med. 1360. Twice Euripides introduces this new image with *kardia*. At *Hel.* 960 Menelaus says that he will speak "what in particular

will touch" (ἀνθάπτω) Theonoë's *kardia*. Medea exults at 1360 that she
has "touched" (ἀνθάπτω) Jason's *kardia*.[34] In both cases the image suggests the arousal of feeling in *kardia* by either the words or actions
of another.

RELATIONSHIP OF PERSON AND KARDIA

In Aeschylus and Sophocles, as in earlier and contemporary poets, we find a
traditional way of regarding person and *kardia*. The two remain distinct.
What is the case with Euripides?

Appendix One examines in detail all the 35 instances of *kardia* in terms
of this relationship. With it as guide, we can make the following observations.

1 *Kardia* appears 9 times as present or active in a person (Category A). Of
   these, 4 are in the vocative as a person directly addresses *kardia*. This usage
   in particular suggests the distinct nature of person and psychic entity.[35] *Kardia* is seen as a location of specific psychological functions. At *Alc.* 837 and
   Med. 1242, we see a person call *kardia* to action. At *IT* 344 and *Or.* 466 a
   person speaks to *kardia*, reacting to feelings present in it. The individual is
   somehow distinct from *kardia* but strongly influenced by its nature.

   In the other five passages, *kardia* is active when it "has beating" (*Bacc.*
   1288). It is described in certain ways. It can be, for example, "gentle" and
   "showing pity" (*IT* 344) or it can have "anger" (*Med.* 590).
2 In four passages a person acts in or with *kardia* (Category B). One can
   "speak" from *kardia* (*IA* 475, Fr. 412). One can act with "courage" of *kardia* (*Med.* 432) or with "raging" *kardia* (*Med.* 432).
3 In 8 passages a person has a direct relationship with *kardia* (Category C).
   Twice someone can "melt" *kardia* (*Hec.* 433, Fr. 908.6). It is a psychic
   entity one can, for example, "stir up" (*Med.* 99) or "stop from distress"
   (*Med.* 245).
4 Four times a person is described in relation to *kardia* (Category D). One
   can be "stung" (δάκνω) in it (*Alc.* 100), for example, or "warmed with
   joy" in it (*El.* 402).
5 In 10 passages outside objects or agents affect *kardia* (Categories E
   and F).

This brief summary of the detailed overview given in Appendix One suggests
again that Euripides views this psychic entity, as he does others, in a traditional
way.[36] Person and *kardia* remain distinct from one another. The person finds
kardia active within, especially as a seat of various emotions. The person can
act in or with *kardia*. Sometimes the person acts directly upon it. Like other
psychic entities, *kardia* proves to be open to the influence of outside objects
and agents.

OVERVIEW OF KARDIA AND KEAR

Based on our discussion of *kardia* and *kear* presented above, we make the following observations.

SPECIFIC FEATURES OF *KARDIA* AND *KEAR*

1 *Kardia* appears 35 times, *kear* only 3.
2 Both psychic terms appear only in the singular.
3 On a continuum from "physical" to "psychological," we find with *kardia* a full range. It exhibits both "physical" and "psychological" aspects.
4 Three times we find *kardia* in a predominantly "physical" context. It "beats" (*Alc.* 1067, *Bacc.* 1288); it receives the "fate" of death (*Hipp.* 841).
5 *Kardia* serves as a seat of emotion.
6 *Kardia* is involved in the emotions of anger, courage, desire, distress, and pain, fear, grief, joy, and love.
7 *Kear* acts as a seat of emotion and is connected with pain.
8 We find the mention of *kardia* in only the goddess Madness (*HF* 833).
9 We do not find *kardia* in moral contexts.
10 Euripides introduces a few new descriptions of *kardia* in traditional and contemporary contexts (see Table 6.1). He offers some new descriptions of *kardia* that suggest a wider range of function for *kardia* (see Table 6.2).
11 Euripides uses *kardia* in 3 major images, namely "armour," "heat," and "touch." The first two occur also in Aeschylus and Sophocles; the third is new.
12 With regard to relationship of person and *kardia* and *kear*, these psychic entities appear to be distinct from the person.

GENERAL FEATURES OF *KARDIA* AND *KEAR*

Just as with *phrēn*, *nous*, and *thumos*, we observe that Euripides' references to *kardia* and *kear* are largely traditional and contemporary. He rarely speaks of the second word for "heart," *kear*, only 3 times in our extant evidence. *Kardia* he refers to 35 times, in numbers similar to *nous* (43) and *thumos* (30). In this use of *kardia* he closely resembles Aeschylus, who mentions it 30 times. Sophocles, in contrast, refers to *kardia* only 6 times.

We see that *kardia* and *kear* are always involved in emotion. The feelings found in *kardia* can be positive: courage, desire, and joy. They are more often negative: anger, distress, and pain, fear, grief, and love. *Kardia* is seen as a very active agent within. Four times it is directly addressed and in two of these instances it is called to action. *Kardia* proves vulnerable to the actions of others. It can be "touched" or "pained."

In some descriptions Euripides suggest a wider range of feeling in *kardia* than is found before. On the whole, however, he very much presents *kardia* and *kear* as they appear in earlier and contemporary poetry.

7 *Psychē*: Traditional Uses

In many instances Euripides refers to *psychē* in ways quite new. He also refers to it in traditional ways. Like Sophocles, who introduces several new uses of *psychē*, Euripides to an even greater degree mentions an extended range of meaning of this psychic term. Aeschylus refers to *psychē* 13 times, always in traditional ways. Sophocles mentions *psychē* 35 times, 14 in traditional ways but 21 in new ways. Euripides speaks of *psychē* 117 times.[1] *Psychē* appears in all of the tragedies. In 61 passages Euripides places *psychē* in traditional contexts; in 56 he places it in new contexts. In this chapter we shall look at the 61 traditional occurrences.

As is well known, *psychē* in Homer does not function as a psychological agent within the living person.[2] Instead, *psychē* is the "breath" that keeps a person alive. It is mentioned only when death threatens. In Homer *psychē* has the meaning of "life-spirit" that animates a person or of "life" within a person. It also principally functions as the "shade" of the person that survives death. We see it featured thus in particular in the First and Second Nekyia of the *Odyssey* (Books 11 and 24).

With the lyric and elegiac poets, Pindar and Bacchylides, *psychē* begins to act as a psychological agent in the living person. It acts as a seat of emotion, namely of courage, endurance, joy, love, and pain. Aeschylus, as mentioned above, refers to *psychē* in principally Homeric ways. It is "life-spirit," "life," or "shade of the dead."[3] Sophocles, when he refers to *psychē* in traditional ways, uses it to signify "life-spirit" or "life." When he uses *psychē* in new ways, Sophocles ascribes to it a full range of psychological activity that includes intellectual, emotional, and moral aspects.[4] Euripides makes *psychē* a permanent psychic entity. It does not, it is true, appear as often as *phrēn* (160 times), but it appears much more often than *nous* (43), *thumos* (30), and *kardia* (35). Let us look first at his traditional uses of this psychic term. We shall suggest these traditional meanings: "life-spirit," "shade of the dead," and "life." Since three meanings may be present in any passage, our use of categories focuses on chief aspects of *psychē* in the various passages. Our classification is necessarily subjective but useful for treating these instances of *psychē*.

LIFE-SPIRIT AND SHADE OF THE DEAD

THE ALCESTIS

Not surprisingly we find *psychē* often mentioned in the *Alcestis*. The play, focusing on the generous surrender of life on the part of a wife for her husband, mentions *psychē* 16 times. Since the *Alcestis* was probably put on in the place of a satyr play, the treatment of its theme is appropriately lightly handled. We do not find here the intensity of drama that is present, for example, in the *Bacchae*, *Hippolytus*, or *Medea*. We encounter exaggerated pathos. Sometimes this appears in the occurrences of *psychē*. Of the 16 occurrences of *psychē*, we find 12 referring to it in a traditional way, 4 in new ways (to be treated in chapter 8). In the 12 traditional occurrences, *psychē* signifies the "life-spirit" of the individual that survives as shade of the dead in Hades.

Alcestis

Four times we hear of the *psychē* of Alcestis. Death will take her *psychē* (54). No rescue for her *psychē* is possible (117). She allowed Admetus to see the light "in place of" her *psychē* (283). She "dared to exchange this *psychē*" for her husband (462).

Admetus

Four times the *psychē* of Admetus is mentioned. Alcestis "gave the dearest in place of" his *psychē* (341). Alcestis died "on behalf of" his *psychē* (620). Admetus is described as "loving" his *psychē* (704). He is said to have "saved his life (βίοτος) and *psychē*" (929).

At 900 we have a reference to the *psychē* of both Alcestis and Admetus: Hades would have had both if he had died with Alcestis.

General

Three times in the *Alcestis* we find general remarks about *psychē*.

Alc. 301. Alcestis expresses her wishes to Admetus before she dies (280-325). At 301 she makes the remark: "for I will never ask you an equal return (for nothing is more valuable [τιμιώτερον] than *psychē*) but what is just." Here we find the notion of the value of *psychē* as "life-spirit." It resembles the statement of Achilles that "all the wealth of Troy" was not "worth" his *psychē* (*Il.* 9.401).

Alc. 712.   Pheres rejects Admetus' criticisms of him for not dying in place of his son. He says: "we must live with one (εἷς) *psychē*, not with two." In a variety of contexts Euripides will use the phrase "one *psychē*" in his different plays.[5] We find the first reference to "one *psychē*" at *Il.* 21.569, where Achilles is said to have just "one *psychē*." The phrase does not occur in Hesiod, lyric and elegiac poets, Pindar, or Bacchylides nor in Aeschylus. Sophocles uses it to describe Antigone at *Ant.* 1069 and *O.C.* 499. Pheres argues that each person has only "one life-spirit," which cannot easily be surrendered.

Alc. 883.   Admetus comments on those who are childless: "I envy the unmarried and childless among mortals. For they are one (εἷς) *psychē*, and to grieve over it is a moderate burden." Euripides will echo this thought about the limited grief of the childless at *Hipp.* 259 and Fr. 908.8 (see below, chapter 8). The loss of these people consists only in their own *psychē*; it is much less than grief caused by family members.

THE OTHER PLAYS

And. 611.   Peleus chastises Menelaus: "you destroyed (ἀπόλλυμι) many (πολύς) and good (ἀγαθός) *psychai*" at Troy. This passage resembles two in Aeschylus where Helen is said to have "destroyed" (ὄλλυμι) many *psychai* at Troy (*Ag.* 1457, 1466). There the verb ὄλλυμι appears in a new way with *psychē*. Before, it described people "losing" their *psychē* at death[6] or *psychē* itself "perishing" (Hes., Fr. 204.10). Both Aeschylus and Euripides describe *psychē* as vulnerable to destruction by another.

These *psychai* that Menelaus has destroyed are called "many" and "good." The first adjective is a traditional one, appearing at *Il.* 1.3 where Achilles' anger sent "many strong *psychai*" to Hades.[7] "Good" (ἀγαθός) is a new adjective that Euripides introduces with *psychē*.[8] Qualities of nobility are here said to reside in *psychai*.

Hec. 22.   This passage resembles *And.* 611. Polydorus' *eidolon* says: "when Troy and the *psychē* of Hector were destroyed" (ἀπόλλυμι). Once again we hear of the destruction of *psychē*.

Hec. 182, 196.   Hecuba says to Polyxena at 182: "alas for your *psychē*!" At 196 Diggle in the OCT and Kovacs in the recent Loeb write μοίρας, but an alternate reading is ψυχᾶς, as follows, when Hecuba again addresses

Polyxena: "I speak words of ill-omen in announcing that the Argives have decided by vote about your *psychē*." If this reference to "*psychē*" instead of "fate" is correct, Hecuba twice laments the destiny of the "life-spirit" of Polyxena.[9]

Hel. 52.   Helen says of herself: "many (πολύς) *psychai* perished (θνήσκω) at the streams of Scamander because of me." This line resembles *And.* 611, with its reference also to "many *psychai*" being "destroyed." It resembles also the description of Helen that Aeschylus gives at *Ag.* 1457 and 1466.[10] Euripides here uses the verb θνήσκω with *psychē*, resembling Sophocles at *Ant.* 559, where the same verb first appears with *psychē*. In that passage Antigone says that her "*psychē* died long ago." Death is often described in terms of *psychē* in earlier and contemporary poets.[11] But we do not hear of *psychē* itself "dying." Both Sophocles and Euripides use θνήσκω in a special way with *psychē*. We know that *psychē* itself does not "die": it leaves the body and survives in Hades. Euripides uses this description of *psychai* to indicate in fact the death of the bodies of heroes at Troy. *Psychē*, however, ceases to be a living presence in these bodies.

Hel. 1431.   Theoclymenus says to Helen: "for Menelaus did not lose (ἀφίημι) his *psychē* here." Menelaus did not release his "life-spirit"; he still lives. Euripides uses here a compound of _ημι to indicate the loss of *psychē*. He will do so again at *Med.* 1219 (μεθίημι), *Or.* 1171 (ἀφίημι), and *Tr.* 1135 (ἀφίημι).[12] We do not find compounds of ἵημι with *psychē* in earlier or contemporary poets.

Hcld. 984.   Eurystheus says to Alcmene: "woman, know clearly that I will not fawn upon you nor say anything else about (περί) my *psychē* from which I would have to incur some reputation for cowardice." Here we find a reference to utterance "about *psychē*," a frequent phrase that Euripides uses.[13] Eurystheus will be reticent about the life-spirit that animates him.

Hipp. 721.   Phaedra says about *psychē*: "for not ever will I disgrace my Cretan home nor will I come before the face of Theseus on account of shameful deeds for the sake of one (εἷς) *psychē*." Phaedra is not clear here about the identity of the owner of the *psychē*.[14] Is it her own "life-spirit" or that of Hippolytus? This ambiguous reference enhances speculation concerning what Phaedra intends to do.

IA 1390.   Iphigenia asks as she sees so many Greeks willing to die for their native land: "will my *psychē*, being one (εἷς), prevent (κωλύω) all these things?"[15] Iphigenia proves willing to sacrifice her "one *psychē*" to serve the interest of others.

IA 1441. Clytemnestra asks Iphigenia: "is it not necessary for me to mourn (πενθέω) your *psychē*?" This passage resembles Sophocles, *O.T.* 94, where Oedipus speaks of bearing "greater grief" for the people of Thebes than for his own *psychē*. Clytemnestra feels that she must grieve over the "life-spirit" of Iphigenia that will soon be lost.

Med. 1219. The Messenger describes the death of Creon: "the ill-fated one gave up (μεθίημι) his *psychē*." As in *Hel.* 1431, we find a compound of ἵημι used to describe the loss of *psychē*. Creon's "life-spirit" departs from his body.

Or. 676. Orestes, addressing Menelaus, asks him to think about Agamemnon: "imagine that the dead person under the earth hears these things and that his *psychē* is flying (ποτωμένη) over you and is speaking (λέγω) what I say." In these lines we find in particular a Homeric picture of *psychē*. At *Od.* 11.222 we hear that, at death, "*psychē*, like a dream, flies off and hovers about (ἀποπέτομαι, ποτάομαι)." Euripides uses the participle of ποτάομαι in the current passage. So too, at *Il.* 16.856 and 22.362, in the case of Patroclus and Hector, "*psychē*, flying (πέτομαι) from the limbs, went to Hades." Frequently we hear also in Homer of the shade of the dead able to speak.[16] Menelaus is to imagine the shade of Agamemnon present just like that of Patroclus speaking to Achilles (*Il.* 9.65–101).[17]

Or. 1046. As Electra and Orestes fear that they are to be killed, Electra says to Orestes: "o dearest, o having (ἔχω) the dearest and sweetest name for your sister and one *psychē*." Part of the text of line 1046 is in question, but the reference to "one *psychē*" is clear.[18] Electra suggests that, although she and Orestes are separate people, "one life-spirit" is shared by them. We can compare Electra's reference to Orestes in Sophocles' play: "o memorial of the *psychē* of the dearest of people to me" (*El.* 1127).

Or. 1163. Orestes, as he assumes that he must die, says: "I, breathing out (ἐκπνέω) my *psychē* in any case, desire to die, doing some harm to my enemies." Euripides uses the verb "breathe forth" to describe death. In earlier and contemporary poetry we find only one such image, at Sim. 553, where the verb ἀποπνέω appears. The original association of *psychē* with "breath" is suggested in this description.[19]

Or. 1171. Orestes affirms that he will not shame his father Agamemnon: "him I will not shame, enduring death as a slave but freely (ἐλευθέρως) I will send forth (ἀφίημι) my *psychē*." Once again we find a compound of ἵημι with *psychē*.[20] As noted under *Hel.* 1431, Euripides first uses this verb and its compounds with *psychē*. Orestes claims that he will "freely" release his "life-spirit" in death.

Or. 1517.   The Phrygian slaves, to assure Orestes that he is speaking the truth, says: "I swear (κατόμνυμι) by my *psyche*, which I would swear well by." Here *psyche* acts as grounds for an oath. The passage resembles Sophocles, *O.C.* 1326, where the *psyche* of Oedipus is called on as the basis of an oath. *Psyche* is considered of high value. It is something one "swears well by," as the Phrygian slave claims.

Pho. 998.   Iphigenia at *IA* 1390 was willing to sacrifice her *psyche* for the Greeks. So too is Menoeceus, son of Creon, at *Pho.* 998. "I will go and save the city, and I will give (δίδωμι) my *psyche* to die (ὑπερθνῄσκω) on behalf of this land."[21] We find individuals "giving" up (δίδωμι) *psyche* also at *Il.* 5.654, 11.445, and 16.625. Menoeceus says that he will offer his "life-spirit and die" for the Thebans.

Pho. 1228.   The Messenger reports how Eteocles addressed the gathered armies: "leaders of the Greeks, who have come here, and people of Cadmus, do not sell (ἀπεμπολάω) your *psychai* for the sake of Polyneices nor for us." We have here an image of "selling" with *psyche*. The passage is similar to Sophocles, *Ant.* 322, where Creon accuses the Guard of "betraying" (προδίδωμι) *psyche* for money. *Psyche* is pictured at *Pho.* 1228 as an item for sale. If it is "sold," *psyche* brings death.[22]

Pho. 1291.   The Chorus, describing how Polyneices and Eteocles will kill each other, say: "a *psyche* of the same family (ὁμογενής)." Euripides introduces a new adjective here with *psyche*: "of the same family." The "life-spirit" in Polyneices and Eteocles is seen as "related."

Pho. 1553.   When Creon hears of the death of Eteocles, Polyneices, and Jocasta, he says: "by what fate, how have three (τρισσός) *psychai* left (λείπω) the light?" Euripides uses a traditional image here of *psyche* "leaving", as found, for example, at *Il.* 16.453.[23] Death is described in terms of the departure of these three "life-spirits."

Supp. 777.   We heard above about the "selling" of *psyche* at *Pho.* 1228. In this passage Adrastus, weeping for the dead, says: "for this alone for mortals is not an expenditure (ἀνάλωμα), once paid out (ἀναλύω), to take again (λαμβάνω), the *psyche* of mortals (βρότειος)." This passage echoes *Il.* 9.408, where *psyche* is described as "not to be seized (λειστή) or grasped (ἑλετή) once it has passed the barrier of the teeth." Euripides introduces a new adjective with *psyche*: βρότειος. This probably means "belonging to mortals" rather than "being mortal." *Psyche* survives death. When it is "paid out," it never is regained. We can compare also the reference Orestes makes to "paying (τίνω) with his dear *psyche*" at *Choe.* 276. Euripides describes *psyche* as an "expenditure" that one can make only once.[24]

Supp. 1024. Evadne makes the assertion to her dead husband: "I will come to the bridal chambers of Persephone, never having betrayed (προδίδωμι) with my *psychē* you, who have died [and are] under the earth." Evadne claims that she has been faithful in her *psychē*, "life-spirit," to her husband. At *Ant.* 322 of Sophocles we hear of someone "betraying" (προδίδωμι) *psychē* for money. Here, with the same verb, we find the picture of someone not "betraying" another with *psychē*.

Tr. 1135. The Messenger describes Astyanax: "falling from the walls he gave up (ἀφίημι) his *psychē*." Again we find a compound of ἵημι describing death, a new use with Euripides.[25] Astyanax "sent forth" his "life-spirit" in death.

Tr. 1214. Hecuba, as she addresses the corpse of Astyanax, says "Helen ... has killed (κτείνω) your *psychē*." Again, as with the reference to *psychē* "dying" at *Hel.* 52, we find death described in terms of the "destruction" of *psychē*. In fact, it is only the body that dies. What is destroyed, however, is *psychē* as a living presence in this body.

Fr. 360.51 (Erechtheus). This fragment reads: "for, in return for one (εἷς) *psychē*, it is not possible that I would not save this city." At *IA* 1390 we heard of a reference to the "one *psychē*" of Iphigenia having an effect on many lives. Here, "one *psychē*" will not prevent an action that would help the city as a whole.

Fr. 370 K 71 (Erechtheus).[26] Athena speaks of certain women: "their *psychai* have not descended (βαίνω) to Hades but I have established their spirit (πνεῦμα) in the aether; they shall be called 'divine Hyacinthids.'" The fragment recalls the descriptions we encountered of *nous* at *Hel.* 1014 as having "immortal *gnōmē* as it falls into the eternal aether."[27] Somehow *psychai* and *pneuma* are related, the latter being what survives. *Psychē*, associated with "breath," may survive as such in special cases. These *psychai* have become also stars, the Hyades.[28]

Fr. 912.9 (Incerta). This fragment contains a prayer to Zeus asking him: "send (πέμπω) into the light the *psychai* of those below, for those seeking to learn beforehand of trials, whence they grow, what is the root of evils, whom of the gods to propitiate to find relief from troubles." Here *psychai* refer to the "shades of the dead." These "shades" are thought to have information that could help the living with important questions about the troubles of life.

In all these passages (27 in number) we have seen *psychē* as "life-spirit" or "shade of the dead." Certainly too the notion of "life" is also often an aspect of the meaning of the term in these instances. We can see that people are convinced that they have "one" *psychē* within of great value. When offered up by some heroic person, such as Iphigenia (*IA* 1390) or Menoeceus (98), "one *psychē*" can do great good for others. In the *Alcestis* we hear frequently of the great value of *psychē* (see, e.g., 301, 341, 620, 704). *Psychē*, once lost, is not to be recovered (*Supp.* 777); it is irretrievable.

Euripides presents a traditional view of *psychē*. He may introduce new adjectives with it or use new verbs in describing it. On the whole, however, what he says in these passages is traditional and familiar.

LIFE

In the following passages the idea of "life" seems to be frequent. We may note again that the notion of "life-spirit" that survives in Hades may also be present.

And. 419.   Andromache says, as she bids her son good-bye: "to all human beings children are (εἰμι) *psychē*. Whoever, being inexperienced, disparages them, he suffers less but is unhappy in his happiness." We can contrast this passage with Hes., *W. & D.* 686, where "money" (χρήματα) is said to be "*psychē* for wretched men." Andromache claims that children are "life" for human beings; this is their great value.

And. 541.   Menelaus tells the child of Andromache as he pleads for his life: "I expended (ἀναλίσκω) a great part (μέγα μόριον) of my *psychē* seizing Troy and your mother." Menelaus has used up a "large share" of his "life" in his former campaign. We heard above of "selling *psychē*" (*Pho.* 1228) and the "expenditure of *psychē*." Here only a portion of *psychē* has been used, but Menelaus feels that his "life within" has been lessened in some way by his activities at Troy.[29]

[Hec. 176].   Part of line 176 and all of 177 are bracketed in Diggle's *OCT* and in Kovacs' recent Loeb.[30] They read: "so that you may know what sort, what sort of report I hear about (περί) your *psychē*." If these lines were genuine, Hecuba would be reporting the news she had about the "life" of Polyxena.

Hel. 946.   As Menelaus and Helen plead for their lives, the Chorus say: "I desire to hear the words of Menelaus, what he will say (ἐρέω) about (περί) his *psychē*." Menelaus will speak about his "life," arguing why he should be spared.

Hcld. 15.   Iolaus describes himself and the children of Heracles: "we escaped; the city is lost but our *psychē* is saved (σώζω)." Here *psychē* indicates the "life" of all the people involved.[31]

Hcld. 296.   The Chorus make general remarks about messengers: "what sort of things do you think that he will tell his masters, how he suffered terribly and how he came to be within a little of wearing out (διακναίω) his *psychē.*" Once again we find the image here of an "expenditure" of *psychē.* The messenger claims almost to have "worn away" his "life." We can compare the reference that Aeschylus makes at *Choe.* 749 to a "wearing away" (τριβή) of *psychē.*

Hcld. 455. Iolaus nobly says to Demophon: "I must not love (φιλέω) my own *psychē.* Let it go." Iolaus says that he ought not to cling to "life"; instead, he will sacrifice it for the children of Heracles.[32] In this generosity of spirit he resembles Iphigenia (*IA* 1390) and Menoeceus (*Pho.* 998).[33]

Hcld. 550. Similar also to Iphigenia and Menoeceus is the Maiden who tells Iolaus: "But if you accept and wish to use my zeal, I give (δίδωμι) my *psychē* willingly (ἑκοῦσα) to these [my brothers], but not under compulsion." Once again we encounter someone willing to sacrifice her "life." She insists that this sacrifice must be a free gift.[34]

[HF 452]. This line is bracketed in Diggle's *OCT.*[35] Megara enters and asks (451–2): "who is the priest, who is the one to slaughter the unfortunate, or who is the murderer (φονεύς) of my wretched (τάλας) *psychē?*" We find here a new use of τάλας with *psychē.*[36] We find too a new noun with *psychē*: "murderer." At *Tr.* 1214 (treated above) Helen was described as "killing" (κτείνω) the *psychē* of Astyanax. The idea in this line 452 is similar: the "life" of the body is destroyed. If this line is genuine, it presents a strong image of the harm another can do to *psychē.*

HF 1146. Heracles says, as he realizes that he has killed his children: "alas, why then do I spare (φείδομαι) my *psychē?*" Solon speaks of the seafarer as "placing no sparing (φειδωλή) of *psychē*" (13 W). Tyrtaeus too calls for soldiers "no longer to spare (φείδομαι) *psychē*" (10.14 W). Sophocles describes Chrysothemis and Electra as those who were "unsparing (ἀφειδέω) of their *psychē*" (*El.* 979). Heracles wonders why he "spares" his own "life," now that he has deprived his children of theirs.

Hipp. 440. The Nurse asks Phaedra, who has been threatening suicide: "and then will you destroy (ὄλλυμι) your *psychē* because of love?" As at *And.* 611 and *Hec.* 22 (see "Life-Spirit"), we find this new use of ὄλλυμι to mean to "destroy." Phaedra threatens to "destroy" her "life," the presence of *psychē* in her body.

Hipp. 726. Later Phaedra says of her *psychē*: "I, released (ἀπαλλάσσω) from *psychē* on this day, will delight Cypris, who destroys (ἐξόλλυμι) me." Here we find the verb ἀπαλλάσσω with *psychē*, one that will appear also at *Med.* 968 (see below). Phaedra will be "released" from "life" when she dies.

Ion 1499.   Creusa tells Ion: "bound by fear, I cast out (ἀποβάλλω) your *psychē*, my child. I killed you unwillingly." Here we have a traditional picture of one person removing the *psychē* of another.[37] Creusa, at least in intent, "cast out" the "life" of Ion.

Med. 226.   Medea in her first speech says: "this unexpected event (ἄελπτον), falling upon me, has destroyed (διαφθείρω) my *psychē*." Just like the references to ἀπόλλυμι and ὄλλυμι at *And.* 611, *Hec.* 22, and *Hipp.* 440, the verb διαφθείρω here indicates the "destruction" of *psychē*. The "life" or "life-spirit" of someone is destroyed within the body. Medea in this case does not refer to "death" as the other passages do. Instead, figuratively, Jason has taken away her *psychē* – that is, the "life" that was joyfully present before.

Med. 968.   Medea says to Jason as she hands over the gifts for his new wife: "I would give in exchange (ἀπαλλάσσω) my *psychē* to free my children from exile, not merely gold." Here we find the same verb ἀπαλάσσω as at *Hipp.* 726 but in a different meaning. There Phaedra was "released" from *psychē*. Here Medea offers to "exchange" her "life" to save her children from being exiled.

[Or. 644].   Diggle in the OCT brackets these lines.[38] In them Orestes says to Menelaus, asking him to repay Agamemnon by saving his son's life: "what you took, give back, having taken from my father. I do not mean money (χρήματα). 'Money' it will be if you save (σώζω) my *psychē*, dearest (φίλτατον) of my possessions." Hesiod at *W. & D.* 686 suggests that "money (χρήματα) is *psychē*" for sailors. They count its value as great as that of "life" and therefore are willing to risk *psychē*. Orestes reverses the picture. *Psychē*, "life" or "life-spirit," is "money," that is, it is of highest value.[39] Orestes calls *psychē* "dearest of my possessions." This resembles Alcestis' statement that "nothing is more valuable than *psychē*" (*Alc.* 301). Menelaus is to "save" Orestes' "life": the verb σώζω appears here as at *Alc.* 929 and *Hcld.* 15. If these lines are genuine, they offer an interesting reversal of what Hesiod has said.[40]

[Or. 847].   Once again in the OCT, lines 847–8 are bracketed.[41] The Chorus answers Electra's question about whether Orestes has fled, driven by madness: "Not at all. He has gone to the people of Argos, about to engage in the present struggle (ἀγών) about (περί) *psychē*, in which it will be necessary for you to live or to die." If the lines are genuine, we have in them Euripides' use of a traditional image, that of a "contest" for *psychē*. At *Il.* 22.161 we hear that Hector and Achilles "ran for the *psychē* of Hector." At Hes., fr. 76.7 a "race is about *psychē*."[42] Sophocles at *El.* 1492 refers to a "contest" (ἀγών)

about the *psychē* of Aegisthus. As we shall see, Euripides uses this image at
Pho. 1330 and Fr. 67 (*Alcmeon*). The "life" of both Orestes and Electra may
be the object of a "current struggle."

Or. 1034.   Electra, as she and Orestes lament their fate, says: "It is not possible not to bemoan sufferings. The dear (φίλος) *psychē* is for all a subject of
pity (οἰκτρόν)." We hear of a "dear" *psychē* at *Pyth.* 3.61 when Pindar addresses it directly: "do not, dear *psychē*, hasten after immortal life." Aeschylus
uses φίλος with *psychē* at *Choe.* 276 when Orestes is to "pay" with his "dear
psychē." Euripides describes "life" as "precious" or "dear." He introduces a
new idea with οἰκτρόν: the "life" in all, especially, when exposed to suffering,
is pitiable.

Pho. 1330.   The Chorus tell Creon: "I think that the contest (ἀγών) about
(περί) *psychē* has already been held (πράττω) for the sons of Oedipus." As in
[*Or.* 847] treated above, we have the image of the "contest for *psychē*."[43] In
this case the "contest" has ended with neither combatant for "life" in possession of the prize.

Tr. 791.   Hecuba laments as Astyanax is led away: "o child, your mother
and I are unjustly stripped (συλάω) of your *psychē*." Euripides uses a new
verb with *psychē* in a traditional image. In Homer we hear of the "robbing"
or "depriving" of *psychē*.[44] Here Andromache and Hecuba are "robbed" of
the "life" of Astyanax.

Tr. 900.   Helen asks Menelaus as he enters: "I wish to ask: 'what are the
judgments (γνῶμαι) of the Greeks and yourself about (περί) my *psychē*?"
Helen wants to learn what has been decided about her "life."

Under the heading "life," we have treated 22 passages. We can see this
meaning as prominent in these instances of *psychē*.[45] The notion of *psychē* as
"life-spirit" may likewise be present. *Psychē* appears to be most valuable and
most valued. What people treasure most can be spoken of in terms of *psychē*,
namely "children" (*And.* 419) and "money" ([*Or.* 644]). *Psychē* is "pitiable"
in all (*Or.* 1034). It is a worthy object of a "contest" ([*Or.* 847], *Pho.* 1330).

In this chapter we have examined 61 passages of Euripides where the meaning of *psychē* appears to be a traditional one. Euripides refers to *psychē* in
ways that would have been familiar to his audience. He introduces some new
features of *psychē* as "shade of the dead," "life-spirit," or "life," but on the
whole his usage is similar to that of earlier and contemporary poets and of
Aeschylus and Sophocles.

8 *Psychē*: Euripidean Uses

In this chapter we shall examine new ways in which Euripides refers to *psychē*. As mentioned at the beginning of chapter 7, *psychē* between the time of Homer and the fifth century gradually appears as a psychological agent in the living person.[1] Three factors are important in this appearance. First, *psychē* seems to have slowly absorbed functions ascribed earlier to other psychic entities, namely to *phrēn* and especially to *thumos* and *kardia*.[2] Second, when Homer speaks of *psychē* as "shade of the dead," he ascribes a range of function to it. The "unburied" shade can recognize a living person, speak, show emotion, and make requests.[3] The "buried" shades, once they have drunk blood, ca n recognize Odysseus, speak, express gladness or grief, prophesy, and inquire about living relations.[4] What seems to have occurred is that *psychē* in the living person gradually came to carry on these intellectual, emotional, and volitional activities.

A third factor, most important for the development of *psychē* by the times of Plato as the seat of personality of the "self" of the individual,[5] lies also in Homer's depiction of the shades in the underworld. What he does in certain passages is to identify *psychē* with the person. He transfers easily from the noun *psychē* to the personal pronoun or to the proper name. The "shade" of Agamemnon, for example, appears at *Od.* 11.387, but then it is "he," having drunk blood, who recognizes Odysseus, answers, recalls his own death, and asks about his son (11.390–456).[6] In such descriptions, part of the formulaic language that Homer repeated, several activities are associated with *psychē*. Gradually *psychai* began to do in living persons what they did in Hades.

Psychē slowly becomes a psychological agent. As it does so, it still appears very often in earlier and contemporary poets in the meaning found in

Homer of "shade of the dead," "life-spirit," and "life." In the lyric and elegiac poets, Pindar and Bacchylides, it becomes a seat of love, joy, endurance,
and pain.

Aeschylus in 13 passages refers to *psychē* in traditional ways.[7] Sophocles
mentions *psychē* 35 times, 14 in traditional ways and the rest in new ways.[8]
He ascribes to *psychē* a wide range of activities that can be described as intellectual, emotional, and moral. Generally in these new uses of *psychē*
Sophocles speaks in a traditional way of person and *psychē* being distinct. In
one passage, however, at *Ph.* 712, the *psychē* of Philoctetes is identified with
Philoctetes himself. As in the Homeric pictures of the shades in the underworld, *psychē* and person appear as one.

Euripides resembles Sophocles in introducing a broad use of *psychē*.
He mentions it much more frequently than either Aeschylus or Sophocles:
117 times. We have seen that in 61 of these instances *psychē* appears to have
a traditional meaning. In 56 the meaning is new.[9]

RANGE

SEAT OF PERSONALITY

Sometimes in Euripides *psychē* appears to be a seat of personality in the person. This may be the case also with other instances that we will term "predominantly intellectual," "emotional," or "moral." This use of *psychē* to
indicate a seat of personality appears already in the lyric and elegiac poets and
in Pindar. Anacreon, for example, speaks of one who is a "charioteer" of his
psychē (360). Theognis says that there is nothing "slavish" in his *psychē*
(530). Simonides mentions "delighting" *psychē* with good things (20.12 W²).
Pindar describes the men of Aetna as "having *psychai* stronger than possessions" (*Nem.* 9.32). He also describes Heracles as "short in stature, unflinching in *psychē*" (*Is.* 4.53 [b]).

Hcld. 530.   The Maiden speaks about her willingness to die: "this *psychē* is
present, willing and not unwilling (ἑκοῦσα κοὐκ ἄκουσα) and I announce
that I will die on behalf of my brothers and myself." In Aeschylus we find a
description of *psychē* as "willing" (θέλουσα) in the suspect passage, *Sept.*
1034. This is the first occurrence of "willing" with *psychē*. Euripides' use of
"not unwilling" is the first such reference with *psychē*.[10] The Maiden refers
to her *psychē* within as being in a "willing" state to face death. It is *psychē*
that she will "give up."[11]

Hipp. 1006.   Hippolytus, making his defence to Theseus, says that he has
never engaged in sexual activity: "nor am I eager to consider these things,
having a virgin (παρθένος) *psychē*." Bacchylides once refers to a "girlish" or

"maiden" (παρθένος) *psyche* when he describes the daughters of Proteus (11.48). Euripides' use of παρθένος is new. Hippolytus sees *psyche* as the seat of a characteristic most important to him: his virginity.

Hipp. 1040.   Theseus, in response to Hippolytus, says: "is this man not an enchanter and sorcerer, who has trusted that he will conquer (κρατέω) my *psyche* by gentleness of temper (εὐοργησία) having dishonoured his father?" Theseus locates the seat of his feelings towards Hippolytus in his *psyche*. In some cases *psyche* might prove vulnerable to "gentleness of temper," but it will not be true in this instance.

Ion 859.   Creusa responds to the news that Xuthus has found a son: "o *psyche*, how shall I keep silent? How will I reveal love hidden in darkness and leave behind shame?" Here we find a direct address to *psyche*, one that Euripides will describe in several plays.[12] We find such an address in earlier and contemporary poets only in Pin., *Pyth.* 3.61, where he urges his *psyche* not to "hasten after immortal life." Aeschylus does not have a direct address of *psyche* but Sophocles does in one passage. At *Tr.* 1260–3 Heracles addresses his "hardy" *psyche*, "calling upon it to keep him from crying out and to complete the "task" of his death as though it were a joy. Creusa in this passage locates *psyche* as the seat of her emotions and thoughts. It may be the source of words that she is trying to stem.

IT 838.   We have another address to *psyche* when Iphigenia embraces Orestes: "o my *psyche*, enjoying good fortune (εὐτυχοῦσα) greater than words, what am I to say?" Euripides introduces a new description of *psyche* here with εὐτυχοῦσα. Iphigenia sees her *psyche* as the location within of her current good fortune. Here, as in *Ion 859*, we see a connection of *psyche* with speech. Words fail Iphigenia; *psyche* could be a source of them.[13]

IT 882.   Another direct address to *psyche* occurs at *IT* 882. Iphigenia, speaking of the necessity of discovering a way of escape, says: "this, this is your need to find, o poor (μέλεος) *psyche*." Euripides, like Sophocles at *Ph.* 712 of Philoctetes, uses a new adjective with *psyche*: μέλεος.[14] Here Iphigenia addresses Orestes, referring to him as "*psyche*."[15] This passage resembles Sophocles, *Ph.* 712, where the Chorus refer to Philoctetes as a *psyche*. In both cases we see in the reference to *psyche* a periphrasis for the person.[16]

Med. 247.   Medea says about women: "it is necessary for us to look (βλέπω) at one *psyche*." As in *IT* 882, *psyche* appears here to stand for the person. A woman's attention has to be focused only on her husband.

Or. 466.   In this passage we also find a direct address to *psychē*. Orestes, recalling the kindness of his grandparents, says: "to whom – o wretched *kardia* and my *psychē* – I paid back no noble return." Orestes locates both *kardia* and *psychē* as the seat of his feelings of remorse in relation to Tyndareus, whose daughter he has killed.[17]

PREDOMINANTLY INTELLECTUAL

And. 160.   Hermione blames Andromache for her troubles: "I am hated by my husband because of your drugs (φάρμακον). For clever (δεινός) for such things is the Asiatic (ἠπειρῶτις) *psychē* of women." Euripides uses two new adjectives of *psychē*. First, he calls it "clever" (δεινός) in using drugs. Second, he refers in general to the "*psychē* of the mainland" – that is, "of Asia." One might suppose that Medea would fall into this category of women, but in the play, *Medea*, her *psychē* is not thus described. Her *nous*, however, is called "subtle" (λεπτός).[18] In this description of the *psychē* of Andromache, *psychē* appears to be a seat of cleverness, used not for admirable ends.

Hec. 87.   As Hecuba fears about the fate of Polyxena, she asks: "wherever can I see (εἰσοράω) the prophetic (θεῖος) *psychē* of Helenus or Cassandra, women of Troy, so that they may interpret my dreams for me?" Euripides introduces a new adjective with *psychē*: "prophetic." We see here a new association of *psychē* in the living person with prophecy. In the *Odyssey* we twice learn of the shade of Teiresias, his *psychē*, uttering prophecies (11.150, 23.251).

In this passage of Euripides, we see too a connection of *psychē* with speech.[19] In earlier and contemporary poets, *psychē* as a "shade of the dead" speaks but not as a psychological agent in the living person.[20] In Sophocles *psychē* is associated with speech in several passages.[21] At *Ant.* 227 it "speaks" (αὐδάω); at *O.C.* 999 it could "refute (ἀντεῖπον). Helenus had received the gift of prophecy in his *psychē*. If he were present he could, Hecuba believes, speak clearly of the future.[22]

HF 626.   Heracles, calming his family, says: "you, my wife, take (λαμβάνω) collectedness (σύλλογον) of *psychē* and cease from fear." Once again we find Euripides using a new expression with *psychē*. It is to have "collectedness." Megara is to calm her thoughts and feelings, gathering them together into serenity.

Or. 1180.   Orestes compliments Electra, who says that she has a proposal to save them: "for I know that understanding (τὸ συνετόν) is present (πάρειμι) in your *psychē*." Here *psychē* is specifically a seat of intelligence. Euripides uses a new noun with it: "understanding."[23]

Tr. 1171. Hecuba says that, if Astyanax had lived, he would have enjoyed "youth," "marriage," and "rule" (1169–70). Then she says: "but now, having seen (εἶδον) and known (γιγνώσκω) them with your *psychē*, child, you do not perceive (οἶδα) them and, having them at home, you enjoy nothing." Astyanax, while alive, dwelt among the blessings he would appreciate more as he grew older. He already "saw" and "knew" these blessings in his *psychē*. Now that he is dead, the blessings remain but he has no awareness of them.[24] Euripides introduces two new ideas here of *psychē* "seeing" and "knowing" in the living person.

Fr. 220 (Antiope). This fragment reads: "many mortals suffer this one evil. Thinking (φρονέω) with judgment (γνώμη), they are not willing to act in accord with (ὑπηρετέω) *psychē*, being conquered in many things by their friends." Euripides here uses an image of "rowing" with the verb ὑπηρετέω. *Psychē* is associated with the positive action of "thinking with judgment." Outside influence prevents people from "rowing with" their inward thoughts. Here we have a clear connection of *psychē* with thinking of a most valuable kind.

Fr. 913 (Incerta). In this fragment we see *psychē* as the recipient of instruction. It reads: "who is so without honour for god and pressed by heavy fate who, on seeing these things, does not teach (προδιδάσκω) his *psychē* beforehand to consider (ἡγέομαι) the god?" Certain circumstances are to lead a person to be reflective and to lead his *psychē* to show reverence for the divine. *Psychē* here is pictured as a seat of thought and reflection.

Fr. 924 (Incerta). Once again we find a person directly addressing his own *psychē*: "do not touch (θιγγάνω) subtle words (μῦθοι), *psychē*. Why do you think (φρονέω) excessive things? Unless you are about to be magnified (sem-nÚnw) by your peers." We see here a connection of *psychē* in the living person with speech.[25] We see too a new association of *psychē* in the living person with "thinking" (φρονέω). This *psychē* is apparently attempting to be clever and subtle in its speech. What it thinks is somehow "excessive." Its motive seems to be to draw praise for itself from contemporaries.

PREDOMINANTLY EMOTIONAL

Anger

In earlier and contemporary poets we find only one reference to *psychē* and anger. Homer pictures the shade of Ajax as "standing apart, angry (κεχολωμένη) because of the victory" that Odysseus achieved in receiving the arms of

Achilles. Sophocles describes Electra as always "begetting wars" in her "sullen (δύσθυμος) *psychē*" (*El.* 219). Euripides now speaks of *psychē* in the living person as capable of this emotion.

Med. 110.   The Nurse in her speech, warning the children about Medea, refers to her *phrēn* (104), *thumos* (108), and *kradia* (99).[26] She "stirs" her *kradia*. She has a "hateful nature of a self-willed *phrēn*." "A cloud of lamentation will kindle in her with greater *thumos*." The Nurse ends her speech with a description of Medea's *psychē*: "whatever will her *psychē*, highspirited (μεγαλόσπλαγχνος), most hard to check (δυσκατάπαυστος), do as it is bitten (δηχθεῖσα) with evils?" Euripides introduces two new adjectives with *psychē*, each five syllables long. Together they sum up the strong-willed and impulsive nature of Medea's *psychē*. The image of *psychē* "bitten by evils" occurs also in Theognis 910. This *psychē* is especially filled with anger. We find this association also in Sophocles when Electra is said "always to beget wars in her *psychē*" (*El.* 219).

The Nurse sees several psychic entities in Medea active in her response to the betrayal by Jason. Each one is of a negative nature, potentially dangerous, especially to the children. Her assessment of Medea's inner nature proves to be correct.

Pho. 1297.   The Chorus speak of Eteocles and Polyneices as they fight one another: "murderous (φονίος) *psychai* with quivering spear will bloody (αἱμάσσω) destructive fallings."[27] *Psychai* here act as the seat of emotion in the two brothers. Euripides uses a new adjective to describe these *psychai*: φονίος, "murderous." Each has one mad aim: to kill the other. They are filled with anger and rage. Both *psychai* too will soon leave in death.

Confidence

Alc. 604.   The Chorus speak in admiration of the way in which Admetus, despite his grief, receives Heracles: "confidence (θράσος) sits on my *psychē* that the god-fearing man [= Admetus] will fare well." Euripides presents a new description of *psychē* in describing it as having "confidence" (θράσος). *Psychē* is a seat of positive emotion in the Chorus.

Courage

In earlier and contemporary poets we find *psychē* associated with courage. Pindar describes Hieron as having a "steadfast (τλήμων) *psychē*" (*Pyth.* 1.48). He also calls Heracles "unflinching" (ἄκαμπτος) in *psychē* (*Is.* 4.53 [b]). Aeschylus associates *psychē* with courage in speaking of "bold judgment of *psychē*" in the Persian leaders and calling them "best in *psychē*" (*Per.* 29, 442).[28] Sophocles likewise associates *psychē* with courage when he has Heracles address his "hardy (σκληρός) *psychē*" (*Tr.* 1260).

Alc. 837.   Heracles addresses his own *psychē*: "o *kardia*, enduring many things, and my *psychē*, now show what sort of son Alcmene bore for Zeus!"[29] Heracles calls upon both *kardia* and *psychē* to be courageous as he begins his journey to Hades to retrieve Alcestis.

Hec. 580.   After the death of Polyxena, the Argives encourage each other to bring gifts to adorn her body: "will you not go, about to give something for the one excessively brave-hearted (εὐκάρδιος) and best (ἄριστος) in *psychē*?" Like Aeschylus, who described the Persian leaders as "best in *psychē*" (*Per.* 442), Euripides uses this description of Polyxena. He also introduces a new picture of her as "excessively brave-hearted in *psychē*." The *psychē* of Polyxena is seen as the seat of her great courage.

Supp. 1103.   Iphis, after Evadne's death, says: "Nothing is sweeter to an old father than a daughter. The *psychai* of men are greater (μείζων) but less sweet (γλυκύς) for caresses." In earlier and contemporary poets we hear of *psychai* greater (κρέσσων) than their possessions at Pin., *Nem.* 9.32. At Soph., *Aj.* 154, we hear of "mighty (μέγας) *psychai*." Euripides seems to refer, by using "greater," to the more valiant spirit that men can show. In Bacch. 5.151 and Sim. 553 we find references to a "sweet" (γλυκύς) *psychē*. A woman's *psychē* has more sweetness in showing affection than a man's. In this passage *psychē* is associated both with courage and with love.

Desire

El. 297, Hipp. 173.   In these two passages we have a new association of *psychē* with desire. At *El.* 297 the Chorus say that they, like Orestes (290–6), wish to hear Electra's story: "and I have the same desire (ἔρος ἔχω) of *psychē* as this one." The wish of the Chorus is centred in their *psychē*. At *Hipp.* 173 the Chorus want to find out why Phaedra is ill: "my *psychē* desires to learn (μαθεῖν ἔραμαι) whatever it is, why the queen's form, changed in colour, has been damaged." *Psychē* here is the seat of a desire for information.

Fear

Tr. 182.   Another new association with *psychē* appears at *Tr.* 182, that of fear. Hecuba tells the Chorus why she has come: "o child, I have come struck (ἐκπλήσσω) with shuddering (φρικά) in my *psychē* that arose early (ὀρθεύουσα)."³⁰ Hecuba's *psychē* has "awakened early." In this *psychē* she feels "struck" with dread or panic – that is, with "shuddering." Euripides locates in *psychē* a severe state of fear. He uses a new participle with *psychē* in describing it as "arising early." We see in this passage a vibrant presence of *psychē* in the living person.

Grief

In five passages Euripides associates *psychē* with grief. In earlier and contemporary poets we find a picture in Homer of the shades of the dead "grieving." Thus we find the participles ἀχνυμένη,³¹ γοόωσα (*Il.* 23.106), μυρομένη (*Il.* 23.106), and ὀλοφυρομένη (*Od.* 11.471). Once in the lyric poets Hipponax describes his *psychē* as "much-enduring" (πολύστονος: 39). Sophocles describes the *psychē* of Oedipus as "groaning" (στένω) for the city, the Thebans, and himself. Euripides speaks of *psychē* in the living person as a location of grief as follows.

Alc. 108.   The Chorus react to the impending death of Alcestis: "you touched (θιγγάνω) my *psychē*, you touched my *phrenes*."³² Both *psychē* and *phrenes* seem to be involved in grief. Euripides here uses *psychē* and *phrenes* almost interchangeably. Sophocles at *Ant.* 317–19 does the same, referring to both *psychē* and *phrenes* as a seat of pain.³³ We see how *psychē* has become a psychological agent in the living person, resembling another psychic entity, namely *phrenes*.

Alc. 354.   Admetus, proposing to make an image of Alcestis to love, says: "I think that this will be a cold delight but none the less I would lessen (ἀναντλέω) the weight (βάρος) of my *psychē*." Euripides introduces here an image of *psychē* as a "ship" from which the "weight" of bilge water is "drawn off" (ἀναντλέω).³⁴ Grief is present to Admetus as a "weight" on *psychē* that he will strive to lessen.

El. 208.   Electra tells the Chorus that her lot is to grieve: "I myself dwell in a poor home, wasting away (τήκω) in my *psychē*, an exile from my father's house." Euripides introduces a new image here of Electra "melting" or "wasting away" (τήκω) in *psychē*.³⁵ She locates her grief in *psychē*.

Hcld. 645.   Euripides here uses the same verb τήκω with *psychē*. Iolaus summons Alcmene to hear news of the children of Heracles: "come out and hear the most dear words of this man. For long being in pain, you have languished (τήκω) in *psychē*, if the return of those who have come would occur." Like Electra, Alcmene has "melted" in her *psychē* with sorrow.

Hipp. 160.   The Chorus wonder if Phaedra is ill because she has received some bad news from Crete: "is her *psychē* bound (δέω) bed-fast (εὐναῖος) with grief (λύπη) over her sufferings?" Euripides presents a new picture of *psychē*. It is "bed-fast," unable through illness to arise. It is filled with grief over sufferings. The state of *psychē* within keeps Phaedra prostrate.

Hope

Hcld. 173.   Euripides introduces a new emotion with *psychē*: hope. Neither Aeschylus nor Sophocles connects *psychē* with this emotion. The Herald warns Demophon not to place his hopes on the future conduct of the children of Heracles: "these, having grown to manhood, would fight poorly with Argives fully armed, if in any way this prospect lifts (ἐπαίρω) you in *psychē*." Demophon is not to be "lifted" in *psychē* with hope.

Joy

In earlier and contemporary poets we find a connection of joy and *psychē* in the picture Homer gives of Achilles' shade rejoicing over the activities of his son: "his *psychē* went, striding in long steps over the field of asphodel" (*Od.* 11.471). Pindar refers to Aeson "rejoicing" (γηθέω) about *psychē*"as he sees his"exceptional son"(*Pyth.* 4.122). Aeschylus speaks of giving pleasure (ἡδονή) to *psychē* day by day" (*Per.* 841). Sophocles speaks of the image of Orestes "bursting upon the *psychē* of Chrysothemis, bringing her great joy" (*El.* 903). Euripides associates joy with *psychē* in two passages.

Ion 1170, Fr. 754 (Hypsipyle).   The Servant describes the guests at the banquet as "filling (πληρόω) their *psychē* with rich food." These people take delight in the bounteous fare they consume. Fr. 754 reads: "lifting one after another prize of flowers with rejoicing (ἡδομένη) *psychē*." Euripides uses a new participle with *psychē*: it is "filled with delight" or "gladness." Like Aeschylus, he associates ἡδονή with *psychē*.

Love

In earlier and contemporary poets love frequently affects *phrenes, thumos, noos,* and *kēr*.[36] In Homer we hear that the shades of the dead "each ask about those dear to him" (*Od.* 11.541). In Anacreon a young boy is described as "charioteer" of his *psychē* (360). Sophocles speaks of love (ἔρος) "distressing (ταράσσω) the *psychai* of the gods above" (Fr. 684). Euripides several times associates *psychē* with love.

Hipp. 255, 259. The Nurse as she tends Phaedra, who is sick, says: "For it is necessary for mortals to mix moderate loves (μετρίας φιλίας) to one another and not to the deep marrow (ἄκρον μυελόν) of *psychē*, but loves (στέργηθα) of *phrenes* should be easily loosed (εὔλυτα), both to be driven away (ὠθέω) and to be tightened (ξυντείνω). For one (εἷς) *psychē* to feel pain (ὠδίνω) over two is a difficult weight (βάρος), as I suffer for this one." As in *Alc.* 108, *psychē* and *phrenes* here are mentioned together and seem to be close in meaning.[37] *Psychē* has become like *phrenes* a seat of love in the living person. Euripides introduces a new image with *psychē*: loves should not penetrate to the "deep marrow" of it.[38] *Psychē* is pictured as having different levels. Love should not be allowed to go too deep.

This passage also speaks of the involvement of *psychē* in pain. For it to "feel pain" (ὠδίνω) is a "difficult weight" (χαλεπόν βάρος). We heard above of the "weight" (βάρος) of *psychē* in grief (*Alc.* 354). Sorrow for another can weigh *psychē* down. The Nurse, describing herself as "one *psychē*," says that she grieves for two, both herself and for Phaedra. Here, as in *IT* 882 and *Med.* 247, we see *psychē* used as a periphrasis for the person.

Hipp. 505. Phaedra, urging the Nurse not to continue further in her shameful suggestions, describes herself: "I am well-tilled (ὑπειργάχομαι) in *psychē* by love (ἔρος)." Euripides introduces an agricultural image here with the verb ὑπειργάχομαι. Phaedra's *psychē* has been made "ready for sowing."[39] "Love" has been the plough that has acted upon *psychē*. Once again *psychē* has become a seat of love in the living person.

Hipp. 527. The Chorus describe Eros: "Eros, Eros, pouring desire in eyes, leading (εἰσάγω) sweet delight (γλυκεῖα χάρις) to the *psychē* of those against whom you wage battle." *Psychē* receives the "sweet delight" that love brings.

Fr. 323 (Danaë). We find the description, probably of a child and his mother: "with a multitude of kisses he took possession of (κτάομαι) my *psychē*." This abundant show of affection wins over *psychē* completely.[40]

Fr. 431 (Hippolytus). This fragment has been ascribed also to Sophocles as Fr. 684 (*Phaedra*). In this fragment we find the verb ταράσσω with *psychai*: love "distresses" the *psychai* of the gods. Euripides' fragment reads: "for Eros comes not only to men and in turn to women but whets (χαράσσω) the *psychai* of the gods." In this fragment we find the reading "whets," χαράσσω, a new one with *psychē*. Love somehow makes the *psychai* of the gods "sharp." As a result, as the fragment goes on to say, even Zeus yields to love.

Madness

Bacc. 1268.   As Agave comes to her senses, Cadmus asks: "is this bewilderment (τὸ πτοηθέν) still present (πάρειμι) in your *psychē?*" Agave responds: "I do not understand their word but I an becoming somehow rational (ἔννους), changing (μεθίστημι) from my former *phrenes.*"[41] Once again, as at *Alc.* 108 and *Hipp.* 255–9, *psychē* and *phrenes* appear to be similar in meaning. Both act as seats of the madness Agave has suffered. Euripides introduces this idea of madness in *psychē.* He uses the phrase τὸ πτοηθέν: Agave is "set aflutter" or "bewildered" in her *psychē.* The phrase recalls the picture of the "bewilderment" (πτοιέω) of the *phrenes* of the suitors at *Od.* 22.298.[42] This condition of *psychē* in Agave was attended by her *phrenes* being also in a distorted condition.

Pain

In earlier and contemporary poets we do not find *psychē* associated often with pain. We have seen, however, that *psychē*, as shade of the dead, is involved greatly in grief.[43] Theognis at 900 describes himself as "bitten (δάκνω) in *psychē* and holding his *thumos* in two directions." We have heard Medea being described as one "bitten (δηχθεῖσα) in *psychē* by evils" (see above, "Anger"). In the questionable line, *Sept.* 1034, of Aeschylus we find a reference to *psychē* "sharing in misfortunes (κακά)." Sophocles associates *psychē* with pain three times. Creon is "bitten (δάκνω) in *psychē*" (*Ant.* 317). "Blasts of wind of *psychē*" hold Antigone, a description of her physical state (*Ant.* 930). Philoctetes' *psychē* is called "wretched" (μελέος) at *Ph.* 712.[44] Euripides associated *psychē* with pain several times.

[HF 1366], Hipp. 259.   Diggle in the OCT brackets *HF* 1366.[45] Heracles in this line asks Theseus: "compel (βιάζω) your *psychē* to share in my sufferings (συμφέρω, κακά)." If the line is genuine, Heracles is asking Theseus to share the terrible misfortunes that have befallen him. *Psychē* would be the location of this shared pain in Theseus. At *Hipp.* 259, as we saw above under "Love," the Nurse says: "for one *psychē* to feel pain (ὠδίνω) over two is a difficult weight, as I suffer for this one." Here *psychē* is explicitly associated with the experience of pain.

Ion 877.   As Creusa decides to tell her past, she says: "my eyes drop tears and my *psychē* feels pain (ἀλγέω), plotted against (κακοβουληθείς) by human beings and gods, whom I will show as thankless betrayers of my bed." In this passage also Euripides describes *psychē* as being "in pain" (ἀλγέω). He also introduces a new description of it as "plotted against."

Ion 1247.   The Chorus wonder what Creusa will suffer after they hear of her attempt to poison Ion: "whatever, o wretched mistress, awaits for you to suffer (πάσχω) in your *psychē*?" Here likewise Creusa is to experience pain in *psychē*.

Med. 474.   When Jason appears, Medea refers to what she has been suffering, locating this as having taken place in her *psychē*.[46] She says: "you did well in coming. For I, having spoken badly of you, will be lightened (κουφίζω) in *psychē* and you, on hearing, will grieve." Medea suggests that she will pour forth from her *psychē* the pain she has been enduring. She will give up its "weight" and become "lightened" in *psychē*.[47]

Tr. 640.   Andromache speaks of the fate of human beings: "but the person who has enjoyed good fortune, having fallen into bad fortune, wanders (ἀλάομαι) in *psychē* because of the former good fortune." Euripides here appears to use the image of *psychē* "wandering" – that is, suffering pain and distress – because it once enjoyed good fortune but has now lost it.[48] Euripides first uses the verb ἀλάομαι with *psychē* in this image of its bewildered state.

Fr. 67.7 (Alcmeon).   Lines 1–4 of this fragment describe the negative effect upon *nous* of fear (φόβος).[49] It keeps *nous* from "saying what it wishes." At lines 6–7 the person says: "nevertheless it is necessary for me to outrun (ὑπερδραμεῖν) this contest (ἀγών), for I see my *psychē* laid on the line as a prize (ἆθλα κειμένην)." This expression with κειμένην is rather unusual. The picture seems to be of *psychē*, caught in a situation of distress, urging the person onwards.

Fr. 822 (Phrixus).   This fragment reads: "For a wife is sweetest for her husband in misfortunes and diseases, if she manages her house well, both being gentle in temper and freeing (μεθίστημι) her *psychē* from desponding (δυσθυμία)." Euripides uses δυσθυμία for the first time with *psychē*. The wife will be a great blessing if she keeps her own *psychē* from despair.

Fr. 908.8 (Incerta).   This fragment speaks of the sorrows that attend having children. At line 6 it mentions a *kardia* that is "wasted away" (τήκω) with "terror" (ὀρρωδία).[50] The fragment asks: "what is this blessing? Is it not sufficient for one (εἷς) *psychē* to be at a loss (ἀλύω) and, for this reason, to have sufferings (πόνος)?" Euripides speaks of this idea of one *psychē* suffering sufficiently at *Alc.* 883 and *Hipp.* 259. Here he describes *psychē* for the first time as being "at a loss."[51] This *psychē* has "sufferings." Once again *psychē* acts as a seat of pain in people.

Fr. *964.6* (Incerta).   This fragment describes someone envisaging disasters beforehand in order that reality might prove to be less painful. He places "misfortunes" (συμφοραί) into *nous* (2); he speaks of imagining evils with *phrēn* (5).[52] A possible reading of lines 5 and 6 is: "in order that, if I were to suffer what I imagined in my *phrēn*, the fresh disaster falling on me would not bite (δάκνω) *psyche*." There is an alternate reading to *psychē*, namely "more" (μᾶλλον). If *psychē* is the correct reading, it would be "bitten" (δάκνω). We can compare *Med.* 110, where Medea is "bitten in *psychē*."[53] *Psychē* would be a seat of distress or pain.

Seat of Pity

Or. 526.   Tyndareus asks Orestes in relation to his murder of Clytemnestra: "what (τίς) *psychē* did you ever have (ἔχω) when your mother showed her breast, beseeching you as a suppliant?" Euripides uses *psychē* in a new way as a seat of pity. Orestes' *psychē* fails to express this emotion. Tyndareus wonders at its absence.

PREDOMINANTLY MORAL

Evil

In earlier and contemporary poets we do not find an association of *psychē* in the living person with negative moral behaviour. Sophocles twice makes this association. At *Ph.* 54 he speaks of Neoptolemus "deceiving" (ἐκκλέπτω) the *psychē* of Philoctetes with words. At 1014–15 the "evil" (κακός) *psychē* of Odysseus "taught" Neoptolemus "to be clever in evil deeds (κακά)." Aeschylus uses κακός to describe the "cowardly *psychē*" of Aegisthus (*Ag.* 1643); Sophocles uses it to indicate Odysseus' evil nature. These two instances are the first occurrences of κακός with *psychē*.

Hcld. 927.   The Chorus, having described the insolence of Lycus, say: "may my thought (*phronēma*) and *psychē* never be insatiate (ἄκόρεστος)." Here we find a mention together of *phronēma* and *psychē*. A similar one appears in Soph., *Ant.* 176, when Creon says: "it is impossible to learn the *psychē*, *phronēma*, and *gnōmē* of every man before he has been seen versed in rule and laws." Euripides links *phronēma* and *psychē*. The two nouns suggest the intelligence of a person and, more fully, his whole inner "life-spirit." Neither should be "insatiate." Euripides uses a new adjective with *psychē*. Ideally, *psychē* must resist excessive desires.

Good

In earlier and contemporary poets we hear once of the "goodness" of *psychē* in Pindar. At *Ol.* 2.70 he describes "those who endured to keep their *psychē* from unjust deeds." Sophocles mentions "goodness" with *psychē* three times. He refers in a positive way to "great (μέγας) *psychai*" at *Ag.* 154. He describes Antigone as "well-intentioned" (εὔνους) at *O.C.* 499. He praises a "more careful (ἐπιμελής) *psychē*" in Fr. 472. Euripides relates *psychē* to "goodness" twice.

Fr. *185* (*Antiope*).   This fragment reads: "you neglect what you ought to think about. For having taken so noble a nature (φύσις γενναία) of *psychē*, you are conspicuous in a form aping women." Here a "noble nature" is ascribed to *psychē*.

Fr. *388* (*Theseus*).   In this fragment we hear: "but there is some other love among mortals of a *psychē* just (δίκαιος), moderate (σώφρων), and good (ἀγαθός)." Three qualities are ascribed to this positive *psychē*. At *And.* 611 Euripides uses ἀγαθός to describe *psychai* whom Menelaus destroyed.[54] That reference and this one here are the first times we find ἀγαθός with *psychē*. The other two descriptions, "just" and "moderate," are likewise new. *Psychē* has become the seat of admirable traits of character.

Holiness

Bacc. 75.   Once Euripides related *psychē* to holiness. Sophocles does likewise at *O.C.* 499 when he praises a *psychē* that "pays" (ἐκτίνω) vows in full. At *Bacc.* 75 the Chorus praise a human being: "o blessed who, being fortunate, knowing the rites of the gods, lives a holy life and hallows (θιασεύω) his *psychē* in Bacchic rites." This person makes his *psychē* holy by taking part in the rites of Dionysus. *Psychē* has become the seat of a person's inner holiness.

GODS

In one fragment only do we hear of the *psychē* of the gods in Euripides. Fr. 431 (*Hippolytus*) mentions Eros "whetting" (χαράσσω) the *psychai* of the gods.[55]

KINDS OF PSYCHĒ

Thus far we have looked at all passages where *psychē* appears in Euripides. In chapter 7 we discussed his traditional usage; in this chapter we shall now look at the adjectives and participles that he uses. These are presented in detail in Appendix Three.

Euripides uses a number of adjectives and one participle that appear already in traditional and contemporary contexts. These include: βρότειος, γλυκύς, εἶς, ἐμός, πολύς, ποτωμένη, σός, and φίλος.[56]

Euripides uses a large number of new adjectives and participles with *psychē*, as Table 8.1 shows. In each case a wider range of function of *psychē* than found before is suggested.

EURIPIDEAN IMAGES

We have seen in our discussion of the instances of *psychē* the appearance of several images. Here we shall look at four major images.

"CONTEST"

[Or. 847], Pho. 1330.   In the suspect line from the *Orestes*, there is a description of Orestes as having gone to the people of Argos, "about to engage in the present struggle (ἀγών) for his *psychē*." At *Pho.* 1330 the Chorus say: "I think that the contest (ἀγών) for *psychē* has been held for the sons of Oedipus." As pointed out in our discussion of these passages, this image is a traditional one. Sophocles likewise uses this image in speaking of a "contest" (ἀγών) for the *psychē* of Aegisthus (*El.* 1492). *Psychē* is seen as a "prize" to be struggled for.[57]

"EXPENDITURE"

And. 541, Hcld. 296, Supp. 777.   In the first passage Menelaus speaks of "expending (ἀναλίσκω) a great part" of his *psychē* in fighting at Troy. In the second we hear of the "wearing out" (διακναίω) of *psychē*. In the third, *psychē* is described as an "expenditure" (ἀνάλωμα) that can be paid out only once. All three passages suggest the image of *psychē* as a commodity within that can be expended. If fully expended, it is lost forever.

"MARROW"

Hipp. 255.   Loves should not, the Nurse asserts, come to the "deep marrow" (μυελόν) of *psychē*. Here we have the image of *psychē* with different levels. It can be involved in emotion in different degrees. If loves penetrate to the "marrow" of *psychē*, it can be very harmful.

"SELLING"

Pho. 1228.   Eteocles calls on the Argives and Thebans not to "sell" (ἀπεμπολάω) their *psychē*. We find this image of "selling *psychē*" also at

Table 8.1
New Adjectives and Participles with *Psychē*

Adjective or participle	Passage	Meaning
ἀγαθός	*And.* 611 Fr. 388 (*Theseus*)	good
ἀκόρεστος	*Hcld.* 927	insatiate
ἄκουσα	*Hcld.* 531	unwilling
δεινός	*And.* 160	clever
δηχθεῖσα	*Med.* 110	bitten
δίκαιος	Fr. 388 (*Theseus*)	just
δυσκατάπαυστος	*Med.* 109	most hard to stop
ἑκοῦσα	*Hcld.* 531 Fr. 360.44 (*Erechtheus*)	willing
εὐναῖος	*Hipp.* 160	bed-fast
αὐτυχοῦσα	*IT* 838	enjoying good fortune
ἡδομένη	Fr. 784 (*Hypsipyle*)	glad, rejoicing
ἠπειρῶτις	*And.* 160	of Asia
θεῖος	*Hec.* 87	prophetic
κακοβουληθείς	*Ion* 877	ill-advised
κειμένη	Fr. 67 (*Alcmeon*)	proposing
μαγαλόσπλαγχνος	*Med.* 109	high-spirited
μείζων	*Hipp.* 1103	greater
μέλεος	*IT* 882	wretched
ὁμογενής	*Pho.* 1291	of the same race
ὀρθεύουσα	*Tr.* 182	arising early
παρθένος	*Hipp.* 1006	virgin
πιστότατος	*Alc.* 900	most faithful
σώφρων	Fr. 388 (*Theseus*)	moderate
τάλας	[*HF* 452]	wretched
τρίσσος	*Pho.* 1553	three
φόνιος	*Pho.* 1297	murderous

Soph., *Ant.* 322, where Creon accuses the Guard of having "betrayed" his *psychē* for "money" (χρήματα). *Psychē* appears to be something that people can choose to "sell," as though it is a personal possession.

RELATIONSHIP OF PERSON AND PSYCHĒ

How does Euripides speak of the relationship of person and *psychē*? Traditionally, as in the case of other psychic entities, person and *psychē* remain distinct. This occurs in earlier and contemporary poets.[58] It is also the case in Aeschylus. In Sophocles a difference appears. In 34 instances he presents the traditional picture but in one, *Ph.* 712, *psychē* and person appear to be identified.

Appendix One lists all the instances of *psychē* (117) in terms of the relationship between this psychic entity and the individual. For *psychē* this description falls into two parts, the first treating traditional uses, the second, new ones. With this Appendix as a guide, we can make the following observations.

1 *Psychē* appears 26 times as either active or described in a person in traditional uses, 24 times in new ones (Category A). In traditional uses it is rarely active. It can, for example, "fly" (*Or.* 676) or "leave the light" (*Pho.* 1553). It is often described. We learn, for example, that it is an object of "pity" (*Or.* 1034) or that "children are *psychē*" (*And.* 419). We hear of a "struggle" ([*Or.* 847]) or a "contest" (*Pho.* 1330) for *psychē*. *Psychē* is something one can swear by (*Or.* 1517).

   In new uses, *psychē* is frequently active. It "desires to learn" (*Hipp.* 173), for example, or "feels pain" (*Ion* 877). It is also frequently described. It is present in a "willing" state (*Hcld.* 530). We hear of a "desire" of *psychē* (*El.* 297) or "collectedness" of it (*HF* 626).

   In two instances of these new uses we find, as in Soph., *Ph.* 712, *psychē* being used as a periphrasis for the person. This occurs at *Hipp.* 259 and *IT* 882.

2 *Psychē* occurs (Category B) twice in traditional uses as an instrument that someone acts with (*Alc.* 712, *Hipp.* 1024). In new uses, it appears once as a location (*Ion* 1247) and twice as an instrument (*Tr.* 1171, Fr. 754).

3 In 18 passages of traditional meanings, a person has a direct relationship with *psychē* (Category C). It is, for example, a psychic entity that one "loves" (*Alc.* 704, *Hcld.* 455), "sends forth" (*Hel.* 1431, *Or.* 1171), or "gives" (*Hcld.* 550, *Pho.* 998).

   In 10 passages of new uses, a person relates directly to *psychē*. It is, for example, a psychic entity that one "has" (*Hipp.* 1006, *Or.* 526), "makes holy" (*Bacc.* 75), or "teaches" (Fr. 913).

4 A person is described in relation to *psychē* only in new uses (Category D). This occurs 7 times. One, for example, "wastes away" (*El.* 208, *Hcld.* 645) in *psychē*, or is "struck" (*Tr.* 182) or "lightened" (*Med.* 474) in it.

5 In 15 passages of traditional meaning, *psychē* is affected by outside objects or agents (Categories E and F). In 12 passages of new uses this is the

case. One of these is significant: at *Med.* 247 we find again a use of *psychē* as a periphrasis for the person when Medea says that women must look at "one *psychē*."

6 One feature is prominent in the new uses of *psychē*. A person frequently addresses it in the vocative.[59] This occurs 7 times. In 6 of these, people address their own *psychē*.[60] These passages suggest a traditional view of the person being distinct from *psychē*. In one instance, *IT* 882, Iphigenia addresses Orestes as "poor *psychē*." This we suggest is an instance of periphrasis where person and *psychē* are identified.

The detailed overview of passages presented in Appendix One and briefly summarized here suggests that to a large extent Euripides referred to the relationship of person and *psychē* in a traditional way. Usually the two remain distinct. In some passages, however, this distinction is lost.[61] We see that, within the person, *psychē* has a rich range of function. It endows people with life; it survives after death. While people are alive it engages in a large number of activities. It has become so prominent a psychic entity that the person can on occasion be identified with it.

OVERVIEW OF PSYCHĒ

From our discussion of *psychē* in chapters 7 and 8 we can make the following observations.

SPECIFIC FEATURES OF *PSYCHĒ*

1 *Psychē* appears most often in the singular (108), with a few references only to the plural (9).

2 On a continuum of "physical" to "psychological" *psychē* appears to lie at the "psychological" end. It differs, however, from other psychic entities in retaining always its meaning as "life," "life-spirit," and "shade of the dead." The original meaning of *psychē* may have been connected with "breath," and this "physical" connotation still appears when we hear of someone "breathing forth" *psychē* (*Or.* 1163).

3 In 61 passages Euripides mentions *psychē* in traditional and contemporary ways. It appears to signify primarily "life-spirit," "shade of the dead," and "life."

4 In 56 passages Euripides introduces new uses of *psychē*. *Psychē* appears as an active psychological agent within the living person. Like *phrēn*, *nous*, *thumos*, *kardia*, and *kear*, it is found in contexts that are intellectual, emotional, and moral.

5 *Psychē* acts several times as a seat of personality.

6 *Psychē* is connected with intellectual functions. It is said to be a source of speech. It is connected with thinking.

7 *Psyche* is associated with a whole range of emotions. These include anger, confidence, courage, desire, fear, grief, and hope. They include also joy, love, madness, pain, and pity.

8 *Psyche* is related to actions evil, good, and holy.

9 We hear of the *psyche* of the gods only once (Fr. 431).

10 Sometimes *psyche* seems very close in meaning to *phrenes*. This occurs at *Alc.* 108, *Bacc.* 1268–70, and *Hipp.* 255–9.

11 Euripides introduces a large number of new adjectives and participles with *psyche*. All of these suggest an expanded meaning of *psyche* (see Table 8.1).

12 Euripides uses four major images of *psyche*. These are: "contest," "expenditure," "marrow," and "selling."

13 With respect to the relationship of person and *psyche*, we find in Euripides a traditional picture of these two being distinct. In three passages, however (*Hipp.* 259, *IT* 882, *Med.* 247), we find an identification of person and *psyche*.

GENERAL FEATURES OF *PSYCHE*

In our examination of the other psychic entities that appear in Euripides – *phrēn, nous, thumos, kardia*, and *kear* – we noted that Euripides' references to them were largely traditional and contemporary. He may introduce new features of them but he usually does so in a context already familiar.

In the case of *psyche* we find that, once again, with half of his references, Euripides appears to be traditional and contemporary. The associations *psyche* had with "life-spirit," "shade of the dead," and "life" reappear.

With the other references to *psyche*, however, Euripides introduces new usages. In this he resembles Sophocles, who likewise has many new uses of *psyche*. Euripides presents *psyche* as a vital psychic entity within. It has a wide range of function. In some passages it seems to be primarily intellectual; in others, emotional or moral. It can also be more, the seat of personality in the individual. In a few cases it has even come to stand for persons themselves.

Homer shows us the shades of the dead, *psychai*, in the First and Second Nekyia (*Odyssey*, Books 11 and 24) acting very much like living persons once they have drunk blood. It was this picture, perhaps, that had a strong bearing on how *psyche* came to be a vibrant psychological agent in the living person. We do not find with *psyche* any restriction in range of function nor any identification with a specific type of intellectual activity (as we do with *phrēn* and *nous*). Instead, *psyche* becomes associated in a very broad way with psychological activity in general.

In his dramas Euripides shows us a new range of meaning of *psyche*. The prominent role that it comes to have in Plato is clearly adumbrated here.

9 Conclusion

In the chapters above we have examined Euripides' use of psychological terminology. Like earlier and contemporary poets and like Aeschylus and Sophocles, he describes psychological activity in terms of multiple psychic entities. In the seventeen extant tragedies and fragments Euripides mentions *phrēn*, *nous*, *prapides*, *thumos*, *kardia*, *kear*, and *psychē*, seven different psychic entities.[1] In this chapter we shall give an overview of these psychic entities, concluding with general observations on Euripides' use of them.

OVERVIEW OF THE PSYCHIC ENTITIES

The following tables, based on the discussion presented in chapters 2–8, illustrate the range of function of the different psychic entities.

Nature of the Psychic Entities

These tables show the range of function of the seven psychic entities that appear in our extant Euripides. (For a detailed overview of each psychic entity, see the final portions of chapters 3–8). *Phrēn* appears most frequently (160 times), having the widest range of function. We do not encounter passages in which the "physical" aspect of *phrēn* is predominant, as happens in Aeschylus (*Eum.* 158) and Sophocles (*Tr.* 931). *Phrenes* alter as a person grows older, generally improving. In the young they are open to criticism.

The intellectual range of *phrēn* is very broad. We see them involved in thinking, pondering, deliberation, and planning. They are described as the

Table 9.1
Phrēn, Nous, Thumos, Psychē

Phrēn	Nous	Thumos	Psychē
Number of Occurences			
160	43	30	117

TRADITIONAL AND CONTEMPORARY USES (WITH SOPHOCLEAN FEATURES)

Phrēn	Nous	Thumos	Psychē
Age			
Young	Young		
Predominantly Physical			
			Several
Predominantly Intellectual			
Mind	Mind: Positive	Seat of Mind	
	Mind: Negative		
	Mind: Attention		
Intelligence	Intelligence		Intelligence
Planning			
Purpose			
Absence / Loss			
Distance			
Damage			
Speech	Speech		
Predominantly Emotial			
		Seat of Emotion	
Anger		Anger	Anger
Calm			
			Confidence
Courage		Courage	Courage
Desire		Desire	Desire
Distress			
Fear	Fear		Fear
Grief			Grief
		Hope	Hope
Joy			Joy
Pleasure			
Love	Love	Love	Love
Madness			Madness
Pain		Pain	Pain
		Passion	
			Pity
Predominantly Moral			
Evil			Evil
Good	Good		Good

Table 9.1 *(Continued)*
Phrēn, Nous, Thumos, Psychē

Phrēn	Nous	Thumos	Psychē
Holiness			Holiness
Justice	Justice	Justice	
Pride			
Prosperity			
Gods (prensent within)			
Yes		Yes	Yes
EURIPIDEAN USES			
Kinds of Psychic Entity			
Many	Few	Several	Many
New Activities			
Intellectual			Intellectual
			Emotional
Emotional			Moral
Divine Aspect			
	Immortal		
EURIPIDEAN IMAGES			
Archery	Archery		
		Breath	
			Contest
			Expenditure
		Lion	
			Marrow
Medical			
Nautical			
Openness			
Sharpness			
			Sell
Sight	Sight		
		Storm	
Touch			

seat of the mind; they are related to the purpose someone may have. If they are "lost" or "damaged," an individual behaves foolishly. They are often associated with speech. Euripides expands the intellectual range of *phrenes* when he speaks of "discernment" and "swiftness" of them.[2]

In their emotional range, *phrenes* are likewise very versatile. As Table 9.1 shows, we have the largest number of emotions found in *phrenes*. They are engaged in anger, fear, grief, joy, love, and pain. *Phrenes* too can be struck with madness, causing the person in whom they are located to behave irrationally.

Table 9.2
Kardia, Kear, and Prapides

Kardia	Kear	Prapides
Number of Occurences		
35	3	5

TRADITIONAL AND CONTEMPORARY USES (WITH EURIPIDEAN FEATURES)

Kardia	Kear	Prapides
Predominantly Physical		
Beating		
Predominantly Intellectual		
		Intelligence
		Mind
Predominantly Emotional		
Seat of Emotion	Seat of Emotion	
Anger		
Courage		
Desire		
Distress		
Fear		
Grief		
Joy		
Love		
EURIPIDEAN USES		
Kinds of Psychic Entity		
Several	None	Two
EURIPIDEAN IMAGES		
Armour		
Heat		
Touch		

Phrenes more than other psychic entities are associated with moral behaviour. They themselves can be "good" or "evil." They are connected with justice, holiness, and pride. To them prosperity can do harm. *Phrenes* are characterized by many adjectives (44 times), far more than most of the psychic entities, and similar only to *psychē* (36 times).

Nous, appearing less often than *phrenes* (143 times), is associated with psychological activity of a valuable kind. Like *phrēn*, it alters with age, becoming weak in the old. *Nous* is associated in particular with the mind and intelligence. As the seat of mind, it appears several times in a positive context. Sometimes it can be a negative presence, as, for example, when it is not "firm" (*IA* 334). As intelligence, *nous* is often said to be something that a person should "have."[3] *Nous* is connected with inner vision that grasps the truth of a situation.[4] *Nous* is not often related to emotion, but we do hear of its connection with love and fear. *Nous* is mentioned in moral contexts in relation to goodness and justice. An important feature that Euripides mentions about *nous* is its divine aspect. He suggests that, after death, it has "immortal gn_m_ as it falls into eternal aether" (*Hel.* 1014). Once he suggests that Zeus may be "the *nous* of mortals" (*Tr.* 886).

Prapides occur only 5 times in Euripides. They are associated with intellectual activity. As in earlier authors they seem to be very similar in function to *phrenes*.[5]

Thumos, appearing 30 times, is rarely associated with intellectual activity, unlike its appearance in Homer. It is connected most often with emotion. Its range of emotion includes anger, courage, desire, hope, love, pain, and passion. It is connected with moral behaviour only once, being mentioned in connection with injustice (*Hcld.* 925).

We find two words for "heart" in Euripides: *kardia* (35 times) and *kear* (3 times). *Kardia* is mentioned in "physical" contexts as the "beating heart" (*Alc.* 1067, *Bacc.* 1288). Most often *kardia* and *kear* are associated with emotion. Their range includes anger, courage, desire, distress, and pain. It includes also fear, grief, joy, and love.

Euripides refers to *psychē* very often: 117 times. Of his references, 61 can be described as traditional. We find the meanings of "life-spirit," "shade of the dead," and "life." In the 56 other mentions of *psychē* Euripides introduces new uses of this psychic term. Like Sophocles, who likewise shows an expanded range of meaning of *psychē*, Euripides speaks of it as having a wide range of psychological activity in the living person.

Psychē functions as a seat of personality in individuals. It is connected with intellectual activity, including "thinking," "knowing," and "speaking."[6] Its emotional range is very broad. It includes anger, confidence, courage, desire, fear, and grief. It also includes hope, joy, love, madness, pain, and pity. In relation to moral behaviour we find *psychē* related to evil, goodness, and holiness. *Psychē* is characterized by many adjectives and participles (36).

Similarities and Differences

Tables 9.1 and 9.2 show some of the ways in which the seven psychic entities both resemble and differ from one another. *Phrēn* and *nous* are alike in altering with age. They are similar too in being associated with intellectual activity. But their activities in chapters 2 and 3 are connected primarily with deliberation, pondering, and reflective thinking. *Nous* functions in a different way. It "sees" and grasps what situations need. If it is positive in nature, what it thinks will prove both true and good.

Phrēn differs from *nous* in being much more involved in emotion. It also is mentioned in moral contexts in Euripides more often than *nous*. *Phrēn* appears in more images than *nous*, but they share in those of "archery" and "sight." With reference to adjectives (see Appendix Three), both *phrēn* and *nous* are called "free";[7] otherwise the adjectives differ,[8] with *phrēn* being characterized by a far greater range of adjectives than *nous*.

Phrēn is like *prapides* in being a seat of intellectual activity. As suggested above, *phrēn* and *prapides* often appear to be quite similar.

Phrēn resembles *thumos* in being a seat of the mind, but *thumos* functions rarely in this capacity. Both *phrēn* and *thumos* have a wide range of emotional functions. Both share in anger, courage, desire, love, and pain. *Phrēn* differs in its involvement in calm, distress, fear, grief, and madness; *thumos*, in its involvement in hope and passion. The adjectives that appear with *phrēn* and *thumos* are different in each case. The images found with *phrēn* and *thumos* likewise differ, *phrēn* appearing in far more than *thumos*.

Phrēn resembles *kardia* and *kear* in the broad range of emotions ascribed to them. *Phrēn* and *kardia* share in anger, courage, desire, distress, fear, grief, joy, and love. *Phrēn* is like *kear* also in sharing in pain. The adjective "top" or "highest" (ἄκρος) appears with both *phrēn* and *kardia*;[9] otherwise the adjectives are different. *Phrēn* shares with *kardia* the image of "touch." Other images differ.

Phrēn and *psychē* are quite different with respect to the 61 traditional occurrences of *psychē*. In these, *psychē* has its own role of "life-spirit," "shade of the dead," and "life." *Phrēn* resembles *psychē* in the new uses that Euripides mentions. Both act as a seat of intelligence in the person. Both share in the emotions of anger, courage, desire, fear, and grief. They share also in joy, love, madness, and pain. *Phrēn* differs in its involvement in calm; *psychē*, in its involvement in hope and pity. *Phrēn* resembles *psychē* in it connection with evil, good, and holy behaviour. *Phrēn* has a wider involvement in moral behaviour. Both *phrēn* and *psychē* are called "good,"[10] "just,"[11] "divine,"[12] and "mortal."[13] All the other adjectives ascribed to each are different. The images associated with *phrēn* and *psychē* are different in each case.

Nous is quite different from *thumos*, especially with its primary function of intellectual activity. These two psychic entities, however, share in the emotion of love. Both are associated with justice. *Nous* is like *psychē* in their association with intelligence. Both share in the emotions of fear and love and in the moral context of gladness. *Nous* is like *kardia* also in that both share in the emotions of fear and love.

Thumos is most like *kardia* and *kear* in the wide range of emotions they are involved in. Both share in anger, courage, desire, love, and pain. *Thumos* differs in its involvement in hope and passion; *kardia*, in its involvement in grief and joy. The two psychic entities are different in the images and qualities ascribed to them.

Thumos resembles *psychē*, as a psychological agent, in the range of emotion it exhibits. Both share in anger, courage, desire, hope, love, and pain. *Thumos* differs in its involvement in passion; *psychē*, in its involvement in confidence, fear, grief, joy, and pity. The two psychic entities differ in the images and qualities that Euripides associates with them.

Kardia and *kear* seem to be very similar, the latter appearing only 3 times. *Kardia* resembles *psychē* in several emotions. Both share in anger, courage, desire, fear, grief, joy, love, and pain. They differ in the images ascribed to them. In terms of qualities that Euripides associates with them, both *kardia* and *psychē* are called "wretched"[14] and "dear."[15]

Relationship among the Psychic Entities

In general in Euripides we encounter the seven psychic entities mentioned by themselves. They may appear together in a passage, but they are not described in terms of one another. We can contrast this situation with that which we find in Homer and later poets, for example, of *phrenes* frequently serving as a location of other psychic entities.[16] Occasionally in Aeschylus and Sophocles we find psychic terms related. Aeschylus speaks of "*phrenes* steering *thumos*" (*Per.* 767).[17] Sophocles appears to suggest at *Ant.* 1090 that *nous* is superior to *phrenes*.[18]

What we do find in three passages of Euripides is the appearance of *phrenes* and *psychē* being treated almost like synonyms. This occurs at *Alc.* 108, *Bacc.*1268–70, and *Hipp.* 255–9. These passages resemble *Ant.* 317–19 of Sophocles, where once again *phrenes* and *psychē* appear to have similar meanings. What is significant here is that *psychē* has become a prominent psychological agent within the person. It has taken on functions ascribed to other psychic entities and, in these instances, has become the equivalent of *phrenes*.

In one passage of the *Medea* we do not find relationships among psychic entities described but we do find the mention of four of them together. The Nurse, in warning the children about Medea, says that Medea "stirs her *kradia*" (99), that she has a "hateful nature of a self-willed *phrēn*" (104), that her *thumos* is becoming "greater" (108), and that her *psychē*, "high-spirited, most difficult to fight against, is bitten with evils" (110). We find here a vivid picture of the inner nature of Medea. These four psychic entities are active in her response to the insults she has received. All will work together, as the play unfolds, in the actions that Medea will devise and carry out.

OBSERVATIONS

Based on our analysis of the seven psychic terms that Euripides uses, we make the following observations of his use of psychological terminology.

1 As with earlier and contemporary poets, Aeschylus and Sophocles, we can speak of a range that psychic terms cover. We suggest that it extends like a continuum from "physical" to "psychological." This continuum for early Greeks was non-divisible and seems to be the same for Euripides. We can describe the various psychic entities in relation to this continuum. For Euripides all psychic entities seem to "lie" at the "psychological" end of

the continuum. *Kardia*, however, occasionally appears to lie at the "physical" end of the continuum. *Psychē*, with both its traditional and new meanings, appears to span the continuum. It is close to the "physical" end as a psychological agent in the living person.

2 Early Greeks did not sharply divide psychological activities, and the ways in which we distinguish "intellectual," "emotional," and "volitional" are not valid for them. This seems still to be the case with Euripides. The categories we introduced were always described as "predominantly" one or another. Several aspects can always be present in any appearance of psychic terms.

3 Early Greeks fuse what we would distinguish as "agent" and "function." We have seen with Euripides that psychic entities may appear to be the seat of a psychological activity or the psychological activity itself. This is particularly true of some instances of *nous* and *thumos*, particularly the latter.[19]

4 Euripides mentions *phrēn* most often of the psychic entities (160 times). In this preference for *phrēn*, Euripides resembles both Aeschylus and Sophocles. We suggested in chapters 2 and 3 that the wide range of intellectual activity and the nature of that activity ascribed to *phrēn* may both account for its frequent appearance in tragedy. First, *phrēn* is associated with deliberation, pondering, and consideration of possibilities of action. Second, *phrenes* are the means that people resort to in times of crisis. At such times they must ponder and reflect. *Nous* could perhaps give them instantly the correct solutions. But *nous* "hides" and fails to function; sometimes it appears to be quite absent.

Phrenes too may have so frequent an appearance because they are associated with a wide range of emotions. Drama presented people responding to difficulties, and their emotional response often was located in *phrenes*. *Phrenes'* connection also with moral activity probably contributes to its being mentioned so often. Drama in particular focuses on moral dilemmas.

5 *Nous* appears 43 times in Euripides. It plays an important role as a seat of mind, attention, and intelligence. Euripides portrays it in particular as a psychic entity that people should "have" or that should be "present" within. *Nous* is perhaps the most valuable of the psychic entities, but it can sometimes fail to act, or it can be of a negative nature. People under such circumstances may act irrationally or find themselves compelled to use *phrenes* instead.

6 With regard to the relationship of person and psychic entities, the usual picture in earlier and contemporary poets, Aeschylus and Sophocles, is for person and psychic entity to remain distinct. Psychological activity is regarded by people as arising from several psychic entities within. People consider these psychic entities to be active within. They remain apart from them. The psychic entities are agents acting. They are locations where people act. They can be instruments they use or accompaniments they act with. Outside objects and agents can act upon these psychic entities within.

Euripides appears to follow this traditional picture of person and psychic entities. In three passages, however, he presents a different picture. At *IT* 882, *Hipp.* 259, and *Med.* 247, person and *psychē* appear to be identified. At *IT* 882 Iphigenia addresses Orestes as a "wretched *psychē*." At *Hipp.* 259 the Nurse speaks of "one *psychē* feeling pain." At *Med.* 247 Medea speaks of women looking at "one *psychē*" – that is, one man. In these passages *psychē* has come to stand for "person."[20] In this use Euripides resembles Sophocles at *Ph.* 712, where Philoctetes and *psychē* appear to be identified.

It is significant that it is *psychē* that comes to be thus identified with the person. As suggested above in chapter 8, the expanded role of *psychē* as a psychological agent in the living person may have appeared partly because of the way in which it is pictured by Homer in the underworld. Once it has drunk blood, *psychē* is able to behave very much like a person. It is capable of intellectual and emotional activity. It is *psychē* that in Plato becomes the seat of personality or "self." In the way in which Euripides pictures *psychē* with its broad range of psychological activities, its future role is already indicated. This is even more the case with these three passages where person and *psychē* appear to be identified.

What can we say of Euripides' use of psychological terminology overall? To a large extent it appears to be traditional. He resembles clearly the ways in which earlier and contemporary poets and also Aeschylus and Sophocles refer to these psychic terms. This is especially true of his references to six psychic entities: *phrēn*, *nous*, *prapides*, *thumos*, *kardia*, and *kear*.

True, within this traditional framework, Euripides does much that is new. He uses new adjectives and participles with psychic terms. He presents psychic entities in various new images. He expands the range of meaning of the terms in familiar contexts.

With *psychē* the case is different. Euripides' references to this psychic entity, while traditional in half the instances, are new in the other half. We cannot know whether the wide role that he ascribes to *psychē* in the living person had become common in the speech and thought of his time. Since Sophocles likewise presents an expanded role of *psychē*, we may suggest that Euripides's "new" uses were already, perhaps, quite widely known. Whatever the truth of the situation, his presentation of *psychē* prepares us well for its prominent role in the late fifth century and particularly in Plato.

This study has examined in detail Euripides' use of psychological terminology. The psychic entities often play an important role as the different dramas unfold. The analysis offered here, we can hope, will contribute to an understanding of these tragedies of Euripides.

APPENDIX A

An Overview of the Psychic Terms

This appendix describes all passages where psychic entities are mentioned in the extant tragedies and fragments.

1   The psychic entities are treated in the order found in the book itself: *phrēn*, *nous*, *prapides*, *thumos*, *kardia*, *kear*, and *psychē*.
2   The seventeen plays are treated in alphabetical order, followed by the fragments. The spurious *Rhesus* is placed after the fragments. The *Cyclops* is not treated.
3   In the case of each psychic entity the following categories are introduced:

   A   Psychic Entity Present or Active in the Person.
   B   A Person Acts in, by, or with the Psychic Entity.
   C   A Person Has a Direct Relationship with the Psychic Entity.
   D   A Person Is Described in Relation to the Psychic Entity.
   E   Outside Objects Present in or Acting on the Psychic Entity.
   F   Outside Agents Acting on or Relating to the Psychic Entity.
   G   Impersonal Expressions Involving the Psychic Entity.

4   Syntax: case and grammatical construction.
5   [ ]: indicates the person in whom the psychic entity is found.
6   Cf.: indicates the same line or lines close by where other psychic entities are mentioned.
7   The abbreviations used in the "Syntax" columns in this appendix and in appendix six are as follows:

abs.:	absolute	adj.:	adjective
acc.:	accusative	art.:	article

comp.: comparison
dat.:   dative
desc.: description
d.o.:   direct object
exclam.: exclamation
gen.:   genitive
ind.:   indicative
ind. obj.: indirect object
inf.:   infinitive
loc.:   locative
nom.:   nominative
obj.:   objective

part.: part affected
part.: participle
perf.: perfect
pl.:   plural
pres.: present
ref.:   reference
resp.: respect
s.:   singular
sep.:   separate
subj.: subjective
voc.:   vocative
w.:   with

I.   *PHRĒN* (CHAPTERS 2 AND 3)

Passage	Description	Syntax
A. *PHRĒN* PRESENT OR ACTIVE IN A PERSON		
1. *Alc.* 797	"the plash [of wine] will unmoor you from your current gloominess and contraction of *phrenes*" [Servant] (μεθορμίζω, ξυνεστός)	Gen. pl./subj. gen.
2. *And.* 181	"in some way jealousy is characteristic of a woman's *phrēn*" [Woman] (ἐπιφθονόν, θῆλυς)	Gen. s./desc.
3. *And.* 361	"I fear one feature of your *phrēn*" [Menelaus] (δέδοικα, σός)	Gen. s./desc.
4. *And.* 365	"the good sense of your *phrēn* has shot forth all its arrows" [Andromache] (τὸ σῶφρον, ἐκτοξεύω)	Gen. s./subj. gen.
5. *And.* 482 (cf. III.1)	"a combined throng of wise men is weaker than a more paltry *phrēn* that has full authority" [Human Being] (φαυλότερος, αὐτοκρατής)	Gen. s./comp.
6. [*Bacc.* 203	"not even if wisdom is found through the highest *phrenes*" (τὸ σοφόν, ἄκρος)	Gen. pl./subj. gen.]
7. *Bacc.* 269	"*phrenes* are not in your words" [Pentheus] (λόγοι)	Nom. pl.
8. *Bacc.* 670 (cf. II.43)	"I fear the swiftness of your *phrenes*" [Pentheus] (τὸ τάχος, δέδοικα)	Gen. pl./subj. gen.
9. *El.* 334	"I am their mouthpiece, these hands, tongue, suffering *phrēn*" [Electra] (ταλαίπωρος)	Nom. s.

Passage	Description	Syntax
10. [*El.* 387	"the flesh, empty of *phrenes*, are statues in the marketplace" [Human Beings] (κεναὶ σάκρες)	Gen. pl./w. adj.]
11. *Hec.* 85	"never so unabatingly has my *phrēn* shuddered, feared" [Hecuba] (φρίσσω, ταρβέω, ἐμός)	Nom. s.
12. *Hcld.* 540	"you were born of the seed of Heracles, of that divine *phrēn*" [daughter of Heracles] (θεῖος)	Gen. s./desc.
13. *Hipp.* 188 (cf. I.62, 154)	"to the second grief of *phrenes* … is added" [Human Beings] (λύπη)	Gen. pl./subj. gen.
14. *Hipp.* 256 (cf. VII.71)	"but love of *phrenes* should be easily loosed, both to be driven away and tightened" [Human Beings] (στέργηθρα, εἴλυτα, ὠθέω, ξυντείνω)	Gen. pl./subj. gen.
15. *Hipp.* 283	"trying to learn the disease of this woman and the wandering of *phrenes*" [Phaedra] (πλάνον)	Gen. pl./subj. gen.
16. *Hipp.* 317	"my *phrēn* has some stain" [Phaedra] (μίασμα)	Nom. s.
17. *Hipp.* 612	"my tongue swore but my *phrēn* is unsworn" [Hippolytus] (ἀνώμοτος)	Nom. s.
18. *Hipp.* 935 (cf. I.19)	"your words, going aside from the mark, outside of *phrenes*" [Theseus] (ἔξεδροι)	Gen. pl./w. adj.
19. *Hipp.* 936 (cf. I.18)	"alas for the mortal *phrēn*! How far will it go? If it swells during the course of a man's life, …" [Human Being] (βροτός, προβαίνω, ἐξογκόω)	Gen. s./exclam.
20. *Hipp.* 983	"father, rage and tension of your *phrenes* are terrible" [Theseus] (μένος, ξυντασίς, σός)	Gen. pl./subj. gen.
21. *Hipp.* 1419 (cf. I.22)	"for the sake of your holiness and your good *phrēn*" [Hippolytus] (ἀγαθός)	Gen. s./w. χάριν
22. *Hipp.* 1454 (cf. I.21)	"alas for your holy and good *phrēn*" [Hippolytus] (ἀγαθός, εὐσεβής, σός)	Gen. s./w. οἴμοι
23. *I.A.* 327 (cf. I.160)	"o gods, for your shameless *phrēn*!" [Menelaus] (ἀναίσχυντος, σός)	Gen. s./exclam.
24. *I.A.* 394	"for they are ready in the foolishness of their *phrenes*" [Suitors of Helen] (μωρία)	Gen. pl./subj. gen.

126   Appendix A

Passage	Description	Syntax
25. *I.T.* 655	"for still my *phrēn* desires two doubtful things" [Chorus] (μέμονα)	Nom. s.
26. [*Med.* 38	"for her *phrēn* is heavy" [Medea] (βαρύς)	Nom. s.]
27. *Med.* 104	"but be on guard against her fierce character and the hateful nature of her self-willed *phrēn*" [Medea] (φύσις, αὐθάδης)	Gen. s./subj. gen.
28. *Med.* 177	"if somehow she might give up her indignant anger and spirit of *phrenes*" [Medea] (βαρύθυμος ὀργά, λῆμα)	Gen. pl./subj. gen.
29. *Med.* 266	"whenever [a woman] has been wronged in love, there are no other *phrenes* more murderous" [Woman] (ἄλλος, μιαιφονώτερος)	Nom. pl.
30. *Med.* 661 (cf. I.68)	"to whom it is not possible to honour friends, opening the bolt of pure *phrenes*" [Human Being] (καθαρός, ἀνοίγω)	Gen. pl./subj. gen.
31. *Med.* 856 (cf. V.12)	"from where will you take the courage of *phrēn* ... to dare this terrible deed?" [Medea] (θράσος)	Gen. s./subj. gen.
32. *Pho.* 746 (cf. I.35)	"choosing out from valour or for good counsel of *phrenes*?" [Seven Captains] (εὐβουλία)	Gen. pl./subj. gen.
33. *Pho.* 1300 (cf. VII.79)	"wretched in that they ever came to a single-combat *phrēn*" [Polyneices and Eteocles] (μονομάχος)	Acc. s./w. ἐς
34. *Pho.* 1740 (cf. I.37)	"alas for the excellence of your *phrenes*" [Antigone] (τὸ χρήσιμον)	Gen. pl./subj. gen.
35. *Supp.* 1062 (cf. I.32)	"by works of Athena or by good counsel of your *phrenes*?" [Evadne] (εὐβουλία)	Gen. pl./subj. gen.
36. *Tr.* 1158	"o having a greater weight of spear than of *phrenes*" [Achaeans] (ὄγκος)	Gen. pl./subj. gen.
37. Fr. 58 *Alexander* (cf. I.34)	"I will die because of the excellence of my *phrenes*" (τὸ χρήσιμον)	Gen. pl./subj. gen.
38. Fr. 400 *Thyestes*	"o mortal affairs, o *phrenes* of women" (γυναικεῖος)	Nom. pl.
39. Fr. 619 *Peleus* (cf. I.144)	"old age is wiser than younger *phrenes* and more firm" (νεώτερος)	Gen. pl./comp.

Passage	Description	Syntax
40. Fr. 640 *Polidos*	"*phrenes* of human beings rage" (μαίνομαι)	Nom. pl.
41. Fr. 659 *Protesilaus* (cf. I.57)	"to another nothing healthy from *phrenes* pleases" (μηδὲν ὑγιές)	Gen. pl./w. ἐκ
42. Fr. 831 *Phrixus*	"but the *phrēn* of those who are not slaves is more free" (ἐλευθερώτερος)	Nom. s.
43. Fr. 1032 Incerta (cf. II.43)	"this speed and the swiftness of *phrenes* has cast many mortals into misfortune in many things" (τὸ λαιψηρόν)	Gen. pl./subj. gen.

B.   A PERSON ACTS IN, BY, OR WITH *PHRĒN*

44. *Alc.* 775	"but receive them with a courteous *phrēn*" [Servant] (δέχομαι, εὐπροσήγορος)	Dat. s./manner
45. *Hec.* 300 (cf. I.50)	"do not in your anger make one who is speaking well an enemy in your *phrēn*" [Hecuba] (ποιέω)	Dat. s./cause
46. *H.F.* 745	"there has come what before the ruler of the land never expected to suffer in *phrēn*" [Lycus] (ἐλπίζω)	Gen. s./w. διά
47. *I.A.* 67	"well in some way Tyndareus outwitted them with a cunning *phrēn*" [Tyndareus] (ὑπέρχομαι, πυκινός)	Dat. s./means
48. *Med.* 316	"I am terrified that in your *phrenes* you are planning some evil" [Medea] (βουλεύω)	Gen. pl./w. ἔσω
49. *Supp.* 217	"having possessed haughtiness in our *phrenes* we seem to be wiser than the gods" [Human Beings] (τὸ γαῦρον, κτάομαι)	Dat. pl./w. ἐν
50. *Supp.* 581 (cf. I.45)	"so that I become angry in *phrenes* because of your boasting" [Theseus] (τυμιάομαι)	Acc. pl./resp.
51. Fr. 598 *Perithous* (cf. I.100)	"speaking not with an untrained *phrēn*" (εἰπών, ἀγύμναστος)	Dat. s./means
52. Fr. 964.5 Incerta (cf. II.39, VII.112)	"If I were to suffer what I imagined in my *phrēn*" (δοξάζω)	Dat. s./loc.

Passage	Description	Syntax

C.   A PERSON HAS A DIRECT RELATIONSHIP WITH *PHRĒN*

53. *Alc.* 327	"he will do these things, if he does not lack in *phrenes*" [Admetus] (ἀμαρτάνω)	Gen. pl./w. verb
54. *Alc.* 346	"nor would I lift up my *phrēn* to sing" [Admetus] (ἐξαίρω, λάσκω)	Acc. s./d.o.
55. *Bacc.* 427 (cf. I.163, III.4)	"to keep a wise *prapis* and *phrēn* from excessive mortals" [Human Beings] (ἀπέχω, σοφός)	Acc. s./d.o.
56. *Bacc.* 944	"I praise you that you changed your *phrenes*" [Pentheus] (μεθίστημι)	Gen. pl./w. verb
57. *Bacc.* 947 (cf. I.41)	"the *phrenes* you had before were not healthy, now you have the sort you should have" [Pentheus] (ὑγίης, οἷος)	Acc. pl./d.o.
58. *El.* 1061	"would that, o mother, you had better *phrenes*" [Clytemnestra] (βελτίων)	Acc. pl./d.o.
59. *Hec.* 590	"I could not wipe out your suffering from my *phrēn* so as not to grieve" [Hecuba] (πάθος, στένω)	Gen. s./sep.
60. *Hel.* 160	"you do not have similar *phrenes* but entirely different ones" [Helen] (ὅμοιος, διάφορος)	Acc. pl./d.o.
61. [*Hel.* 732	"to have evil *phrenes*" [Human Beings] (κακός)	Acc. pl./d.o.
62. *Hel.* 1192 (cf. I.13, 91, 109, 121, 125, 154)	"do you destroy your *phrenes* with grief?" [Helen] (λύπη, διαφθείρω, σός)	Acc. pl./d.o.
63. *H.F.* 212 (cf. I.147)	"if Zeus has just *phrenes* in regard to us" [Zeus] (δίκαιος)	Acc. pl./d.o.
64. *Hipp.* 390	"so that I once again depart from *phrenes*" [Phaedra] (πίπτω)	Gen. pl./w. verb
65. *Hipp.* 474	"cease from evil *phrenes*" [Phaedra] (λήγω, κακός)	Gen. pl./w. verb
66. *Hipp.* 701	"for in light of our fortunes we possess [a reputation for] *phrenes*" [Human Beings] (κτάομαι)	Acc. pl./d.o.

Passage	Description	Syntax
67. *Hipp.* 775 (cf. I.128, 143)	"casting forth painful love from her *phrenes*" [Phaedra] (ἀπαλλάσσω, ἔρως)	Gen. pl./sep.
68. *Hipp.* 1120 (cf. I.30)	"for no longer do I have an untroubled *phrēn*" [Chorus] (καθαρός)	Acc. s./d.o.
69. *I.T.* 1322	"do not turn your *phrēn* there" [Thoas] (τρέπω, σός)	Acc. s./d.o.
70. *Or.* 1021 (cf. I.83, 143)	"I stand apart from your *phrenes*" [Electra] (ἐξίστημι)	Gen. pl./w. verb
71. *Or.* 1176 (cf. I.138–9, 158, II.32, VII.111)	"it is sweet ... to delight *phrēn* with winged words and without expense" [Orestes] (τέρπω)	Acc. s./d.o.
72. *Or.* 1204	"o you, who possess the *phrenes* of a man" [Electra] (κτάομαι, ἄρσην)	Acc. pl./d.o.
73. *Pho.* 1285	"I have a trembling with shuddering, trembling *phrēn*" [Chorus] (τρομερός)	Acc. s./d.o.
74. *Tr.* 417	"for you do not have ready *phrenes*" [Cassandra] (ἄρτιος)	Acc. pl./d.o.
75. *Tr.* 662	"if I will open my *phrēn* to my current husband" [Andromache] (ἀναπτύσσω)	Acc. s./d.o.
76. Fr. 212 *Antiope* (cf. II.17)	"what need is there of a beautiful woman unless she has good *phrenes*?" (χρηστός)	Acc. pl./d.o.
77. Fr. 362.6 *Erechtheus*	"first it is necessary to have gentle *phrenes*" (ἤπιος)	Acc. pl./d.o.
78. Fr. 548 *Oedipus* (cf. II.43)	"it is necessary to watch *nous, nous*. What need is there of fair form when someone does not have good *phrenes*?" (καλός)	Acc. pl./d.o.
79. Fr. 776 *Phaëthon*	"they have blind *phrenes*" (τυφλός)	Acc. pl./d.o.
80. Fr. 781.56 *Phaëthon*	"sacrificing to the gods, she holds her *phrenes* there" (ἔχω)	Acc. pl./d.o.
81. Fr. 1079 Incerta (cf. I.104–5, 114, 144)	"whenever someone ... confuses and calms *phrēn*" (ταπάσσω, γαληνίζω)	Acc. s./d.o.

Passage	Description	Syntax

D.   A PERSON IS DESCRIBED IN RELATION TO *PHRĒN*

82. *Bacc.* 33	"they dwell in the hills, frantic in *phrenes*" [Women of Thebes] (παράκοπος)	Gen. pl./w. adj.
83. *Bacc.* 359 (cf. I.70, 134)	"even before, you stood apart from your *phrenes*" [Pentheus] (ἐξίστημι)	Gen. pl./w. verb
84. *Bacc.* 1270	"I am becoming somehow rational, changing from my former *phrenes*" [Agave] (μεθίστημι, τῶν πάρος)	Gen. pl./w. verb
85. *Hec.* 359	"I would chance to receive masters, cruel in *phrenes*" [Polyxena] (τυγχάνω, ὠμός)	Acc. pl./resp.
86. *Hel.* 501	"for no man is so barbarous in *phrenes*" [Human Being] (βάρβαρος)	Acc. pl./resp.
87. *Hcld.* 709	"what thing are you planning, not being within your *phrenes*?" [Iolaus] (οὐκ ἔνδον, σός)	Gen. pl./w. ἔνδον
88. *H.F.* 1122 (cf. I.157)	"not in any way do I recall having been frenzied in *phrenes*" [Heracles] (βακχεύω)	Acc. pl./resp.
89. *Hipp.* 462	"how many men, being well endowed with *phrenes*" [Human Beings] (ἔξω εὖ)	Gen. pl./desc.
90. *Hipp.* 689	"for he, sharpened in his *phrenes* with anger" [Hippolytus] (συνθήγω, ὀργή)	Acc. pl./resp.
91. *Hipp.* 1012 (cf. I.62, 109, 121, 125)	"I was foolish, no rather, nowhere in *phrenes*" [Hippolytus] (οὐδαμοῦ)	Gen. pl./w. οὐδαμο
92. *Hipp.* 1230 (cf. I.99)	"maddened in *phrenes*" [Horses] (μαργάω)	Acc. pl./resp.
93. *I.A.* 359	"having taken delight in your *phrenes*" [Agamemnon] (ἥδομαι)	Acc. pl./resp.
94. *I.A.* 1359	"may you be blessed for your *phrenes*" [Achilles] (ὀνίνημι)	Gen. pl./w. verb
95. *Med.* 143	"soothed in no way in her *phrēn* by the words of any of her friends" [Medea] (παραθαλπομένη)	Acc. s./resp.

Passage	Description	Syntax
96. *Or.* 216	"for I forget, deprived of my former *phrenes*" [Orestes] (ἀπολείπω, τῶν πρίν)	Gen. pl./w. verb
97. *Or.* 1604	"not [holy] in *phrenes*" [Menelaus] (ἁγνός)	Acc. pl./resp.
98. *Tr.* 682	"nor am I deceived in my *phrenes*" [Andromache] (κλέπτομαι)	Acc. pl./resp.
99. *Tr.* 992 (cf. I.92)	"you were impassioned in *phrenes*" [Helen] (μαργάω)	Acc. pl./resp.
100. Fr. 344 *Dictys* (cf. I.50)	"young man, in labours not untrained in *phrenes*" (ἀγύμναστος)	Acc. pl./resp.

E.   OUTSIDE OBJECTS PRESENT IN OR ACTING ON *PHRĒN*

101. *Alc.* 878	"you remind me of what has wounded my *phrenes*" [Admetus] (ἑλκόω)	Acc. pl./d.o.
102. *Hcld.* 483 (cf. I.156)	"some additional pain is vexing your *phrēn*" [Iolaus] (πῆμα, δάκνω, σός)	Acc. s./d.o.
103. *H.F.* 776	"gold and good fortune draw mortals away from *phrenes*" [Human Beings] (χρυσός, εὐτυχία)	Gen. pl./sep.
104. *H.F.* 836 (cf. I.81, 105, 114, 144)	"child-killing turmoils of *phrenes*" [Heracles] (ταραγμοί)	Gen. pl./obj. gen.
105. *H.F.* 1091 (cf. I.81, 104, 114, 144)	"for in the wave and terrible distress of *phrenes* I have fallen" [Heracles] (κλύδων, τάραγμα)	Gen. pl./obj. gen.
106. *Hipp.* 511 (cf. I.120, 123)	"charms of love ... nor with harm to your *phrenes*" [Phaedra] (φίλτρα, βλάβη)	Gen. pl./obj. gen.
107. *Hipp.* 574	"what report frightens you, rushing in on *phrenes*?" [Phaedra] (φήμα, ἐπίσσυτος)	Acc. pl./w. adj.
108. *Hipp.* 926	"there ought to be for mortals some reliable test of their friends and discernment of *phrenes*" [Human Beings] (διάγνωσις)	Gen. pl./obj. gen.

Passage	Description	Syntax
109. *Hipp.* 1014 (cf. I.62, 91, 121, 125)	"since monarchy has corrupted the *phrenes* of mortals whom it pleases" [Human Beings] (μοναρχία, διαφθείρω)	Acc. pl./d.o.
110. *Hipp.* 1104	"how greatly do thoughts of the gods, when they enter my *phrenes*, relieve my griefs" [Chorus] (μελεδήματα, λύπη)	Acc. pl./w. verb
111. *Hipp.* 1390	"your nobility of *phrenes* destroyed you" [Hippolytus] (τὸ εὐγενές, ἀπόλλυμι)	Gen. pl./subj. gen.
112. *Ion* 927	"for a wave of evils just now exhausts my *phrēn*" [Servant] (κῦμα, κακά, ὑπεξαντλέω)	Dat. s./w. verb
113. *Ion* 1180	"in order that these people may come more quickly to pleasures of *phrenes*" [Human Beings] (ἡδοναί)	Gen. pl./obj. gen.
114. *Ion* 1538 (cf. I.81, 104–5, 144)	"it destroys my *phrēn*" [Ion] (ταράσσω)	Acc. s./d.o.
115. *I.A.* 1580 (cf. I.151, 155)	"pain not small entered my *phrēn*" [Messenger] (ἄλγος)	Dat. s./ind. obj.
116. *I.T.* 1181	"they cast sweet bait for my *phrenes*" [Iphigenia] (δέλεαρ)	Gen. pl./obj. gen.
117. *Med.* 55	"the affairs of masters turning out badly … touch *phrenes*" [Good Slaves] (ξυμφορά, ἀνθάπτω)	Gen. pl./w. verb
118. *Med.* 599	"nor prosperity that torments my *phrēn*" [Medea] (κνίζω, ἐμός)	Acc. s./d.o.
119. *Med.* 1052	"even to admit soft words to my *phrēn*" [Medea] (λόγοι, προσίημι)	Dat. s./ind. obj.
120. *Med.* 1265	"what heavy anger falls to you in your *phrenes*" [Medea] (χόλος, προσπίτνω)	Gen. pl./w. verb
121. *Or.* 297 (cf. I.62, 91, 109, 125)	"strengthen and comfort the horror and the destruction of my *phrenes*" [Orestes] (ἰσχαίνω, παραμυθέομαι, διαφθειρέν)	Gen. pl./obj. gen.
122. *Supp.* 1162 (cf. I.132, 159)	"[this most distressing word] has touched my *phrenes*" [Child] (ἔπος, θιγγάνω)	Gen. pl./w. verb
123. *Tr.* 6	"never has good-will departed from my *phrenes*" [Poseidon] (εὔνοια, ἀφίστημι, ἐμός)	Gen. pl./w. verb

Passage	Description	Syntax
124. *Tr.* 52 (cf. I.106, 127)	"for associations of kindred are no small charm of *phrenes*" [Gods and Human Beings] (ὁμιλίαι, φίλτρον)	Gen. pl./obj. gen.
125. Fr. 551 *Oedipus* (cf. I.62, 91, 109, 121)	"envy, which corrupts the *phrēn* of many mortals" (φθόνος, δαιφθείρω)	Acc. s./d.o.
126. Fr. 573 *Oinomaus* (cf. V.32)	"[complaints and downpourings of tears] ... lighten the pains of *phrenes*" (ὀδυρμοί, δακρύων, ἐπιρροαί, ἀλγηδών, κουφίζω)	Gen. pl./subj. gen.
127. Fr. 652 *Protesilaus* (cf. I.106, 124)	"what sort of charm of *phrēn*?" (φίλτρον)	Gen. s./obj. gen.
128. Fr. 1054 *Incerta* (cf. I.67, 143)	"for love is untrustworthy and generally lives in the most evil of *phrenes*" (ἔρως, οἰκέω, κάκιστος)	Gen. pl./partitive
129. [*Rh.* 79	"suspicion is very much in my *phrēn*" [Chorus] (ὕποπτον, ἐμός)	Dat. s./loc.]
130. [*Rh.* 266	"surely may foolish thoughts cling to the *phrēn* of shepherds" [Human Beings] (σκαιά, πρόσκειμαι, ἀγρώτης)	Dat. s./w. verb]
131. [*Rh.* 863	"I fear him and it distresses in some way my *phrenes*" [Hector] (θράσσω)	Acc. pl./d.o.]

F.   OUTSIDE AGENTS ACTING ON OR RELATING TO *PHRĒN*

132. *Alc.* 108 (cf. I.122, 159, VII.113)	"you [Chorus B] touched my *psychē*, you touched my *phrenes*" [Chorus A] (θιγγάνω)	Gen. pl./w. verb
133. *Alc.* 674	"[Admetus], do not provoke the *phrenes* of your father" [Pheres] (παροξύνω)	Acc. pl./d.o.
134. *Bacc.* 850 (cf. I.70, 83)	"first, [Dionysus], set him outside of *phrenes*, placing a light-minded madness" [Pentheus] (ἐξίστημι)	Gen. pl./w. verb
135. *El.* 1059	"but I [Clytemnestra] will grant the delight to your *phrēn*" [Electra] (ἡδύ, προστίθημι, σός)	Dat. s./ind. obj.

Passage	Description	Syntax
136. *Hec.* 746	"do I [Hecuba] reckon the *phrenes* of this man as tending to the hostile?" [Agamemnon] (ἐκλογίζομαι, τὸ δυσμενές)	Acc. pl./d.o.
137. *Hcld.* 356	"you [Iolaus] will not alarm my *phrenes* with your loud boasts" [Chorus] (φοβέω, ἐμός)	Acc. pl./d.o.
138. *Hcld.* 663 (cf. I.71, 139, 158)	"what misfortune prevents him [Hyllus], appearing here, from delighting *phrēn*?" [Alcmene] (τέρπω, ἐμός)	Acc. s./d.o.
139. *Hcld.* 939 (cf. I.71, 138, 158)	"they [Hyllus and Iolaus] ordered me to bring this man to you wishing to delight your *phrēn*" [Alcmene] (τέρπω, σός)	Acc. s./d.o.
140. *Hipp.* 238	"who of the gods reins you back and strikes your *phrenes*, child?" [Phaedra] (παρακόπτω)	Acc. pl./d.o.
141. *Hipp.* 365	"may I [Chorus] perish before I share your *phrenes*" [Phaedra] (κατανύω, σός)	Gen. pl./w. verb
142. *Hipp.* 685	"did I [Phaedra] not perceive your *phrēn* beforehand" [Nurse] (προνοοῦμαι, σός)	Gen. s./w. verb
143. *Hipp.* 765 (cf. I.67, 128, 161)	"Aphrodite has broken her *phrenes* with the terrible disease of unholy loves" [Phaedra] (κατακλάω, ἔρωτες)	Acc. pl./d.o.
144. *Hipp.* 969 (cf. I.81, 104–5, 114)	"when Cypris distresses their young *phrēn*" [Young Men] (ταράσσω, ἡβῶσα)	Acc. s./d.o.
145. *Hipp.* 1262	"what shall we [Chorus] do to please your *phrēn*?" [Theseus] (χαρίζομαι, σός)	Dat. s./w. verb
146. *Hipp.* 1268	"Cypris, you take captive the unbending *phrēn* of gods and mortals" [Gods and Human Beings] (ἄγω, ἄκαμπτος)	Acc. s./d.o.
147. *Hipp.* 1298 (cf. I.63)	"but I [Artemis] have come for this, to show the just *phrēn* of your son" [Hippolytus] (ἐκδείκνυμι, δίκαιος)	Acc. s./d.o.
148. *Hipp.* 1337	"so that she [Phaedra] persuaded your *phrēn*" [Theseus] (πείθω, σός)	Acc. s./d.o.
149. *Hipp.* 1448	"do you [Hippolytus] leave me with my *phrēn* unclean?" [Theseus] (ἐκλείπω, ἄναγνος, ἐμός)	Acc. s./d.o.

Passage	Description	Syntax
150. *Ion* 1271	"for I [Ion] measured your *phrenes* among allies" [Creusa] (ἀναμετρέω, σός)	Acc. pl./d.o.
151. *I.A.* 1434 (cf. I.115, 155)	"I [Clytemnestra] have cause so as to pain your *phrēn*" [Iphigenia] (ἀλγέω)	Acc. s./d.o.
152. *I.T.* 815	"you [Orestes] come near to my *phrenes*" [Iphigenia] (χρίμπτω, ἐμός)	Gen. pl./w. ἐγγύς
153. *Med.* 1373	"they [gods] know obviously enough your detestable *phrēn*" [Medea] (οἶδα, ἀπόπτυστος, σός)	Acc. s./d.o.
154. [*Or.* 545 (c.f. I.13, 62)	"I [Orestes] fear to speak before you in what I cannot but grieve you and your *phrēn*" [Tyndareus] (λυπέω, σός)	Acc. s./d.o.]
155. *Or.* 608 (cf. I.115, 151)	"you [Orestes] answer in such a way as to pain me in my *phrēn*" [Tyndareus] (ἀλγέω)	Acc. s./resp.
156. *Pho.* 383 (cf. I.102)	"in order that I [Jocasta] not pain your *phrēn*" [Polyneices] (δάκνω, σός)	Acc. s./d.o.
157. *Tr.* 408 (cf. I.88)	"if Apollo had not made you rave in your *phrenes*" [Cassandra] (ἐκβακχεύω)	Acc. pl./resp.
158. [*Tr.* 635 (cf. I.71, 138–9)	"so that I [Andromache] may cast delight to your *phrēn*" [Hecuba] (τέρψις)	Dat. s./ind. obj.]
159. *Tr.* 1216 (cf. I.122, 132)	"you [Hecuba] have touched, you have touched my *phrenes*" [Chorus] (θιγγάνω)	Gen. pl./w. verb
160. Fr. 436 *Hippolytus* (cf. I.23)	"o queen *aidos*, would that you took out the shamelessness from *phrenes*" (τὸ ἀναίσχυντον)	Gen. pl./w. verb
161. Fr. 644 *Polyidos* (cf. I.143)	"someone evil … makes the *phrenes* of better people sick" (νοσέω)	Acc. pl./d.o.
162. *Erechtheus* 370K.60 (*Selected Fragmentary Plays*, vol. 1) (cf. I.163)	"have you [Poseidon] not touched my *phrēn*?" [Athena] (ἅπτω, ἐμός)	Gen. s./w. verb
163. [*Rh.* 916 (cf. I.162)	"you [son of Philammon] touched my *phrēn*" [Muse] (ἅπτω, ἐμός)	Gen. s./w. verb]

Passage	Description	Syntax

G. IMPERSONAL EXPRESSIONS INVOLVING *PHRĒN*

Passage	Description	Syntax
164. *Med.* 677 (cf. I.55)	"for there is need of a wise *phrēn*" [Human Beings] (δεῖ, σοφός)	Gen. s./w. δεῖ

II. *NOUS* (CHAPTER 4)

Passage	Description	Syntax

A. *NOUS* PRESENT OR ACTIVE IN A PERSON

Passage	Description	Syntax
1. *And.* 231	"it is necessary for children in whom there is *nous* to avoid the ways of their evil mothers" [Children] (ἔνειμι)	Nom. s.
2. *And.* 237	"may your *nous* not dwell with me, woman!" [Andromache] (ξυνοικέω)	Nom. s.
3. *And.* 667	"while *nous* is in you" [Peleus] (ἔνειμι)	Nom. s.
4. *Hec.* 603	"these are comments my *nous* has shot in vain" [Hecuba] (τοξεύω)	Nom. s.
5. [*Hel.* 122	"I myself saw with my eyes and *nous* saw" [Teucer] (ὁράω)	Nom. s.]
6. *Hel.* 1014	"the *nous* of the dead does not live but it has immortal *gnōmē* as it falls into eternal aether" [Human Beings] (ζάω, ἔξω, ἐμπεσών)	Nom. s.
7. *Hipp.* 920	"to teach those in whom *nous* is not present to think" [Human Beings] (ἔνειμι)	Nom. s.
8. *Ion* 742 (cf. I.8, 43)	"the feature of the foot is slowness, that of the *nous*, speed" [Servant] (ταχύ)	Gen. s./subj. gen.
9. *I.A.* 334	"a *nous* which is not firm is an unjust possession, one not reliable for its friends" [Human Beings] (βεβαιός, κτῆμα)	Nom. s.
10. *I.A.* 1139 (cf. II.31)	"this *nous* itself does not have *nous*" [Agamemnon] (ἔχω)	Nom. s.
11. *Med.* 529	"your *nous* is subtle" [Medea] (εἰμι, λεπτός)	Nom. s.

Passage	Description	Syntax
12. *Tr.* 886	"Zeus, whether necessity of nature or *nous* of mortals" [Human Beings] (βροτός)	Nom. s.
13. *Tr.* 988	"your *nous* seeing him [Paris] was made Kypris" [Helen] (ποιέω)	Nom. s.
14. *Tr.* 1052	"that depends on how the *nous* of lovers turns out" [Human Beings] (ἐκβαίνω)	Nom. s.
15. Fr. 25.4 Aiolos	"*nous* is not in us but we imagine that we think well" [old men] (ἔνειμι)	Nom. s.
16. Fr. 149 Andromeda	"youth arouses me and boldness more than *nous*" (θράσος)	Gen. s./comp.
17. Fr. 212 Antiope (cf. I.76)	"if *nous* is present" (ἔνειμι)	Nom. s.
18. Fr. 710 Telephus	"*nous* is not in you" (ἔνειμι)	Nom. s.
19. Fr. 909.6 Incerta (cf. II.37)	"for the eye is not to judge but *nous*" (εἰμι)	Nom. s.
20. Fr. 1018 Incerta	"for our *nous* is in each a god" (εἰμι)	Nom. s.

B.   A PERSON ACTS IN, BY, OR WITH *NOUS*

21. [*Or.* 909	"whoever planning noble things with *nous*" [Human Beings] (βουλεύω)	Dat. s./w. σύν]

C.   A PERSON HAS A DIRECT RELATIONSHIP WITH *NOUS*

22. *And.* 252	"I say you do not have the *nous* you ought to have had" [Hermione] (ἔχω)	Acc. s./d.o.
23. *And.* 944	"but never, never ... should men having *nous* ... allow women to visit their wives" [Men] (ἔχω)	Acc. s./d.o.
24. *Bacc.* 252	"I feel contempt, seeing your old age not having *nous*" [Cadmus] (ἔχω)	Acc. s./d.o.
25. *Bacc.* 271	"the bold person ... becomes a bad citizen, not having *nous*" [Human Beings] (ἔχω)	Acc. s./d.o.

Passage		Description	Syntax
26.	[*Hel.* 731	"I would be numbered among the noble slaves, not having the name 'free' but the *nous*" [Messenger] (ἔχω, ἐλεύθερος)	Acc. s./d.o.]
27.	*Hipp.* 105	"may you be fortunate, having the *nous* which you ought to have" [Hippolytus] (ἔχω)	Acc. s./d.o.
28.	*Ion* 251	"I held my *nous* there, being somehow here" [Creusa] (ἔχω)	Acc. s./d.o.
29.	*Ion* 1370	"directing my *nous* there" [Ion] (δίδωμι)	Acc. s./d.o.
30.	*I.A.* 374	"it is necessary for a leader of a city to have *nous*" [Human Being] (ἔχω)	Acc. s./d.o.
31.	*I.A.* 1139 (cf. II.10)	"this *nous* itself does not have *nous*" [Agamemnon] (ἔχω)	Acc. s./d.o.
32.	*Or.* 1181 (cf. I.71, VII.111)	"hear now and hold your *nous* here" [Orestes] (ἔχω)	Acc. s./d.o.
33.	*Pho.* 360	"he sports with words but he holds his *nous* there" [Human Being] (ἔχω)	Acc. s./d.o.
34.	*Pho.* 1418	"not having his *nous* towards [Polyneices] himself" [Eteocles] (ἔχω)	Acc. s./d.o.
35.	*Tr.* 652	"having my *nous* as a good teacher at home, I sufficed for myself" [Andromache] (ἔχω)	Acc. s./d.o.
36.	Fr. 256 Archelaus	"blessed is he who, having *nous*, honours god" (ἔχω)	Acc. s./d.o.
37.	Fr. 909.5 Incerta (cf. II.19)	"for one possessing *nous*" (κτάομαι)	Acc. s./d.o.
38.	Fr. 934 Incerta	"of the one having *nous*" (ἔχω)	Acc. s./d.o.
39.	Fr. 964.2 Incerta (cf. I.52, VII.112)	"I thrust misfortunes in my thoughts and *nous*" (βάλλω)	Acc. s./w. εἰς

D.   A PERSON IS DESCRIBED IN RELATION TO *NOUS*

None

Passage	Description	Syntax

E. OUTSIDE OBJECTS AFFECT *NOUS*

40. Fr. 67.4 *Alcmeon* (cf. VII.97)	"fear ... prevents the *nous* from speaking what it wishes" (φόβος, ἀπείργω)	Acc. s./d.o.
41. Fr. 265 *Augē*	"wine set me apart from *nous*" (οἶνος, ἐξίστημι)	Gen. s./sep.

F. OUTSIDE AGENTS RELATING TO *NOUS*

42. Fr. 144 *Andromeda*	"do not inhabit my *nous*" (οἰκέω, ἐμός)	Acc. s./d.o.

G. IMPERSONAL EXPRESSIONS WITH *NOUS*

43. Fr. 548 (cf. I.78)	"it is necessary to watch *nous, nous*" (θεάομαι)	Acc. s./d.o.

III. *PRAPIDES* (CHAPTER 4)

Passage	Description	Syntax

A. *PRAPIDES* PRESENT OR ACTIVE IN A PERSON

1. *And.* 480 (cf. I.5)	"a double judgement at the helm" [Human Beings] (γνώμη, πηδάλιος)	Gen. s./subj. gen.
2. Fr. 27.2 *Aiolos*	"with versatility of *prapides* he conquers the terrible tribes of the sea and the offspring of earth and air" (ποικιλία, δαμνάω)	Gen. pl./subj. gen.
3. Fr. 901.1 Incerta	"often a thought came to me in *prapides*" (φροντίς, διέρχομαι)	Gen. pl./subj. gen.

C. A PERSON HAS A DIRECT RELATIONSHIP WITH *PRAPIDES*

4. *Bacc.* 427	"to keep a wise *prapis* and *phrēn* from excessive mortals" [Human Beings] (ἀπέχω, σοφός)	Acc. s./d.o.

D. A PERSON IS DESCRIBED IN RELATION TO *PRAPIDES*

5. *Bacc.* 999	"he is sent with raging *prapis* and frenzied spirit" [Pentheus] (στέλλω, μανεῖσα)	Dat. s./manner

IV. *THUMOS* (CHAPTER 5)

Passage	Description	Syntax

A.   *THUMOS* PRESENT OR ACTIVE IN A PERSON

1. *Alc.* 829	"in spite of *thumos* I was drinking" [Heracles] (βίᾳ)	Gen. s./w. βίᾳ
2. *And.* 1072	"my prophetic *thumos*, how it expects some [disaster]" [Peleus] (προσδοκάω, πρόμαντις)	Nom. s.
3. *Hcld.* 925 (cf. VII.67)	"she [Athena] checked the *hybris* of a man whose *thumos* was violent at the cost of justice" [Eurystheus] (εἰμι, βίαιος)	Nom. s.
4. *Hipp.* 1087	"if it is your *thumos*" [Theseus] (εἰμι understood)	Nom. s.
5. *I.A.* 919 (cf. IV.21)	"my lofty-spirited *thumos* is lifted on high" [Achilles] (αἴρω, ὑψηλόφρων)	Nom. s.
6. *Med.* 310	"you married your daughter to whom your *thumos* led you" [Creon] (ἄγω)	Nom. s.
7. [*Med.* 1056	"do not, *thumos*, do not do these things" [Medea] (ἐργάζω)	Voc. s.]
8. *Med.* 1079 (cf. IV.11)	"but *thumos* is stronger than my plans, *thumos* which is responsible for the greater evils for mortals" [Medea] (κρείσσων, αἴτος)	Nom. s.]
9. [*Or.* 702 (cf. IV.11)	"in them is pity, in them is great *thumos*" [Argives] (ἔνειμι, μέγας)	Nom. s.]
10. *Pho.* 454	"check your terrible look and breaths of *thumos*" [Eteocles] (πνοή, ἔχω)	Gen. s./subj. gen.
11. Fr. 257 *Archelaus* (cf. IV.8, 9)	"the great *thumos* has destroyed many mortals" (ὄλλυμι, μέγας)	Nom. s.
12. Fr. 362.34 *Erechtheus*	"for a womanly-minded *thumos* does not belong to a wise man" (εἰμι understood, γυναικόφρων)	Nom. s.
13. Fr. 718 *Telephus*	"it is time for you to have judgement stronger than *thumos*" (γνώμη)	Gen. s./comp.
14. Fr. 1039 *Incerta*	"the *thumos* in pain does not have stability" (ἔχω, ἀλγῶν, ἀσφάλεια)	Nom. s.

Passage	Description	Syntax

B. A PERSON ACTS IN, BY, OR WITH *THUMOS*

15. *Med.* 108 (cf. VII.77)	"it is clear that a cloud of lamentation ... will quickly flare up with greater *thumos*" [Medea] (ἀνάπτω, μείζων)	Dat. s./manner
16. *Med.* 865	"you will not be able ... to stain your murderous hand with bold *thumos*" [Medea] (τλήμων)	Dat. s./manner
17. *Supp.* 556	"it is necessary, if we are treated unjustly, to endure moderately, not with *thumos*" [Human Beings] (φέρω)	Dat. s./manner

C. A PERSON HAS A DIRECT RELATIONSHIP WITH *THUMOS*

18. *Bacc.* 620	"breathing out *thumos*" [Pentheus] (ἐκπνεύω)	Acc. s./d.o.
19. *H.F.* 1211	"check the *thumos* of a fierce lion" [Heracles] (κατέχω)	Acc. s./d.o.
20. *Hipp.* 1328	"fulfilling her *thumos*" [Kypris] (πληρόω)	Acc. s./d.o.
21. *I.A.* 125 (cf. IV.5)	"and how will Achilles ... not raise *thumos*?" [Achilles] (ἐπαίρω)	Acc. s./d.o.
22. *Med.* 1152	"but cease from your *thumos*" [Creon's Daughter] (παύω)	Gen. s./w. verb
23. [*Rh.* 786	"they breathed out *thumos*" [Horses] (πνέω)	Acc. s./d.o.]

D. A PERSON IS DESCRIBED IN RELATION TO *THUMOS*

24. *El.* 578	"not for adornments nor for golden chains am I set aflutter in *thumos*" [Electra] (ἐκπόταομαι)	Acc. s./resp.
25. *El.* 578	"for I am persuaded in *thumos* by your signs" [Electra] (πείθω)	Acc. s./resp.
26. *Med.* 8 (cf. IV.31)	"smitten in *thumos* with love of Jason" [Medea] (πλήσσω)	Acc. s./resp.
27. *Med.* 879	"shall I not be released from *thumos*?" [Medea] (ἀπαλάσσω)	Gen. s./w. verb

Passage	Description	Syntax

E. OUTSIDE OBJECTS AFFECT *THUMOS*

28. *Supp.* 480   "for hope is an untrustworthy thing, which has   Acc. s./d.o.
engaged many cities in conflict, leading *thumos* into
excess" [Human Beings]
(ἐλπίς, ἄγω)

F. OUTSIDE AGENTS ACT ON *THUMOS*

29. *Hec.* 1055   "but I will stand aside from his boiling Thracian   Dat. s./w. verb
thumos, most difficult to fight against" [Hecuba]
(ἀφίστημι, ζέων, θρᾷξ, δυσμαχώτατος)

30. *Hipp.* 1114   "fate might give ... a *thumos* unmixed with pains"   Acc. s./d.o.
[Chorus]
(παρέχω, ἀκήρατος, ἄλγος)

31. *Med.* 640   "may terrible Kypris never ... striking my *thumos* for   Dat. s./w. verb
(cf. IV.26)   other beds" [Chorus]
(ἐκπλήσσω)

G. IMPERSONAL EXPRESSIONS WITH *THUMOS*

None

V. *KARDIA* (CHAPTER 6)

Passage	Description	Syntax

A. *KARDIA* PRESENT IN A PERSON

1. *Alc.* 837   "o *kardia* enduring many things and my *psychē*, now   Voc. s.
(cf. V.5, 8,   show what sort of son" [Heracles]
9, VII.63)   (δείκνυμι, τλᾶσα)

2. *Bacc.* 1288   "speak, for my *kardia* beats in relation to what is   Nom. s.
(cf. V.34)   coming" [Agave]
(ἔξω, πήδημα)

3. *Hcld.* 583   "may there be to you whatever my *kardia* beforehand   Nom. s.
is foiled of" [Maiden]
(σφάλλω, ἐμός)

4. [*Hipp.* 912   "for the *kardia*, longing to hear all things, is caught   Nom. s.]
being curious, even in misfortunes"
[Human Beings]
(ἁλίσκομαι, οθοῦσα, κλύειν, λίχνος)

Passage	Description	Syntax
5. *I.T.* 344 (cf. V. I, 8, 9, 21)	"o wretched *kardia*, before you were gentle to strangers always showing pity, measuring out tears ... whenever you took Greeks into your hands" [Iphigenia] (εἰμι, λαμβάνω, τάλας, γαληνός, φιλοκτίρμων, ἀναμετρουμένη δακρύ)	Voc. s.
6. *Med.* 590	"who even now cannot bring yourself to set aside the great anger of your *kardia*" [Medea] (μεθίημι, χόλος)	Gen. s./subj. gen.
7. *Med.* 1042	"for *kardia* has gone" [Medea] (οἴχομαι)	Nom. s.
8. *Med.* 1242 (cf. V.1, 5, 9)	"but come, arm yourself, o *kardia*" [Medea] (ὁπλίζω)	Voc. s.
9. *Or.* 466 (cf. V.1, 5, 8, 21, VII.78)	"to them, o wretched *kardia* and my *psychē*, I have paid back no noble return" [Orestes] (ἀποδίδωμι, τάλας)	Voc. s.

B.   A PERSON ACTS IN *KARDIA*

10. *I.A.* 475	"I swear ... to speak to you clearly the things from my *kardia*" [Menelaus] (ἐρέω)	Gen. s./w. ἀπό
11. *Med.* 432 (cf. V.36)	"but you sailed from your father's halls with raging *kradia*" [Medea] (πλέω, μαινομένα)	Dat. s./manner
12. *Med.* 858 (cf. I.31)	"from where will you take ... courage of hand and *kardia* to dare this terrible deed?" [Medea] (θράσος)	Dat. s./manner
13. [*Rh.* 770	"I, with thoughtful *kardia*, ceasing from sleep" [charioteer] (λήγω, μελοῦσα)	Dat. s./manner]
14. Fr. 412.3 *Ino*	"who will speak the things from his *kardia*" (ἐρέω)	Gen. s./w. ἀπό

C.   A PERSON HAS A DIRECT RELATIONSHIP WITH *KARDIA*

15. *Hec.* 433 (cf. V.21)	"I have melted my *kardia* with the laments of my mother and I am melting her with my mourning" [Polyxena] (τήκω, θρῆνος, γόος)	Gen. s./w. verb
16. *Hec.* 1129	"casting out from your *kardia* this barbarian impulse" [Polymestor] (ἐκβάλλω)	Acc. s./d.o.

Passage	Description	Syntax
17. *H.F.* 833	"but keeping your *kardia* untouched" [Madness] (συλλαμβάνω, ἄτεγκτός)	Acc. s./d.o.
18. *I.A.* 1173	"what *kardia* do you think that I shall have?" [Clytemnestra] (ἔχω, τίς)	Acc. s./d.o.
19. *Med.* 99	"your mother is stirring up her *kradia*" [Medea] (κινέω)	Acc. s./d.o.
20. *Med.* 245	"a man ... stops his *kardia* from distress" [A Man] (παύω, ἄση)	Acc. s./d.o.
21. Fr. 908.6 Incerta (cf. V.5, 9, 15, VII.85)	"I melt my wretched *kardia* with terror" (τήκω, ὀρρωδία, τάλας)	Acc. s./d.o.
22. Fr. 1063.12 Incerta	"whoever of us holds *kardia* out of doors" (ἔχω)	Acc. s./d.o.

D.   A PERSON IS DESCRIBED IN RELATION TO *KARDIA*

23. *Alc.* 1100 (cf. V.27, 28)	"I will be stung in my *kardia* with grief" [Admetus] (δάκνω, λύπη)	Acc. s./resp.
24. *El.* 402	"we are warmed with joy in our *kardia*" [Chorus] (θερμαίνω, χαρά)	Acc. s./resp.
25. *Hec.* 1026	"you will fall aslant from your dear *kardia*" [Polymestor] (ἐκπίπτω, λέχριος, φίλος)	Gen. s./w. adj.
26. *Hipp.* 27	"Phaedra, seeing him, was held in her *kardia* with terrible love" [Phaedra] (κατέχω, ἔρος)	Acc. s./resp.
27. [*Rh.* 596 (cf. V.23, 28)	"stung in your *kardia* with grief" [Odysseus and Diomedes] (δάκνω, λύπη)	Acc. s./resp.]

E.   OUTSIDE OBJECTS AFFECT *KARDIA*

28. *Hec.* 235 (cf. V.23, 27)	"things not grievous or paining their *kardia*" [Free People] (δηκτήριος)	Gen. s./w. adj.
29. *Hec.* 242	"for it touched me, not at the surface of my *kardia*" [Odysseus] (ψαύω, ἄκρος)	Gen. s./w. verb
30. *Hel.* 960 (cf. V.37)	"what will touch your *kardia*" [Theonoë] (ἀνθάπτω, σός)	Gen. s./w. verb

Passage	Description	Syntax
31. *Hipp.* 841	"whence the deadly fate came against your *kardia*" [Phaedra] (βαίνω, τύχα, σός)	Acc. s./d.o.
32. Fr. 573.4 *Oinomaus* (cf. I.126)	"these ... release too great sufferings from the *kardia*" (πόνοι, λύω)	Gen. s./sep.
33. Fr. 1038.2 Incerta	"wandering stands near *kardia*" (προσίστημι, πλάνος)	Dat. s./w. verb

F.   OUTSIDE AGENTS AFFECT *KARDIA*

34. *Alc.* 1067 (cf. V.2)	"she makes my *kardia* beat" [Admetus] (θολόω)	Acc. s./d.o.
35. *Bacc.* 1321	"who, being offensive, distresses your *kardia*?" [Cadmus] (ταράσσω, σός)	Acc. s./d.o.
36. *Hipp.* 1274 (cf. V.11)	"Eros ... charms the one with maddened *kradia*" [Human Beings] (θέλγω, μαινομένα)	Dat. s./desc.
37. *Med.* 1360 (cf. V.30)	"I have touched your *kradia*" [Jason] (ἀνθάπτω, σός)	Gen. s./w. verb

VI.   *KEAR* (CHAPTER 6)

Passage	Description	Syntax

A.   *KEAR* PRESENT IN A PERSON

1. *Med.* 911	"your *kear* has changed to the better" [Medea] (μεθίστημι, σός)	Nom. s.

F.   AN OUTSIDE AGENT AFFECTS *KEAR*

2. *Med.* 398	"not any of them will pain my *kear* and enjoy it" [Medea] (ἀλγύνω, ἐμός)	Acc. s./d.o.
[3. *H.F.* 1003 Too Fragmentary	"Pallas Athena brandishing a spear ... *kear*"?	?]

VII. *PSYCHĒ* (CHAPTERS 7 AND 8)

TRADITIONAL USES OF *PSYCHĒ* (CHAPTER 7)

Passage	Description	Syntax
A. *PSYCHĒ* PRESENT OR ACTIVE IN A PERSON		
1. *Alc.* 283	"I ... have caused you to behold this light in place of my *psychē*" [Alcestis] (ἀντί, ἐμός)	Gen. s./w. ἀντί
2. *Alc.* 301	"for nothing is more valuable than *psychē*" [Human Beings] (τιμώτερον)	Gen. s./comp.
3. *Alc.* 462	"you dared to exchange your own husband from Hades in place of your *psychē*" [Alcestis] (ἀντί, σός)	Gen. s./w. ἀντί
4. *Alc.* 883	"for they are one *psychē*" [Human Beings] (εἷς)	Nom. s.
5. *And.* 419	"to all human beings children are *psychē*" [Human Beings] (εἰμι)	Nom. s.
6. *Hec.* 22 (cf. VII.53)	"when Troy and the *psychē* of Hector were destroyed" [Hector] (ἀπόλλυμι)	Nom. s.
[7. *Hec.* 176	"what sort of report I hear about your *psychē*" [Polyxena] (φάμα, σός)	Gen. s./w. περί
8. *Hec.* 182	"alas for your *psychē*" (σός)	Gen. s./
9. *Hec.* 196	"the Argives have decided by vote about your *psychē*" [Polyxena] (ἀγγέλλω, σός)	Gen. s./w. περί
10. *Hel.* 52	"many *psychai* perished ... because of me" [Helen] (θνῄσκω, πολύς)	Nom. pl.
11. *Hel.* 946	"what he will say about his *psychē*" [Menelaus] (ἐρέω)	Gen. s./w. περί
12. *Hcld.* 15 (cf. VII.29, 57)	"but our *psychē* is saved" [Children of Heracles] (σώζω)	Nom. s.
13. *Hcld.* 984	"nor say anything else about my *psychē*" [Eurystheus] (λέγω, ἐμός)	Gen. s./w. περί
14. *Hipp.* 721	"nor will I come ... on account of shameful deeds for the sake of one *psychē*" [Phaedra] (ἀφικνέομαι, εἷς)	Gen. s./w. οὕνεκα

Passage	Description	Syntax
15. *Hipp.* 726	"I, released from *psychē* on this day" [Phaedra] (ἀπαλάσσω)	Gen. s./w. verb
16. *I.A.* 1390	"will my *psychē*, being one, prevent all these things?" [Iphigenia] (κωλύω, ἐμός, εἷς)	Nom. s.
17. *Or.* 676	"imagine … that his *psychē* is flying over you and is speaking what I say" [Agamemnon] (λέγω, ποτωμένη)	Acc. s./s. of inf.
18. [*Or.* 847	"about to engage in the present struggle for his *psychē*" [Orestes] (ἄγων, δίδωμι)	Gen. s./w. περί]
19. *Or.* 1034	"the dear *psychē* is for all an object of pity" [Human Beings] (οἰκτρόν, φίλος)	Nom. s.
20. *Or.* 1517	"I swear by my *psychē*, which I could swear well by" [Phrygian] (κατόμνυμι, ἐμός)	Acc. s./w. verb
21. *Pho.* 1330	"the contest about *psychē* has already been held for the sons of Oedipus" [Polyneices and Eteocles] (πράττω, ἄγων)	Gen. s./w. περί
22. *Pho.* 1553	"by what fate have these three *psychai* left the light?" [Jocasta, Polyneices, and Eteocles] (λείπω, τρισσός)	Nom. pl.
23. *Tr.* 791	"your mother and I are unjustly stripped of your *psychē*" [Astyanax] (συλάω, σός)	Acc. s./w. verb
24. *Tr.* 900	"what are the judgements of the Greeks about my *psychē*?" [Helen] (γνῶμαι, ἐμός)	Gen. s./w. περί
25. Fr. 360.51 *Erechtheus* (cf. VII.83)	"for in return for one *psychē*, it is not possible that I would not save the city" (ἀντί, εἷς)	Gen. s./w. ἀντί
25a. Fr. 370K.71 *Erechtheus* (*Selected Fragmentary Plays,* vol. 1)	"their *psychai* have not descended to Hades" [Hyacinthids] (βαίνω)	Nom. pl.

B.   A PERSON ACTS IN, BY, OR WITH *PSYCHĒ*

| 26. *Alc.* 712 | "we must live with one *psychē*, not with two" [Human Beings] (ζάω, εἷς, δύο) | Dat. s./manner |

Passage	Description	Syntax
27. *Supp.* 1024	"never having betrayed with my *psychē* you who have died" [Evadne] (προδίδωμι, ἐμός)	Dat. s./means

C.   A PERSON HAS A DIRECT RELATIONSHIP WITH *PSYCHĒ*

28. *Alc.* 704	"consider that if you love your own *psychē*, all people love theirs" [Admetus] (φιλέω)	Acc. s./d.o.
29. *Alc.* 929 (cf. VII.12, 57)	"but you saved your life and your *psychē*" [Admetus] (βίοτος, σώζω)	Acc. s./d.o.
30. *And.* 541	"I expended a great portion of my *psychē*" [Menelaus] (ἀναλίσκω, μόριον)	Gen. s./partitive
31. *Hel.* 1431 (cf. VII.41, 45)	"for Menelaus did not lose his *psychē* here" [Menelaus] (ἀφίημι)	Acc. s./d.o.
32. *Hcld.* 296	"he came within a little of wearing out his *psychē*" [Messenger] (διακναίω)	Acc. s./d.o.
33. *Hcld.* 455	"I must not love my own *psychē*" [Iolaus] (φιλέω, ἐμός)	Acc. s./d.o.
34. *Hcld.* 550	"I give up my *psychē* willingly to these [my brothers]" [Maiden] (δίδωμι, ἐμός)	Acc. s./d.o.
35. *H.F.* 1146	"why then do I spare my own *psychē*?" [Heracles] (φείδομαι, ἐμός)	Gen. s./w. verb
36. *Hipp.* 440	"and then will you destroy your *psychē* because of love?" [Phaedra] (ὄλλυμι)	Acc. s./d.o.
37. *Med.* 968	"I would give in exchange my *psychē* to free my children from exile" [Medea] (ἀπαλλάσσω)	Gen. s./w. verb
38. *Med.* 1219	"the ill-fated one gave up his *psychē*" [Creon] (μεθίημι)	Acc. s./d.o.
39. *Or.* 1046	"having ... one *psychē*" [Orestes] (ἔχω, εἷς)	Acc. s./d.o.
40. *Or.* 1163	"I, breathing out my *psychē*" [Orestes] (ἐκπνέω)	Acc. s./d.o.
41. *Or.* 1171 (cf. VII.31, 45)	"but freely I will send forth my *psychē*" [Orestes] (ἀφίημι)	Acc. s./d.o.

Passage	Description	Syntax
42. *Pho.* 998	"I will give my *psychē* to die on behalf of this land" [Menelaus] (δίδωμι)	Acc. s./d.o.
43. *Pho.* 1228	"do not sell your *psychaï*" [Greeks] (ἀπεμπολάω)	Acc. pl./d.o.
44. *Supp.* 777	"for this alone for mortals is an expenditure, once paid out, to take again, the *psychē* of mortals" [Human Beings] (λαμβάνω, βρότειος)	Acc. s./d.o.
45. *Tr.* 1135 (cf. VII.31, 41)	"who, falling from the walls, gave up his *psychē*" [Astyanax] (ἀφίημι, προβάλλω)	Acc. s./d.o.
[46. *Rh.* 183	"it is necessary to labour for worthy objects in hazarding *psychē*" [Human Beings] (προβάλλω)	Acc. s./d.o.]

D.   A PERSON IS DESCRIBED IN RELATION TO *PSYCHĒ*

None

E.   OUTSIDE OBJECTS AFFECT *PSYCHĒ*

47. *Med.* 226	"this unexpected event ... has destroyed my *psychē*" [Medea] (διαφθείρω)	Acc. s./d.o.

F.   OUTSIDE OBJECTS ACTING ON OR RELATING TO *PSYCHĒ*

48. *Alc.* 54	"not in truth would you [Death] take more than one *psychē*" [Alcestis] (λαμβάνω, εἷς)	Acc. s./d.o.
49. *Alc.* 117	"but there is no place where one might send a ship ... to save the *psychē* of the wretched woman" [Alcestis] (παραλύω)	Acc. s./d.o.
50. *Alc.* 341	"you [Alcestis] giving the dearest in return for my *psychē*, saved me" [Admetus] (ἀντιδίδωμι, ἐμός)	Gen. s./w. verb
51. *Alc.* 620	"she [Alcestis] died on behalf of your *psychē*" [Admetus] (προθνῄσκω, σός)	Gen. s./w. verb
52. *Alc.* 900	"Hades would have had two most faithful *psychai*, instead of one" [Admetus] (ἔχω, δύο, εἷς, πιστότατος)	Acc. pl./d.o.

Passage	Description	Syntax
53. *And.* 611 (cf. VII.6)	"you [Menelaus] destroyed many good *psychai*" [Greeks] (ἀπόλλυμι, πολύς, ἀγαθός)	Acc. pl./d.o.
[54. *H.F.* 452	"who is the murderer of my wretched *psychē*?" [Megara] (φονεύς, ἐμός, τάλας)	Gen. s./obj. gen.]
55. *Ion* 1499	"bound by fear I [Creusa] cast out your *psychē*" [Ion] (ἀποβάλλω, σός)	Acc. s./d.o.
56. *I.A.* 1441	"is it not necessary for me [Clytemnestra] to mourn your *psychē*?" [Iphigenia] (πενθέω, σός)	Acc. s./d.o.
[57. *Or.* 644 (cf. VII.12, 29)	"if you [Menelaus] save my *psychē*, dearest of all my possessions" [Orestes] (σώζω, ἐμός)	Acc. s./d.o.]
58. *Or.* 662	"give [Menelaus] my *psychē* to my wretched father [and that of my sister]" [Orestes and?] (δίδωμι, ἐμός)	Acc. s./d.o.
59. *Pho.* 1291 (cf. VII.79)	"will two sons bloody ... a *psychē* of the same family?" [Polyneices and Eteocles] (αἱμάσσω, ὁμογενής)	Acc. s./d.o.
60. *Tr.* 1214	"she [Helen] has killed your *psychē*" [Astyanax] (κτείνω)	Acc. s./d.o.
61. *Fr.* 912.9 Incerta	"send [Zeus] into the light of the *psychai* of those below" (πέμπω)	Acc. pl./d.o.
[62. *Rh.* 965	"I will beseech the nymph below to release the *psychē* of this man" [Rhesus] (ἀνίημι)	Acc. s./d.o.]

EURIPIDEAN USES OF *PSYCHĒ* (CHAPTER 8)

Passage	Description	Syntax

A.   *PSYCHĒ* PRESENT OR ACTIVE IN A PERSON

63. *Alc.* 837 (cf. V.1)	"o *kardia*, enduring many things, and my *psychē*, now show what sort of son" [Heracles] (δείκνυμι, ἐμός)	Voc. s.
64. *And.* 160	"for clever for such things is the Asiatic *psychē* of women" [women of Asia] (δεινός, ἠπειρῶτις)	Nom. s.

Passage	Description	Syntax
65. *El.* 297	"and I have the same desire of *psychē* as this one" [Chorus] (ἔχω, ἔρος)	Gen. s./subj. gen.
66. *Hcld.* 530 (cf. VII.83)	"this *psychē* is present, willing and not unwilling" [Maiden] (πάρειμι, κουσα, ἄκουσα)	Nom. s.
67. *Hcld.* 927 (cf. IV.3)	"may my *phronēma* and *psychē* never be insatiate" [Chorus] (εἰμι, ἀκόρεστος)	Nom. s.
68. *H.F.* 626	"you, my wife, take collectiveness of *psychē*" [Megara] (λαμβάνω, σύλλογος)	Gen. s./subj. gen.
69. *Hipp.* 160	"is her *psychē* bound bed-fast with grief over her sufferings?" [Phaedra] (δέω, εὐναῖος)	Nom. s.
70. *Hipp.* 173	"my *psychē* desires to learn" [Chorus] (ἔραμαι)	Nom. s.
71. *Hipp.* 255 (cf. I.14)	"for it is necessary for mortals to mix moderate loves for one another and not to the deep marrow of *psychē*" [Human Beings] (ἀνακρίνομαι, φιλία, μυελόν)	Gen. s./subj. gen.
72. *Hipp.* 259	"for one *psychē* to feel pain over two is a difficult weight, as I grieve over this one" [Nurse] (ὠδίνω, εἷς)	Nom. s.
73. *Ion* 859	"o *psychē*, how shall I keep silent?" [Creousa] (σιγάω)	Voc. s.
74. *Ion* 877	"my *psychē* feels pain, plotted against by human beings and by gods" [Creousa] (ἀλγέω, κακοβουληθείς)	Nom. s.
75. *I.T.* 838 (cf. VII.107)	"o my *psychē*, engaging good fortune greater than words, what am I to say?" [Iphigenia] (φημί, εὐτυχοῦσα)	Voc. s.
76. *I.T.* 882	"this, this is your need to find, o wretched *psychē*" [Orestes] (χρέος, μέλεος)	Voc. s.
77. *Med.* 110 (cf. IV.15)	"whatever will her *psychē*, high-spirited, most hard to check, do as it is bitten with evils?" [Medea] (ἐργάζομαι, μεγαλόσπλαγχνος, δυσκατάπαυστος, δηχθεῖσα)	Nom. s.
78. *Or.* 466 (cf. V.9)	"to whom, o wretched *kardia* and my *psychē*, I paid back no noble return" [Orestes] (ἀποδίδωμι, ἐμός)	Voc. s.
79. *Pho.* 1297 (cf. I.33, VII.59)	"murderous *psychai* ... will bloody destructive fallings" [Polyneices and Eteocles] (αἱμάσσω, φόνιος)	Nom. pl.

Passage	Description	Syntax
80. *Supp.* 1103	"the *psychai* of men are greater, but less sweet for caresses" [Men] (μείζων, γλυκύς)	Nom. pl.
81. Fr. 185 *Antigone*	"having taken so noble a nature of *psychē*" (φύσις)	Gen. s./subj. gen.
82. Fr. 308.1 *Bellero-phontes*	"hasten, o *psychē*" (σπεύδω)	Voc. s.
83. Fr. 360.44 *Erechtheus* (cf. VII.25, 66)	"there is no one who will cast out the laws of parents without my *psychē* being willing" (ἑκοῦσα)	Gen. s./w. ἄτερ
84. Fr. 388 *Theseus*	"but there is another love among mortals of a *psychē* just, moderate, and good" (ἔρως, δίκαιος, σώφρων, ἀγαθός)	Gen. s./obj. gen.
85. Fr. 908.8 *Incerta* (cf. V.21)	"is it not sufficient for one *psychē* to be at a loss and for this reason to have sufferings?" (ἀλύω, ἔχω, πόνος, εἷς)	Acc. s./subj. of inf.
86. Fr. 924 *Incerta*	"do not touch subtle words, *psychē*. Why do you think excessive things? Unless you are about to be magnified among your peers" (θιγγάνω, φρονέω, μέλλω, σεμνύνω)	Voc. s.
[87. *Rh.* 345	"I will speak what is dear to my *psychē* to say" [Chorus] (προσφιλές, λέγω)	Dat. s./w. προσφιλές]

B.   A PERSON ACTS IN, BY, OR WITH *PSYCHĒ*

88. *Ion* 1247	"whatever awaits for you to suffer in *psychē*?" [Creousa] (πάσχω)	Dat. s./loc.
89. *Tr.* 1171	"but having seen and known them with your *psychē*" [Astyanax] (εἶδον, γιγνώσκω, σός)	Dat. s./means
90. Fr. 754 *Hypsipyle*	"lifting one after another prize of flowers with rejoicing *psychē*" (αἴρω, ἡδομένη)	Dat. s./manner

C.   A PERSON HAS A DIRECT RELATIONSHIP WITH *PSYCHĒ*

91. *Alc.* 354	"I would lessen the weight of *psychē*" [Admetus] (ἀπαντλέω, βάρος)	Gen. s./subj. gen.
92. *Bacc.* 75	"o blessed who ... hallows his *psychē* in Bacchic rites" [Human Beings] (θιασεύω)	Acc. s./d.o.

Passage	Description	Syntax
[93. *H.F.* 1366	"compel your *psychē* to share in my sufferings" [Theseus] (βιάζω)	Acc. s./d.o.]
94. *Hipp.* 1006	"having a virgin *psychē*" [Hippolytus] (ἔχω, παρθένος)	Acc. s./d.o.
95. *Ion* 1170	"they filled their *psychē* with rich food" [Guests] (πληρόω)	Acc. s./d.o.
96. *Or.* 526	"what *psychē* did you leave?" [Orestes] (ἔχω, τίς)	Acc. s./d.o.
97. Fr. 67 *Alcmeon* (cf. II.40)	"for I see my *psychē* laid on the line as a prize" (κειμένη, ἐμός, ἆθλον)	Acc. s./d.o.
98. Fr. 220 *Antiope*	"thinking with judgement they are not willing to act in accord with *psychē*" (ὑπηρετέω)	Dat. s./w. verb
99. Fr. 822 *Phrixus*	"a wife ... freeing her *psychē* from despondency" (μεθίστημι, δυσθυμία)	Acc. s./d.o.
100. Fr. 913 Incerta	"who, seeing these things, does not teach his *psychē* beforehand to consider the gods" (προδιδάσκω, ἡγέομαι)	Acc. s./d.o.

D.　A PERSON IS DESCRIBED IN *PSYCHĒ*

101. *El.* 208 (cf. VII.103)	"wasting away in my *psychē*" [Euripides] (τήκω)	Acc. s./resp.
102. *Hec.* 580	"will you not go, about to give something for me excessively brave-hearted and best in *psychē*?" [Polyxena] (δίδωμι)	Acc. s./resp.
103. *Hcld.* 645 (cf. VII.101)	"for long being in pain, you have languished in *psychē*" [Alcmene] (τήκω)	Acc. s./resp.
104. *Hipp.* 505	"for I am well-tilled in *psychē* by love" [Phaedra] (ὑπεργάζομαι, ἔρως)	Acc. s./resp.
105. *Med.* 474	"I will be lightened in *psychē*" [Medea] (κουφίζω)	Acc. s./resp.
106. *Tr.* 182	"I have come, struck with shuddering in my *psychē* that arose early" [Hecuba] (ἐκπλήσσω, φρικά, ὀρθρεύουσα)	Acc. s./resp.
107. *Tr.* 640 (cf. VII.75)	"but the person ... wanders in *psychē* from the former good fortune" [Human Being] (ἀλάομαι)	Acc. s./resp.

Passage	Description	Syntax

E.   OUTSIDE OBJECTS AFFECT *PSYCHĒ*

108. *Alc.* 604	"confidence sits on my *psychē* that the god-fearing man will fare well" [Human Being] (θράσος, ἧμαι, ἐμός)	Dat. s./w. πρός
109. *Bacc.* 1268	"is this bewilderment still present in your *psychē*?" [Agave] (πτοηθέν, σός)	Dat. s./loc.
110. *Hcld.* 173	"if in any way this prospect lifts you in *psychē*" [Athenians] (τοῦτο, ἐπαίρω)	Acc. s./resp.
111. *Or.* 1180 (cf. I.71, II.32)	"for I know that understanding is in your *psychē*" [Electra] (πάρειμι, συνετόν, σός)	Dat. s./loc.
112. Fr. 964.6 Incerta (cf. I.52, II.39)	"the fresh disasters, falling on me, would not bite *psychē*" (δάκνω, νεῶρες)	Acc. s./d.o.

F.   OUTSIDE AGENTS AFFECT *PSYCHĒ*

113. *Alc.* 108 (cf. I.132)	"you touching my *psychē*, you touched my *phrenes*" [Chorus] (τιγγάνω)	Gen. s./w. verb
114. *Hec.* 87	"wherever can I [Hecuba] see the prophetic *psychē* of Helenus" [Helenus] (εἰσοράω, θεῖος)	Acc. s./d.o.
115. *Hipp.* 527 (cf. VII.119)	"Love … leading sweet delight to the *psychē*" [Human Beings] (εἰσάγω, χάρις)	Dat. s./ind. obj.
116. *Hipp.* 1040	"who [Hippolytus] has trusted that he will conquer my *psychē* by gentleness of temper" [Theseus] (κρατέω, ἐμός)	Acc. s./d.o.
117. *Med.* 247	"it is necessary for us [women] to look at one *psychē*" [Man] (βλέπω, εἷς)	Acc. s./d.o.
118. Fr. 323 Danaë	"he took possession of my *psychē*" (κτάομαι, ἐμός)	Acc. s./d.o.
119. Fr. 431 Hippolytus (cf. VII.115)	"Love … whets the *psychai* of the gods above" (χαράσσω)	Acc. pl./d.o.

Psychic Terms in Each Tragedy

The psychic terms have been classified according to the categories introduced in each chapter.

ABBREVIATIONS

Trad./Con.	Traditional and Contemporary Uses
S. Images	Euripidean Images
S. Uses	Euripidean Uses

ALCESTIS

Line	Category	Sub-category	App. A
PHRĒN (CHAPTERS 2 AND 3)			
108	Trad./Con.	Grief	I.132
	E. Images	Touch	
327	Trad./Con.	Absence/Loss	I.53
346	Trad./Con.	Joy, Speech	I.54
674	Trad./Con.	Anger	I.133
775	E. Use	Emotional	I.44
797	E. Use	Emotional	I.1
878	Trad./Con.	Grief	I.101
	E. Images	Medical	

Line	Category	Sub-category	App. A
NOUS (CHAPTER 4)			
None			
THUMOS (CHAPTER 6)			
829	Trad./Con.	Seat of Emotion	IV. 1
KARDIA (CHAPTER 6)			
837	Trad./Con.	Seat of Emotion	V.1
1067	Trad./Con.	Physical	V.34
1100	Trad./Con.	Grief	V.23
PSYCHĒ (CHAPTERS 7 AND 8)			
54	Traditional	Life-Spirit	VII.48
108	E. Uses	Grief	VII.13
117	Trad./Con.	Life-Spirit	VII.49
283	Trad./Con.	Life-Spirit	VII.1
301	Trad./Con.	Life-Spirit	VII.2
341	Trad./Con.	Life-Spirit	VII.50
354	E. Uses	Grief	VII.91
462	Trad./Con.	Life-Spirit	VII.3
604	E. Uses	Confidence	VII.108
620	Trad./Con.	Life-Spirit	VII.51
704	Trad./Con.	Life-Spirit	VII.28
712	Trad./Con.	Life-Spirit	VII.26
837	E. Uses	Courage	VII.63
883	Trad./Con.	Life-Spirit	VII.4
900	Trad./Con.	Life-Spirit	VII.52
929	Trad./Con.	Life-Spirit	VII.29

ANDROMACHE

Line	Category	Sub-category	App. A
PHRĒN (CHAPTERS 2 AND 3)			
181	E. Uses	Emotional	I.2
361	Trad./Con.	Intelligence	I.3
365	Trad./Con. E. Images	Intelligence Archery	I.4
482	Trad./Con.	Mind	I.5
NOUS (CHAPTER 4)			
231	Trad./Con.	Intelligence	II.1
237	Trad./Con.	Mind: Negatives	II.2
252	Trad./Con.	Intelligence	II.22
667	Trad./Con.	Intelligence	II.3
944	Trad./Con.	Intelligence	II.23
PRAPIDES (CHAPTER 4)			
480 ·	Trad./Con.	Intelligence	III.1
THUMOS (CHAPTER 5)			
None			
KARDIA (CHAPTER 6)			
None			
PSYCHĒ (CHAPTERS 7 AND 8)			
160	E. Uses	Intellectual	VII.64
419	Trad./Con.	Life	VII.5
541	Trad./Con.	Life	VII.30
611	Trad./Con.	Life-spirit	VII.53

BACCHAE

Line	Category	Sub-category	App. A

PHRĒN (CHAPTERS 2 AND 3)

Line	Category	Sub-category	App. A
33	Trad./Con.	Madness	I.92
[203	Trad./Con.	Intelligence	I.6]
269	Trad./Con.	Speech, Intelligence	I.7
359	Trad./Con.	Distance, Madness	I.83
427	Trad./Con.	Intelligence	I.55
670	E. Uses	Intellectual	I.8
850	Trad./Con.	Distance	I.134
944	Trad./Con.	Mind	I.56
947	Trad./Con. E. Images	Mind Medical	I.57
1270	Trad./Con.	Mind	I.84

NOUS (CHAPTER 4)

252	Trad./Con.	Age, Intelligence	II.24
271	Trad./Con.	Intelligence	II.25

PRAPIDES (CHAPTER 4)

427	Trad./Con.	Mind: Raging	III.5
999	Trad./Con.	Mind: Positive	III.4

THUMOS (CHAPTER 5)

620	Trad./Con. E. Images	Hope Breath	IV.18

KARDIA (CHAPTER 6)

1288	Trad./Con.	Physical	V.2
1321	Trad./Con.	Distress	V.35

PSYCHĒ (CHAPTERS 7 AND 8)

75	E. Uses	Holiness	VII.92
1268	E. Uses	Madness	VII.109

ELECTRA

Line	Category	Sub-category	App. A
PHRĒN (CHAPTERS 2 AND 3)			
334	Trad./Con.	Distress	I.9
[387	Trad./Con.	Absence/Loss	I.10]
1059	Trad./Con.	Joy/Pleasure	I.135
603	Trad./Con.	Moral: "Good"	I.58
NOUS (CHAPTER 4)			
None			
THUMOS (CHAPTER 5)			
117	Trad./Con.	Desire	IV.24
	E. Uses	Emotion	
578	Trad./Con.	Seat of Mind	IV.25
KARDIA (CHAPTER 6)			
402	Trad./Con.	Joy	V.24
	E. Images	Heat	
PSYCHĒ (CHAPTERS 7 AND 8)			
208	E. Uses	Grief	VII.101
297	E. Uses	Desire	VII.65

HECUBA

Line	Category	Sub-category	App. A
PHRĒN (CHAPTERS 2 AND 3)			
85	Trad./Con.	Fear	I.11
300	Trad./Con.	Anger	I.45
359	Trad./Con.	Moral: "Evil"	I.85
590	Trad./Con.	Grief	I.59
746	Trad./Con.	Mind	I.136

Line	Category	Sub-category	App. A
NOUS (CHAPTER 4)			
[603	Trad./Con.	Mind: Positive	II.4
THUMOS (CHAPTER 5)			
1055	Trad./Con.	Anger	IV.29
KARDIA (CHAPTER 6)			
235	Trad./Con.	Distress/Pain	V.28
242	Trad./Con.	Seat of Emotion	V.29
433	Trad./Con.	Grief	V.14
1026	Trad./Con.	Desire	V,25
1129	Trad./Con.	Seat of Emotion	V.15
PSYCHĒ (CHAPTERS 7 AND 8)			
22	Trad./Con.	Life-Spirit	VII.6
87	E. Uses	Intellectual	VII.114
[176	Trad./Con.	Life	VII.7
182	Trad./Con.	Life-Spirit	VII.8
196	Trad./Con.	Life-Spirit	VII.9
580	E. Uses	Courage	VII.102

HELEN

Line	Category	Sub-category	App. A
PHRĒN (CHAPTERS 2 AND 3)			
160	Trad./Con.	Intelligence	I.60
501	Trad./Con.	Moral: "Evil"	I.86
[732	Trad./Con.	Moral: "Evil"	I.61]
1192	Trad./Con.	Grief	I.62
NOUS (CHAPTER 4)			
[122	Trad./Con. E. Images	Mind: Positive Sight	II.5]
[731	Trad./Con.	Mind: Positive	II.26]

Line	Category	Sub-category	App. A
1014	E. Uses	Divine Agent	II.6

THUMOS (CHAPTER 5)

None

KARDIA (CHAPTER 6)

Line	Category	Sub-category	App. A
960	Trad./Con. E. Images	Seat of Emotion Touch	V.30

PSYCHĒ (CHAPTERS 7 AND 8)

Line	Category	Sub-category	App. A
52	Trad./Con.	Life-Spirit	VII.10
946	Trad./Con.	Life	VII.11
1431	Trad./Con.	Life-Spirit	VII.31

HERACLIDAE

Line	Category	Sub-category	App. A

PHRĒN (CHAPTERS 2 AND 3)

Line	Category	Sub-category	App. A
356	Trad./Con.	Fear	I.137
483	Trad./Con. E. Images	Pain Medical	I.102
540	Trad./Con.	Mind	I.12
663	Trad./Con.	Joy/Pleasure	I.138
709	Trad./Con.	Distance	I.87
939	Trad./Con.	Joy/Pleasure	I.139

NOUS (CHAPTER 4)

None

THUMOS (CHAPTER 5)

Line	Category	Sub-category	App. A
925	Trad./Con.	Mind: "Unjust"	IV.3

KARDIA (CHAPTER 6)

Line	Category	Sub-category	App. A
583	Trad./Con.	Joy	V.3

Line	Category	Sub-category	App. A

PSYCHĒ (CHAPTERS 7 AND 8)

Line	Category	Sub-category	App. A
15	Trad./Con.	Life	VII.12
173	E. Uses	Hope	VII.110
296	Trad./Con.	LIfe	VII.32
455	Trad./Con.	Life	VII.33
530	E. Uses	Seat of Personality	VII.66
550	Trad./Con.	Life	VII.34
645	E. Uses	Grief	VII.103
927	E. Uses	Evil	VII.67
984	Trad./Con.	Life-Spirit	VII.13

HERCULES FURENS

Line	Category	Sub-category	App. A

PHRĒN (CHAPTERS 2 AND 3)

Line	Category	Sub-category	App. A
212	Trad./Con.	Moral: Justice Gods	I.63
745	Trad./Con.	Pain	I.46
776	Trad./Con.	Distance, Moral: Prosperity	I.103
836	Trad./Con.	Madness	I.104
1091	Trad./Con. E. Images	Madness Nautical	I.105
1122	Trad./Con.	Madness	I.88

NOUS (CHAPTER 4)

None

THUMOS (CHAPTER 5)

Line	Category	Sub-category	App. A
1121	Trad./Con.	Passion	IV.19

KARDIA (CHAPTER 6)

Line	Category	Sub-category	App. A
833	Trad./Con. Gods	Grief	V.16

Line	Category	Sub-category	App. A
KEAR (CHAPTER 6)			
1003	unclear		VI.3
PSYCHĒ (CHAPTERS 7 AND 8)			
[452	Trad./Con.	Life	VII.54]
626	E. Uses	Intellectual	VII.68
1146	Trad./Con.	Life	VII.35
[1366	E. Uses	Pain	VII.93]

HIPPOLYTUS

Line	Category	Sub-category	App. A
PHRĒN (CHAPTERS 2 AND 3)			
188	Trad./Con.	Grief	I.13
238	Trad./Con.	Damage	I.140
256	Trad./Con.	Love	I.14
283	Trad./Con. E. Images	Damage Medical	I.15
317	Trad./Con.	Moral: Holiness	I.16
365	Trad./Con.	Intelligence	I.141
390	Trad./Con.	Intelligence	I.64
462	Trad./Con.	Intelligence	I.89
474	Trad./Con.	Moral: "Evil"	I.65
511	Trad./Con.	Damage, Love	I.106
574	Trad./Con.	Fear	I.107
612	Trad./Con.	Mind	I.17
685	Trad./Con.	Purpose	I.142
689	Trad./Con. E. Images	Anger "Sharpness"	I.90
701	Trad./Con.	Intelligence	I.66
765	Trad./Con. E. Images	Love Medical	I.143
775	Trad./Con.	Love	I.67
926	E. Uses	Intellectual	I.108
935	Trad./Con.	Speech	I.18

Line	Category	Sub-category	App. A
936	Trad./Con. E. Images	Moral: "Evil" Medical	I.19
969	Trad./Con.	Age, Love	I.144
983	Trad./Con.	Anger	I.20
1012	Trad./Con.	Distance	I.91
1014	Trad./Con.	Damage	I.109
1104	Trad./Con.	Grief	I.110
1120	Trad./Con.	Distress	I.68
1230	Trad./Con.	Madness	I.92
1262	Trad./Con.	Joy/Madness	I.145
1268	Trad./Con. Trad./Con.	Love Gods	I.146
1298	Trad./Con.	Moral: Justice	I.147
1337	Trad./Con.	Mind	I.148
1390	Trad./Con.	Moral: "Good"	I.111
1419	Trad./Con.	Moral: "Good"	I.21
1448	Trad./Con.	Moral: "Holiness"	I.149
1454	Trad./Con.	Moral: "Good"	I.22

NOUS (CHAPTER 4)

105	Trad./Con.	Intelligence	II.27
920	Trad./Con.	Intelligence	II.7

THUMOS (CHAPTER 5)

1087	Trad./Con.	Desire	IV.4
1114	Trad./Con.	Pain	IV.30
1328	Trad./Con.	Desire	IV. 20

KARDIA (CHAPTER 6)

27	Trad./Con.	Love	V.26
841	Trad./Con.	Physical	V.31
[912	Trad./Con.	Desire	V.4]

PSYCHĒ (CHAPTERS 7 AND 8)

160	E. Uses	Grief	VII.69
173	E. Uses	Desire	VII.70

Line	Category	Sub-category	App. A
255	E. Uses	Love	VII.71
	E. Images	Marrow	
259	E. Uses	Pain	VII.72
440	Trad./Con.	Life	VII.36
505	E. Uses	Love	VII.104
527	E. Uses	Love	VII.115
721	Trad./Con.	Life-Spirit	VII.14
726	Trad./Con.	Life	VII.15
1006	E. Uses	Seat of Personality	VII.94
1040	E. Uses	Seat of Personality	VII.116

ION

Line	Category	Sub-category	App. A

PHRĒN (CHAPTERS 2 AND 3)

Line	Category	Sub-category	App. A
927	Trad./Con.	Pain	I.112
	E. Images	Nautical	
1180	Trad./Con.	Joy/Pleasure	I.109
1271	Trad./Con.	Intelligence	I.150
1538	Trad./Con.	Distress	I.114

NOUS (CHAPTER 4)

Line	Category	Sub-category	App. A
251	Trad./Con.	Mind: Attention	II.28
742	Trad./Con.	Mind: Positive	II.8
1370	Trad./Con.	Mind: Attention	II.29

THUMOS (CHAPTER 5)

None

KARDIA (CHAPTER 6)

None

PSYCHĒ (CHAPTERS 7 AND 8)

Line	Category	Sub-category	App. A
859	E. Uses	Seat of Personality	VII.73
877	E. Uses	Pain	VII.74

Line	Category	Sub-category	App. A
1170	E. Uses	Joy	VII.95
1247	E. Uses	Pain	VII.88
1499	Trad./Con.	Life	VII.55

IPHIGENIA AT AULIS

Line	Category	Sub-category	App. A

PHRĒN (CHAPTERS 2 AND 3)

Line	Category	Sub-category	App. A
67	Trad./Con.	Intelligence	I.47
327	Trad./Con.	Moral: "Evil"	I.23
359	Trad./Con.	Joy/Pleasure	I.93
194	E. Uses	Intelligence	I.24
1359	Trad./Con.	Purpose	I.94
1434	Trad./Con.	Pain	I.151
1580	Trad./Con.	Pain	I.111

NOUS (CHAPTER 4)

Line	Category	Sub-category	App. A
334	Trad./Con.	Mind: Negative, Justice	II.9
374	Trad./Con.	Intelligence	II.30
1139	Trad./Con.	Intelligence	II.10, 31

THUMOS (CHAPTER 5)

Line	Category	Sub-category	App. A
125	Trad./Con. E. Images	Anger Breath	IV.21
919	Trad./Con.	Courage	IV.5

KARDIA (CHAPTER 6)

Line	Category	Sub-category	App. A
475	Trad./Con.	Seat of Emotion	V.10
1173	Trad./Con.	Seat of Emotion	V.17

PSYCHĒ (CHAPTERS 7 AND 8)

Line	Category	Sub-category	App. A
1390	Trad./Con.	Life-Spirit	VII.16
1141	Trad./Con.	Life-Spirit	VII.56

IPHIGENIA IN TAURIS

Line	Category	Sub-category	App. A

PHRĒN (CHAPTERS 2 AND 3)

Line	Category	Sub-category	App. A
655	Trad./Con.	Desire	I.25
815	Trad./Con.	Intelligence	I.152
1181	Trad./Con.	Intelligence	I.116
1322	Trad./Con.	Intelligence	I.69

NOUS (CHAPTER 4)

None

THUMOS (CHAPTER 5)

None

KARDIA (CHAPTER 6)

Line	Category	Sub-category	App. A
344	E. Uses	Kinds of	V.5

PSYCHĒ (CHAPTERS 7 AND 8)

Line	Category	Sub-category	App. A
838	E. Uses	Seat of Personality	VII.75
882	E. Uses	Seat of Personality	VII.76

MEDEA

Line	Category	Sub-category	App. A

PHRĒN (CHAPTERS 2 AND 3)

Line	Category	Sub-category	App. A
[38	Trad./Con.	Anger	I.26]
55	Trad./Con. E. Images	Grief Touch	I.117
104	Trad./Con.	Mind	I.27
143	Trad./Con.	Calm	I.95
177	Trad./Con.	Anger	I.28
266	Trad./Con.	Moral: "Evil"	I.29
316	Trad./Con.	Planning, Moral: "Evil"	I.48
599	Trad./Con.	Moral: Prosperity	I.118

Line	Category	Sub-category	App. A
661	Trad./Con. E. Images	Love "Openness"	I.30
677	Trad./Con.	Mind	I.164
856	Trad./Con.	Courage	I.31
1052	Trad./Con.	Speech	I.119
1265	Trad./Con.	Anger	I.120
1373	Trad./Con.	Moral: "Evil"	I.153

NOUS (CHAPTER 4)

529	Trad./Con.	Mind: Negative	II.11

THUMOS (CHAPTER 5)

8	Trad./Con.	Love	IV.26
108	Trad./Con. E. Images	Passion Storm	IV.15
310	Trad./Con.	Desire	IV.6
640	Trad./Con.	Love	IV.31
865	Trad./Con.	Courage	IV.16
879	Trad./Con.	Anger	IV.27
[1056	Trad./Con.	Seat of Emotion	IV.7]
[1079	Trad./Con. E. Uses	Seat of Emotion Responsible for evils	IV.8]
1152	Trad./Con.	Anger	IV.22

KARDIA (CHAPTER 6)

99	Trad./Con.	Anger	V.18
245	Trad./Con.	Distress/Pain	V.19
432	Trad./Con.	Love	V.11
590	Trad./Con.	Anger	V.6
858	Trad./Con.	Courage	V.12
1042	Trad./Con.	Courage	V.7
1242	Trad./Con. E. Images	Courage Armour	V.8
1360	Trad./Con. E. Images	Seat of Emotion Touch	V.37

Line	Category	Sub-category	App. A
KEAR (CAPTER 6)			
398	Trad./Con.	Pain	VI.2
911	Trad./Con.	Thought	VI.1
PSYCHĒ (CHAPTERS 7 AND 8)			
110	E. Uses	Life-Spirit	VII.77
226	Trad./Con.	Anger	VII.47
247	E. Uses	Life	VII.117
474	E. Uses	Seat of Personality	VII.105
968	Trad./Con.	Life	VII.37
1219	Trad./Con.	Life-Spirit	VII.38

ORESTES

Line	Category	Sub-category	App. A
PHRĒN (CHAPTERS 2 AND 3)			
216	Trad./Con.	Absence/Loss	I.96
297	Trad./Con.	Damage, Madness, Fear	I.121
[545	Trad./Con.	Grief	I.154]
608	Trad./Con.	Pain	I.155
1021	Trad./Con.	Distance	I.70
1176	Trad./Con.	Joy/Pleasure	I.71
1204	Trad./Con.	Intelligence	I.72
1604	Trad./Con.	Moral: Holiness	I.97
NOUS (CHAPTER 4)			
[909	Trad./Con.	Mind: Positive	II.21]
1181	Trad./Con.	Mind: Attention	II.32

Line	Category	Sub-category	App. A

THUMOS (CHAPTER 5)

Line	Category	Sub-category	App. A
[702	Trad./Con.	Seat of Emotion	IV.9]

KARDIA (CHAPTER 6)

Line	Category	Sub-category	App. A
466	Trad./Con. E. Uses	Seat of Emotion Kind of	V.9

PHOENICIAN WOMEN

Line	Category	Sub-category	App. A

PHRĒN (CHAPTERS 2 AND 3)

Line	Category	Sub-category	App. A
383	Trad./Con.	Pain	I.156
746	Trad./Con.	Planning	I.32
1285	Trad./Con.	Fear	I.73
1300	Trad./Con.	Purpose	I.33
1740	Trad./Con.	Moral: "Good"	I.34

NOUS (CHAPTER 4)

Line	Category	Sub-category	App. A
360	Trad./Con.	Mind: Attention	II.33
1418	Trad./Con.	Mind: Attention	II.34

THUMOS (CHAPTER 5)

Line	Category	Sub-category	App. A
454	Trad./Con. E. Images	Anger Breath	IV.10

KARDIA (CHAPTER 6)

None

PSYCHĒ (CHAPTERS 7 AND 8)

Line	Category	Sub-category	App. A
998	Trad./Con.	Life-Spirit	VII.42
1228	Trad./Con. E. Images	Life-Spirit Sell	VII.43

Line	Category	Sub-category	App. A
1291	Trad./Con.	Life-Spirit	VII.59
1297	E. Uses	Anger	VII.79
1330	Trad./Con. E. Images	Life Contest	VII.21
1553	Trad./Con.	Life-Spirit	VII.22

SUPPLIANT WOMEN

Line	Category	Sub-category	App. A

PHRĒN (CHAPTERS 2 AND 3)

Line	Category	Sub-category	App. A
217	Trad./Con.	Moral: Pride	I.49
581	Trad./Con.	Anger	I.50
1062	Trad./Con.	Planning	I.35
1162	Trad./Con. E. Images	Grief Touch	I.122

NOUS (CHAPTER 4)

None

THUMOS (CHAPTER 5)

Line	Category	Sub-category	App. A
480	Trad./Con.	Hope	IV.28
556	Trad./Con.	Anger	IV.17

KARDIA (CHAPTER 6)

None

PSYCHĒ (CHAPTERS 7 AND 8)

Line	Category	Sub-category	App. A
777	Trad./Con. E. Images	Life-Spirit Expenditure	VII.44
1024	Trad./Con.	Life-Spirit	VII.27
1103	E. Uses	Love, Courage	VII.80

TROJAN WOMEN

Line	Category	Sub-category	App. A

PHRĒN (CHAPTERS 2 AND 3)

Line	Category	Sub-category	App. A
6	Trad./Con.	Mind	I.123
52	Trad./Con.	Love	I.124
	Trad./Con.	Gods	
408	Trad./Con.	Madness	I.157
417	Trad./Con.	Absence/Loss	I.74
[635	Trad./Con.	Joy	I.158]
662	Trad./Con.	Love	I.75
	E. Images	"Openness"	
682	Trad./Con.	Intelligence	I.98
992	Trad./Con.	Love, Madness	I.99
1158	Trad./Con.	Intelligence	I.36
1216	Trad./Con.	Grief	I.159
	E. Images	Touch	

NOUS (CHAPTER 4)

Line	Category	Sub-category	App. A
652	Trad./Con.	Mind: Positive, "Goods"	II.35
886	E. Uses	Divine Aspect	II.12
988	Trad./Con.	Love	II.13
	E. Images	Sight	
1052	Trad./Con.	Love	II.14
	E. Images	Nautical	

THUMOS (CHAPTER 5)

None

KARDIA (CHAPTER 6)

None

PSYCHĒ (CHAPTERS 7 AND 8)

Line	Category	Sub-category	App. A
182	E. Uses	Fear	VII.106
108	E. Uses	Pain	VII.107
640	Trad./Con.	Life	VII.23
791	Trad./Con.	Life	VII.24
900	Trad./Con.	Life-Spirit	VII.45
1135	E. Uses	Intelligence	VII.89
1214	Trad./Con.	Life-Spirit	VII.90

FRAGMENTS

Line	Category	Sub-category	App. A

PHRĒN (CHAPTERS 2 AND 3)

Line	Category	Sub-category	App. A
58 *Alexander*	Trad./Con.	Moral: "Good"	I.37
212 *Antiope*	Trad./Con.	Moral: "Good"	I.76
344 *Dictys*	Trad./Con.	Intelligence	I.100
362.6 *Erechtheus*	Trad./Con.	Mind	I.77
400 *Thyestes*	Trad./Con.	Love	I.38
436 *Hippolytus*	Trad./Con.	Moral: "Evil"	I.160
548 *Oedipus*	Trad./Con.	Moral: "Good"	I.78
551 *Oedipus*	Trad./Con.	Moral: "Evil"	I.125
573 *Oinomaus*	Trad./Con.	Pain	I.126
598 *Pirithous*	Trad./Con.	Speech	I.51
619 *Peleus*	Trad./Con.	Age	I.39
640 *Polyidos*	Trad./Con.	Madness	I.40
644 *Polyidos*	Trad./Con.	Moral: "Good"	I.161
652 *Protesilaus*	Trad./Con.	Love	I.127
659 *Protesilaus*	Trad./Con.	Speech	I.41
776 *Phaëthon*	E. Uses E. Images	Intellectual Sight	I.79
781.56 *Phaëthon*	Trad./Con.	Mind	I.80
831 *Phrixus*	Trad./Con.	Mind	I.42
964.5 Incerta	Trad./Con.	Mind	I.52

Line	Category	Sub-category	App. A
1032 Incerta	E. Uses	Intellectual	I.43
1054 Incerta	Trad./Con.	Love, Moral: "Evil"	I.128
1079 Incerta	Trad./Con.	Grief, Calm	I.81
370K.60 Erechtheus	Trad./Con.	Grief	I.162

NOUS (CHAPTER 4)

Line	Category	Sub-category	App. A
25.4 Aiolos	Trad./Con.	Age, Intelligence	II.15
67.4 Alcmeon	Trad./Con.	Fear, Speech	II.40
144 Andromeda	Trad./Con.	Mind: Positive	II.42
149 Andromeda	Trad./Con.	Intelligence	II.16
212 Antigone	Trad./Con.	Mind: Positive	II.17
256 Erechtheus	Trad./Con.	Intelligence	II.36
265 Aug_	Trad./Con.	Intelligence	II.41
548 Oedipus	Trad./Con.	Mind: Positive	II.43
710 Telephus	Trad./Con.	Intelligence	II.18
909.5 Incerta	Trad./Con.	Intelligence	II.37
909.6 Incerta	Trad./Con.	Intelligence	II.19
934 Incerta	Trad./Con.	Intelligence	II.38
964.2 Incerta	Trad./Con.	Mind: Positive	II.39
1018 Incerta	E. Uses	Divine Agent	II.20

Line	Category	Sub-category	App. A

PRAPIDES (CHAPTER 4)

27.1 *Aiolos*	Trad./Con.	Intelligence	III.2
901.1 Incerta	Trad./Con.	Intelligence	III.3

THUMOS (CHAPTER 5)

257 *Archelaus*	Trad./Con.	Passion	IV.11
362.34 *Erechtheus*	E. Uses	Emotion	IV.12
718 *Telephus*	Trad./Con.	Passion	IV.13
1039 Incerta	Trad./Con.	Pain	IV.14

KARDIA (CHAPTER 6)

412.3 *Ino*	Trad./Con.	Seat of Emotion	V.20
573.4 *Oinomaus*	Trad./Con.	Distress/Pain	V.32
908.6 Incerta	Trad./Con.	Fear	V.21
1038.2 Incerta	Trad./Con.	Distress/Pain	V.33
1063.12 Incerta	Trad./Con.	Love	V.22

PSYCHĒ (CHAPTERS 7 AND 8)

67 *Alcmeon*	E. Uses E. Images	Pain Contest	VII.97
185 *Antigone*	E. Uses	Good	VII.81
220 *Antigone*	E. Uses	Intellectual	VII.98
308.1 *Beller- ophone*	E. Uses	Seat of Personality	VII.82

Line	Category	Sub-category	App. A
323 *Danaë*	E. Uses	Love	VII.118
360.44 *Erechtheus*	E. Uses	Seat of Personality	VII.83
360.51 *Erechtheus*	E. Uses	Life-Spirit	VII.25
370K.71 *Erechtheus*	Trad./Con.	Life-Spirit	II.25a
388 *Theseus*	Trad./Con.	Good	VII.84
431 *Hippolytus*	E. Uses	Love, Gods	VII.119
754 *Hypsipyle*	E. Uses	Joy	VII.90
822 *Phrixus*	E. Uses	Pain	VII.99
908.8 Incerta	E. Uses	Pain	VII.85
912.9 Incerta	Trad./Con. E. Images	Life-Spirit Contest	VII.64VII. 61
913 Incerta	E. Uses	Intellectual	VII.100
924 Incerta	E. Uses	Seat of Personality, Intelligence	VII.86
964.6 Incerta	E. Uses	Pain	VII.112 2

[RHESUS]

Line	Category	Sub-category	App. A
PHRĒN (CHAPTERS 2 AND 3)			
79	New Uses	Intellectual	I.129
266	New Uses	Intellectual	I.130
863	Trad./Con.	Distress	I.131
916	Trad./Con.	Grief	1.163
	Image	Touch	
NOUS (CHAPTER 4)			
None			
THUMOS (CHAPTER 5)			
786	Trad./Con.	Anger	IV.23
	Image	Breath	
KARDIA (CHAPTER 6)			
596	Trad./Con.	Grief	V.27
770	Trad./Con.	Seat of Emotion	V.13
PSYCHĒ (CHAPTERS 7 AND 8)			
183	Trad./Con.	Life-Spirit	VII.46
345	New Uses	Intellectual	VII.87
965	Trad./Con.	Life-Spirit	VII.62

APPENDIX C

Adjectives and Participles with Psychic Terms

PHRĒN (CHAPTERS 2 AND 3)

Adjective or participle	Passage	App. A	Meaning
ἀγαθός	*Hipp.* 1419	I.21	good
	Hipp. 1454	I.22	good
ἀγύμναστος	*Fr.* 598 *Pirithous*	I.51	untrained, unexercised
ἄκαμπτος	*Hipp.* 1268	I.146	unbending
ἄκρος	[*Bacc.* 203]	I.6	highest, top
ἄλλος	*Med.* 266	I.29	other
ἄναγνος	*Hipp.* 1448	I.149	unholy
ἀναίσχυντος	*I.A.* 327	I.23	shameless
ἀνώμοτος	*Hipp.* 612	I.17	unsworn
ἀπότυστος	*Med.* 1373	I.153	detestable, abominable
ἄρσην	*Or.* 1204	I.72	male
ἄρτιος	*Tr.* 417	I.74	ready, complete
αὐθάδης	*Med.* 104	I.27	self-willed, stubborn
αὐτοκρατής	*And.* 482	I.5	having full authority
βαρύς	[*Med.* 38]	I.26	heavy, grievous
βελτίων	*El.* 1061	I.58	better

Adjective or participle	Passage	App. A	Meaning
βροτός	Hipp. 936	I.19	mortal
γυναικεῖος	Fr. 400 Thyestes	I.38	of women
διάφορος	Hel. 160–1	I.60	different
δίκαιος	H.F. 212 Hipp. 1298	I.63 I.147	just
ἐλευθερώτερος	Fr. 832 Phrixus	I.42	more free
ἐμός	Hec. 85 Hcld. 356 Hcld. 663 Hipp. 1448 I.T. 815 Med. 599 Tr. 6 [Rh. 79] [Rh. 916] 370K.60 Erechtheus	I.11 I.137 I.138 I.149 I.152 I.118 I.123 I.129 I.163 I.162	my
εὐπροσήγρος	Alc. 775	I.44	courteous
εὐσεβής	Hipp. 1454	I.22	holy
ἡβῶσα	Hipp. 969	I.144	young, youthful
ἤπιος	Fr. 362.6 Erechtheus	I.77	gentle, mild
θεῖος	Hcld. 540	I.12	divine
θήλυς	And. 181	I.2	of a woman
καθαρός	Hipp. 1120 Med. 661	I.68 I.30	untroubled, clear pure, holy
κακός	[Hel. 732] Hipp. 474	I.61 I.65	evil
καλός	Fr. 548 Oedipus	I.78	good, noble
μιαιφονώτερος	Med. 266	I.29	more murderous, more blood-stained
μονομάχος	Pho. 1300	I.33	single-combat
νεώτερος	Fr. 619 Peleus	I.39	younger
οἷος	Bacc. 947	I.57	the sort of
ὅμοιος	Hel. 160–1	I.60	similar
πυκινός	I.A. 67	I.47	cunning, clever

Adjective or participle	Passage	App. A	Meaning
σός	And. 361	I.3	your
	El. 1059	I.135	
	Hcld. 483	I.102	
	709	I.87	
	939	I.139	
	Hel. 1192	I.62	
	Hipp. 365	I.141	
	685	I.142	
	983	I.20	
	1262	I.145	
	1337	I.148	
	1454	I.22	
	Ion 1271	I.150	
	I.A. 327	I.23	
	I.T. 1322	I.69	
	Med. 1373	I.153	
	[Or. 545]	I.154	
	Pho. 383	I.156	
σοφός	Bacc. 427	I.55	wise
	Med. 677	I.164	
ταλαίπωρος	El. 334	I.9	suffering, wretched
τρομερός	Pho. 1285	I.73	trembling
τυφλός	Fr. 776 Phaëthon	I.79	blind
ὑγιής	Bacc. 947	I.57	healthy
φαυλότερος	And. 482	I.5	more paltry
χρηστός	Fr. 212 Antigone	I.76	good, noble

NOUS (CHAPTER 4)

Adjective or participle	Passage	App. A	Meaning
βέβαιος	I.A. 334	II.9	firm, steady
ἐλεύθερος	[Hel. 731]	II.26	free
ἐμός	Fr. 144 Andromeda	II.42	my
ἐμπεσών	Hel. 1015	II.6	falling
ἰδών	Tr. 988	II.13	seeing

Adjective or participle	Passage	App. A	Meaning
λεπτός	Med. 529	II.11	subtle
σός	And. 237	II.2	your
	Tr. 988	II.13	

PRAPIDES (CHAPTER 4)

Adjective or participle	Passage	App. A	Meaning
μανεῖσα	Bacc. 999	III.5	raging
πηδάλιος	And. 480	III.1	at the helm
σοφός	Bacc. 427	III.4	wise

THUMOS (CHAPTER 5)

Adjective or participle	Passage	App. A	Meaning
αἴτιος	[Med. 1079]	IV.8	responsible
ἀκήρατος	Hipp. 1114	IV.30	unmixed
ἀλγών	Fr. 1039 Incerta	IV.14	in pain
βίαιος	Hcld. 925	IV.3	violent
γυναικόφρων	Fr. 326.34 Erechtheus	IV.12	womanly-minded
δυσμαχώτατος	Hec. 1055	IV.29	most difficult to fight
ζέων	Hec. 1055	IV.29	boiling
Θρᾷξ	Hec. 1055	IV.29	Thracian
κρείσσων	[Med. 1079]	IV.8	stronger
μέγας	[Or. 702] Fr. 257 Archelaus	IV.9 IV.11	great
μείζων	Med. 108	IV.15	greater
πρόμαντις	And. 1072	IV.2	prophetic
τλήμων	Med. 865	IV.16	bold
ὑψηλόφρων	I.A. 919	IV.5	lofty-minded

KARDIA (CHAPTER 6)

Adjective or participle	Passage	App. A	Meaning
ἄκρος	Hec. 242	V.29	top, surface
ἀναμετρουμένη δακρύ	I.T. 346	V.5	measuring out tears
ἄτεγκτος	H.F. 833	V.16	untouched
γαληνός	I.T. 345	V.5	gentle
ἐμός	Hcld. 583	V.3	my
λίχνος	[Hipp. 912]	V.4	curious
μαινομένα	Hipp. 1274	V.36	raging, mad
	Med. 432	V.11	
μελοῦσα	[Rh. 770]	V.13	caring
ποθοῦσα κλύειν	[Hipp. 912]	V.4	desiring to hear
σός	Bacc. 1321	V.35	your
	Hel. 960	V.30	
	Hipp. 841	V.31	
	Med. 1360	V.37	
τάλας	I.T. 344	V.5	wretched
	Or. 466	V.9	
	Fr. 908.6 Incerta	V.21	
τίς	I.A. 1173	V.17	what
τλῆσα	Alc. 837	V.1	enduring
φιλοκτίρων	I.T. 345	V.5	showing pity
φίλος	Hec. 1026	V.25	dear

KEAR (CHAPTER 6)

Adjective or participle	Passage	App. A	Meaning
ἐμός	Med. 398	VI.2	my
σός	Med. 911	VI.1	your

PSYCHĒ (CHAPTERS 7 AND 8)

Adjective or participle	Passage	App. A	Meaning
ἀγαθός	And. 611 Fr. 388 Theseus	VII.53 VII.84	good
ἀκόρεστος	Hcld. 927	VII.67	insatiable
ἄκουσα	Hcld. 531	VII.66	unwilling
βρότειος	Supp. 777	VII.44	of mortals
γλυκύς	Supp. 1103	VII.80	sweet
δεινός	And. 160	VII.64	clever
δηχθεῖσα	Med. 110	VII.77	bitten
διαβάντε	Alc. 900	VII.52	crossing
δίκαιος	Fr. 388 Theseus	VII.84	just
δύο	Alc. 712 Alc. 900	VII.26 VII.52	two
δυσκατάπαυστος	Med. 109	VII.77	most hard to stop
εἷς	Alc. 54 Alc. 712 Alc. 883 Alc. 900 Hipp. 259 Hipp. 721 I.A. 1390 Med. 247 Or. 1046 Fr. 360.51 Erechtheus Fr. 908.8 Incerta	VII.48 VII.26 VII.4 VII.52 VII.72 VII.14 VII.16 VII.117 VII.39 VII.25 VII.85	one
ἑκοῦσα	Hcld. 531 Fr. 360.44 Erechtheus	VII.66 VII.83	willing

Adjective or participle	Passage	App. A	Meaning
ἐμός	Alc. 283	VII.1	my
	Alc. 341	VII.50	
	Alc. 604	VII.108	
	Alc. 837	VII.63	
	Hcld. 455	VII.33	
	Hcld. 550	VII.34	
	Hcld. 984	VII.13	
	[H.F. 452]	VII.54	
	H.F. 1146	VII.35	
	Hipp. 1040	VII.116	
	I.A. 1390	VII.16	
	Or. 446	VII.78	
	[Or. 644]	VII.57	
	Or. 662	VII.58	
	Or. 1517	VII.20	
	Supp. 1024	VII.27	
	Tr. 900	VII.24	
	Fr. 67	VII.97	
	Alcmeon		
	Fr. 323	VII.118	
	Danaë		
εὐναῖος	Hipp. 160	VII.69	bed-fast
εὐτυχοῦσα	I.T. 838	VII.75	enjoying good fortune
ἡδομένη	Fr. 784	VII.90	glad, rejoicing
	Hypsipyle		
ἠπειρῶτις	And. 160	VII.64	of Asia
θεῖος	Hec. 87	VII.114	prophetic
κακοβουληθείς	Ion 877	VII.77	ill-advised
κειμένη	Fr. 67	VII.97	prosperity
	Alcmeon		
μεγαλόσπλαγχνοος	Med. 109	VII.77	high-spirited
μείζων	Supp. 1103	VII.80	greater
μέλεος	I.T. 882	VII.76	wretched
ὁμογενής	Pho. 1291	VII.59	of the same race
ὀρθεύσουσα	Tr. 182	VII.106	arising early
παρθένος	Hipp. 1006	VII.94	virgin
πιστόταος	Alc. 900	VII.52	most faithful
πολύς	And. 611	VII.53	much (many)
	Hel. 52	VII.10	
ποτωμένη	Or. 676	VII.17	flying

Adjective or participle	Passage	App. A	Meaning
σός	*Alc.* 462	VII.3	your
	Alc. 620	VII.51	
	Bacc. 1268	VII.109	
	Hec. 176	VII.7	
	Hec. 182	VII.8	
	Hec. 196	VII.9	
	Ion 1499	VII.55	
	I.A. 1441	VII.56	
	Or. 1180	VII.111	
	Tr. 791	VII.23	
	Tr. 1171	VII.89	
σώφρων	Fr. 388 *Theseus*	VII.84	moderate
τάλας	[*H.F.* 452]	VII.54	wretched
τίς	*Or.* 526	VII.96	what
τρίσσος	*Pho.* 1553	VII.22	three
φίλος	*Or.* 1034	VII.19	dear
φόνιος	*Pho.* 1297	VII.79	murderous

Cognate Verbs, Adverbs, Adjectives, and Nouns

PHRĒN

Verb	Adverb	Adjective (-phrēn)	Adjective (other)	Noun
SIMPLE VERBS, ADVERBS, ADJECTIVES, NOUNS				
φρονέω (e.g., to consider, ponder, regard, desire, to be intelligent, minded, disposed, to have feeling)			φρόνιμος (wise, prudent) φροντιστέος (needing to take thought)	φρόνημα (thought, understanding) φρόνησις (thought, understanding) φροντίς (thought, intelligence) φραδή (thought, understanding)
φράζω (e.g., to show, display, observe, think, plan, to be inclined)				
φρενόω (to make wise, instruct)				
φροντίζω (to think, reflect)				
COMPOUND VERBS, ADVERBS, ADJECTIVES, NOUNS				
-φρον, -φραιν, -φραξ				
ἀφρονέω (to be foolish)	ἀφροντίστως (foolishly)	ἄφρων (heedless, foolish, insensible)	ἄφροντις (foolish) ἄφραστος (inexpressible)	ἀφροσύνη (foolishness)

PHRĒN (cont'd)

Verb	Adverb	Adjective (-phrēn)	Adjective (other)	Noun
ἐκφροντίζω (to think over, ponder)		δύσφρων (ill-disposed, malignant)		δυσφροσύνη (anxiety, worry)
	εὐφρόνως (joyfully)	εὔφρων (cheerful, joyful)		εὐφροσύνη (joy, gladness)
καταφρονέω (to think little of, despise)				
συσσωφρονέω (to share in moderation)				
σωφρονέω (to be moderate, wise)	σωφρόνως (modestly, wisely)	σώφρων (prudent, wise, moderate)		σωφροσύνη (moderation, sound thought)
	σωφρονεστέρος (moderately)			
σωφρονίζω (to come to senses, be moderate)				
ὑπερφρονέω (to be haughty, proud)				
φρεν-			φρενήρης (sound of mind)	

PHRĒN (cont'd)

Verb	Adverb	Adjective (-phrēn)	Adjective (other)	Noun
REMAINING -*PHRĒN* ADJECTIVES				
αἰδόφρων		respectful, compassionate		
ἀρτίφρων		sound of mind		
γυναικόφρων		of a woman's mind		
δολιόφρων		deceitful in mind		
ἔμφρων		rational, sensible		
κοινόφρων		like-minded with		
μελεόφρων		miserable-minded		
ὀνειρόφρων		versed in dreams		
ὀξύφρων		sharp-minded		
παράφρων		out of one's wits		
ποικιλόφρων		wily-minded		
κακόφρων		thinking evil		
πρόφρων		eager, kind		
σιδηρόφρων		iron-minded		
ταλαίφρων		wretched, suffering in mind		
ὑπέρφρων		excessively proud		
ὑψηλόφρων		high-spirited, haughty		
φιλόφρων		kindly-minded, affable		

PHRĒN (cont'd)

Verb	Adverb	Adjective (-phrēn)	Adjective (other)	Noun
ὠμόφρον		savage-minded		

NOUS

Verb	Adverb	Adjective (-nous)	Adjective (other)	Noun

SIMPLE VERBS, ADVERBS, ADJECTIVES, NOUNS

νοέω
(to think, intend, perceive)

νουθετέω
(to advise)

νουθέτημα
(advice)

νουθέτησις
(advice)

COMPOUND VERBS, ADVERBS, ADJECTIVES, NOUNS

ἀγνοέω
(to be ignorant of)

ἄγνοια
(ignorance)

ἄνοια
(foolishness, folly)

Verb	Adverb	Adjective (-nous)	Adjective (other)	Noun
				διάνοια (thought, opinion)
		δύσνους (of hostile mind)		δύσνοια (ill-will)
ἐννοέω (to understand)		ἔννους (intelligent)		ἔννοια (thought, plan)
ἐπινοέω (to think, plan)				ἐπίνοια (thought, purpose)
		εὔνους (well-intentioned, of good-will)		εὔνοια (kindness, good-will)
μετανοέω (to change mind, repent)				
				ξύννοια (thought, reflection)
παρανοέω (to be deranged)				παράνοια (derangement)
προνοέω (to foresee)				πρόνοια (foresight, foreknowledge)
συννοέω (to ponder, reflect)				
ὑπονοέω (to suspect)				ὑπόνοια (suspicions, supposition)

THUMOS

Verb	Adverb	Adjective (-thumos)	Adjective (other)	Noun

SIMPLE VERBS, ADVERBS, ADJECTIVES, NOUNS

θυμόω
(to be angry, indignant)

COMPOUND VERBS, ADVERBS, ADJECTIVES, NOUNS

-θυμ-

ἀθυμέω
(to lose spirit, fail in spirit)

ἀθυμία
(lack of spirit)

δυσθυμέω
(to be melancholy)

δυσθυμία
(despondency, despair)

ἐνθύμιος
(taken to heart)

ἐνθύμησις
(thought, pondering)

ἐπιθυμέω
(to desire)

ἐπιθυμία
(desire)

εὐθυμέω
(to be of good cheer, delight)

ὀξυθυμέω
(to show sharp anger)

ὀξύθυμος
(of sharp temper)

ὀξυθυμία
(sharp anger)

προθυμέομαι
(to be eager for, to desire)

πρόθυμος
(eager, willing)

προθυμία
(willingness, eagerness)

THUMOS (cont'd)

Verb	Adverb	Adjective (-thumos)	Adjective (other)	Noun
		ἄθυμος (lazy)		ἀθυμία (laziness)

REMAINING -THUMOS ADJECTIVES AND ADVERBS

Verb	Adverb	Adjective (-thumos)	Adjective (other)	Noun
βαρύθυμος			heavy-spirited, indignant	

KARDIA

Verb	Adverb	Adjective (-kardios)	Adjective (other)	Noun
	εὐκαρδίως (bravely)	εὐκάρδιος (of stout or brave heart)		

COMPOUND VERBS, ADVERBS, ADJECTIVES, NOUNS

Verb	Adverb	Adjective (-psychos)	Adjective (other)	Noun

SIMPLE VERBS, ADVERBS, ADJECTIVES, NOUNS

Verb	Adverb	Adjective (-psychos)	Adjective (other)	Noun
				ψῦχος (cold)

-ψυχ

COMPOUND VERBS, ADVERBS, ADJECTIVES, NOUNS

Verb	Adverb	Adjective (-psychos)	Adjective (other)	Noun
ἀναψύχω (to cool, refresh, console)				ἀναψυχή (cooling, refreshing, consolation)
		ἄψυχος (lifeless, inanimate)		ἀψυχία (faint-heartedness)
		ἔμψυχος (living)		
		εὔψυχος (of good spirit, courageous)		εὐψυχία (courage, high-spirit)
				παραψυχή (cooling, refreshing, consolation)
φιλοψυχέω (to love one's life, be cowardly)		φιλόψυχος (loving one's life, cowardly)		

PSYCHĒ (cont'd)

Verb	Adverb	Adjective (-psychos)	Adjective (other)	Noun
ψυχ-				
			ψυχαγωγός (leading *psychai*)	
				ψυχοπομπός (guidance of *psychai*)
ψυχορραγέω (to let *psychē* break loose)			ψυχορραγής (letting *psychē* break loose)	

APPENDIX E

Hēpar and *Splanchna*[1]

HĒPAR

In Euripides there are twelve references to *hēpar*. In every case it is the physical "liver."[2] Only at *Rh.* 425 is it associated with "grief" (λύπη).[3]

SPLANCHNA

Splanchna occurs nine times. In four passages it signifies "viscera" or "internal organs."[4] In other passages emotional or intellectual elements seem to be present.

Alc. 1009. Heracles tells Admetus that one should speak frankly to a friend "and not have reproaches (μορφάς) in silence under *splanchna.*" Here *splanchna* serve as the location of thoughts and feelings.

Hipp. 118. The Servant remarks about Hippolytus: "if someone being young, bearing a vehement *splanchnon*, speaks foolish things, pretend not to hear him." *Splanchnon* serves as the seat of a person's character.

Or. 1201. Electra, speaking of Menelaus, says to Orestes: "And I think that, even if it at first he was greatly distressed, he will in time soften (μαλάσσω) his *splanchnon.*" In this case *splanchnon* appears to be the location of Menelaus' rage and distress.

Fr. 858 (Incerta) speaks of a "hot-tempered (θερμόβουλος) *splanchnon.*" Again *splanchnon* is associated with deep feeling.

In these five passages described above *splanchnon* or *splanchna* function as a seat of strong emotion. In *Alc.* 1009 and *Med.* 220 it has as well a broader sense of seat of character or thought. The *splanchna* do not appear to function as psychological agents but to act as the location of feeling within the person.[5]

Notes

1 We shall include passages from the *Rhesus*, mainly in the Notes and at the end of Appendices 1–3.
2 See the excellent table describing the plays in C. Collard, *Euripides* (Oxford 1981), *Greece and Rome Surveys* 14, 2.
3 See, e.g., the work of Adkins, Austin, Biraud, Böhme, Bremmer, Caswell, Cheyns, Claus, Dihle, von Fritz, Furley, Gelzer, Harrison, Jahn, Jarcho, Larock, Lesher, Lynch and Miles, Nehring, Onians, Padel, Pellicia, Plamböck, Rohde, de Romilly, Russo and Simon, Rüsche, Schmitt, Snell, Vivante, and Warden.
4 My articles are as follows:

Phrēn in Homer: see *Psychological Activity*; in Hesiod: *RBPh* 67 (1989), 5–17; in the lyric and elegiac poets: *Glotta* 66 (1988), 26–61; in Pindar and Bacchylides: *Glotta* 67 (1989), 148–89.

Thumos in Homer: *IF* 85 (1980), 135–50; in Hesiod: *Emerita* 61 (1993), 16–40; in the lyric and elegiac poets: *SIFC* 12 (1994), Part One, 12–37, Part Two, 149–74; in Pindar and Bacchylides: *RBPh* 71 (1993), 46–68.

Noos in Homer: *SIFC* 7 (1989), 152–95; in Hesiod: *Glotta* 68 (1990), 68–85; in the lyric and elegiac poets: *Emerita* 57 (1989), 129–68; in Pindar and Bacchylides: *Glotta* 68 (1990), 179–202.

Kradiē in Homer: *Euphrosyne* 23 (1995), 9–25; *Kēr* in Homer: *Euphrosyne* 24 (1996), 1–22; *ētor* in Homer: *Emerita* 62 (1994), 11–29; *Kradiē, Kēr, ētor* in poetry after Homer: *RBPh* 73 (1995), 13–34.

Prapides in Homer: *Glotta* 65 (1987), 182–93.

Psychē in Homer and Hesiod: *SIFC* 6 (1988), 151–80; in the lyric and elegiac poets: *Parola del Passato* 144 (1989), 241–62; in Pindar and Bacchylides: *SIFC* 9 (1991), 163–83.

See also my book, *Psychological and Ethical Ideas: What Early Greeks Say* (1995), chaps. 2 and 3, which offers a treatment of all the psychic terms in both the early Greek poets and the Presocratic philosophers.

5 On this question of "self," B. Snell argued that no notion of "self" was present (see especially *Discovery* and *Der Weg*). His views have been frequently challenged, especially by Claus, 1–47; Harrison, 79–80; D. Gill, S.J., "Two-Decisions: *Iliad* 11.401 and *Agamemnon* 192–230," in *Studies Presented to Sterling Dow* (Durham, NC, 1984); Lloyd-Jones, *Justice*, 9–23; Pellicia, de Romilly, *Patience*, 23–45; T. Rosenmeyer, "Wahlakt und Entscheidungsprozess in der antiken Tragödie," *Poetica* 10 (1978), 1–24; W. Schadewaldt, *Von Homers Welt und Werk*[2] (Stuttgart 1951), 234–66; R.W. Sharples, " 'But Why Has My Spirit Spoken with Me Thus?': Homeric Decision-Making," *G&R* 30 (1930), 1–7; B. Williams, *Shame and Necessity* (Berkeley 1993), 21–49. See further discussion (with bibliography) in my article, " 'Self' and Psychic Entities in Early Greek Epic," *Eos* 81 (1993), 1–12; *Psychological Activity*, 1–10, and the new book of C. Gill, *Personality in Greek Epic, Tragedy and Philosophy: The Self in Dialogue* (New York 1996), which treats in detail the question of "self."

6 On *psychē* see: Adkins, 62–4; J. Burnet, "The Socratic Doctrine of the Soul" in *Essays and Addresses* (London 1929), 121–62; Claus, 1–7, 156–80; Furley, 1; Guthrie, vol. 3, 467–9; Jaeger, vol. 2, 40–2; A.G. Taylor, *Socrates* (New York 1952), 131–8.

7 On the question of conscious choice of terms see the work of Jahn, who questions its presence. See also my articles "The Mind and Heart of Zeus in Homer and the *Homeric Hymns*," *ABG* 37 (1994), 101–26, and "The Mind and Heart of Zeus in the Poetry of Hesiod," *ABG* 38 (1995), 34–47, where I suggest that it is present to some extent.

8 With reference to Aeschylus, his usage of psychological terminology in the six plays of undisputed authorship will be referred to under his name. Since the authorship of the *Prometheus Bound* is much disputed, this play will be referred to simply as the *P.V.*, and its references will be treated separately.

CHAPTER TWO

1 In Aeschylus we find *phrēn* 104 times, *nous* 3, *thumos* 20, *kardia* 30, *kear* 7, *ētor* 1, *prapides* 3, and *psychē* 13 in the tragedies and fragments, omitting the *Prometheus Bound*. In the *Prometheus Bound* we encounter *phrēn* 13 times, *nous* 2, *thumos* 3, *kardia* 1, *kear* 7, *ētor* 0, *prapides* 0, and *psychē* 1.

2 In the seven tragedies and fragments of Sophocles *phrēn* occurs 74 times, *nous* 38, *thumos* 35, *kardia* 6, *kear* 5, and *psychē* 35.

3 On *phrēn* in early Greek literature and in tragedy see Biraud, Böhme, Bremmer, Cheyns, *Cah. Inst. Ling. de Louvain*, 1980, Claus, Furley, Gelzer, Harrison, S. Ireland and F.L. Steel, "*Phrenes* as an Anatomical Organ in the Works of Homer," *Glotta* 53 (1975), 183–94, Jahn, Jarcho, Larock, Luck, Marg, Meissner, 12–14, 42–51, 76–97, 107–25, Onians, Padel, *Mind*, 20–3, Pellicia, Plamböck, Russo and Simon, Snell, "*Phrenes – Phronēsis*," *Glotta* 55 (1977), 34–64 (= *Der Weg*, 53–90), Solmsen, Sullivan, see above chap. 1, n 4, *Ideas*, 36–53, *Aeschylus*, chaps. 2–3, *Sophocles*, chaps. 2–3, Vivante, Webster, *JHS* 77 (1957), 149–54.

4 See further below on love's influence upon *phrēn*.

5 The verb ταράσσω will appear in relation to *phrēn* also at *HF* 836, 1091, *Ion* 1538, and Fr. 1079 (Incerta).

6 Note that Aeschylus and Sophocles each refer to *phrenes* in ways that strongly suggest their physical nature. See *Eum.* 158 and *Tr.* 931, where *phrenes* are located near the liver.

7 See further on *prapides* in chap. 4.

8 See, e.g., *Od.* 3.266, 11.367, 14.421, 24.194; *Theog.* 429.

9 Cf. too Sophocles' reference to Thebes "being sick" (νοσέω) from Creon's *phrēn* (*Ant.* 1015).

10 Both Dodds and Roux (*ad* 943–4) point out the ambiguous meaning in the description of Pentheus' change of *phrenes*. In the action of the play Pentheus understands the reference in relation to his carrying the thyrsus, but its meaning is more far-ranging in relation to the play as a whole.

11 On *psychē* in this passage see below, chap. 8.

12 See *Pyth.* 3.59, frs. 61.4 and 222.3.

13 Barrett and Halleran, *ad* 612, mention the passages from Aristophanes: *Thes.* 275, *Frogs* 101–2, 1471.

14 See Halleran, *ad* 612, for this point.

15 See especially the picture of Penelope (*Od.* 2.93, 24.128) and the suitors (*Od.* 17.66). See too Pin., *Nem.* 10.29 and Scol. 889.

16 See, e.g., *Il.* 4.104, 12.173; *Od.* 1.42; Pin., *Pyth.* 4.219.

17 We find another reference to *phrēn* being persuaded at *P.V.* 131.

18 On the references to *thumos* in l. 108 and *psychē* in l. 110, see below chaps. 5 and 8.

19 Cf. the reference to αὐθαδία at *O.T.* 550, where its presence without *nous* is judged of little value.

20 Note the references to *nous* in l. 2 and *psychē* in l. 6 (as an alternate reading) of this fragment. See below chaps. 4 and 8.

21 For this use of *phrēn* as a "way of thinking," cf. *Hipp.* 365, where the Chorus hope to perish before they "share" (κατανύω) in Phaedra's *phrenes*.

22 Here I interpret *phrēn* as a subjective genitive: "good sense belongs" to it. Stevens (following Kamerbeek), *ad* 364–5, takes the reference to *phrēn* as a genitive of separation: "good sense has fled from your *phrēn*." There are no parallels, however, for the verb being taken in this way.

23 The text is daggered in Diggle because of a problem in metre. See further discussion in Dodds and Roux, *ad* 427–8.

24 See further on *prapis* in this passage in chap. 4 below.

25 We can contrast the absence of wisdom that Teiresias suggests is to be found in what Pentheus says: "*phrenes* are not in your words" (*Bacc.* 269).

26 This use of *phrenes* as "seat of intelligence" occurs as well at *Hipp.* 462, where men "well-endowed with *phrenes*" are mentioned, and also at *Ion* 1271, where Ion speaks of "measuring" (ἀναμετρέω) Creusa's *phrenes*.

27 See Alcaeus 39; Stesichorus S88.19; Theog. 1388; Bacch. fr. 1.1.

28 We can compare the reference to the young man "not untrained (ἀγύμναστος) in *phrenes*" in Fr. 344 (*Dictys*).

29 On the text see Platenauer, *ad* 815.

30 On *phrenes* as a seat of memory cf. Aesch., *Choe.* 450, *Eum.* 275, and Soph., *Phil.* 1325 and Fr. 597.

31 See *Il.* 6.61, 10.45; Arch. 96 W; Theog. 87.

32 See *Od.* 13.327, 15.421; *H. Ven.* 38; Hes., *W. & D.* 55, *Theog.* 889.

33 Cf. the reference in *Alc.* 604 to "confidence" (θάρσος) being in *psychē* that Admetus "will do noble deeds." See below, chap. 8.

34 See further on this passage in chap. 3.

35 See, e.g., *Il.* 17.470; *Od.* 1.444, 14.337, Phocylides 8 (G–P); Sol. 33 W; Theog. 161–4, 1052; Pin., *Nem.* 1.27.

36 See below, chap. 3 on "moral" instances of *phrēn*.

37 At *Supp.* 1062 Iphis asks Evadne how she will win victory over other women, "whether by works of Athena or good counsel (εὐβουλία) of *phrenes*." Here again Euripides uses this term in relation to *phrenes*.

38 See, e.g., *Il.* 14.141, 24.201; *Od.* 21.288; Arch. 191 W; Sol. 33 W.

39 See below on this passage under "Madness."

40 Lee, *ad* 417, points out that ἄρτιος is found only here in extant Greek tragedy.

41 At *El.* 387, bracketed in Diggle, we read: "flesh (σάρκες) empty (κεναί) of *phrenes*, are statues in the market place." Again the absence of *phrenes* makes rational behaviour impossible.

42 Cf. *Bacc.* 947 and 1270, treated under "Mind," for other references to "former *phrenes*."

43 For the verb ἐξίστημι see also *Bacc.* 850 and *Or.* 1021.

44 On ἐλαφρὰ λύσσα see Dodds and Seaford, *ad* 850–3.

45 This image of "charm" or "drug" (φάρμακον) will recur at *Hipp.* 479 and 506–15. See Halleran, *ad* 388–90. See also below on *Hipp.* 511.

46 See further on "damage" in the next category.

47 The text of 1014 is in question. See the full discussion of Barrett, *ad* 1014–15. Kovacs in the new Loeb edition brackets 1012–15.

48 See other references to the verb διαφθείρω in *Hel.* 1192, *Hipp.* 390, *Or.* 297, and Fr. 551 (*Oedipus*).

49 On the meaning of the verb in this passage see Biehl, West, and Willinck, *ad* 1021.

50 See, e.g., *Il.* 13.394, 15.128, 16.403; *Od.* 2.243, 18.327, 22.298; Arch. 172 W; Anacreon 346.12; Theog. 593, 657; Pin., *Ol.* 7.30.

51 Cf. *Hipp.* 390 above, where Phaedra mentions her resistance to a "charm" or "drug."

52 See also this verb at *Hipp.* 390 and Fr. 551 (*Oedipus*).

53 See my article, "The Relationship of Speech and Psychic Entities in Early Greek Poetry," *Prometheus* 22 (1996), 1–13, and the discussion of Sansone, 83–92.

54 See, e.g., *Il.* 2.213, 14.92, 17.260; Arch. 120 W; Pin., *Pyth.* 6.36, *Is.* 6.71.

55 See, e.g., *Il.* 10.139, 19.121; *Od.* 15.445; Pin., *Pyth.* 1.12.

56 On this meaning of *phrenes* in this passage see Dodds, *ad* 266–9.

57 On *Bacc.* 269 see also above, n 25. Contrast the person in Fr. 598 (*Pirithous*) who speaks "not with an untrained (ἀγύμναστος) *phrēn.*"

58 Cf. the reference to *phrenes* as a source of speech in Fr. 659 (*Protesilaus*): "to another nothing healthy (ὑγιές) from *phrenes* pleases, by speaking to persuade those nearby with evil daring." Speech here comes from *phrenes*, which contain "diseased" thoughts of some kind.

59 Zeus also "rages (μαίνομαι) with baneful *phrenes*" (*Il.* 8.360); Achilles has "raging" (μαινομένη) *phrenes* (*Il.* 24.114, 135).

60 Contrast *Il.* 2.241, where "anger" (χόλος) is said not to be in Achilles' *phrenes.*

61 In the verb παροξύνω there may be an image of "sharpening," as in *Hipp.* 689 (see below).

62 The codices read φρενί, a reading accepted by Tierney and also Kovacs in the recent Loeb and which I follow. Diggle in the *OCT* prints φρενός, and the text would mean: "in the anger of your *phrēn.*" On the reading see further discussion in Tierney, *ad* 300.

63 See Halleran, *ad* 689, for other instances in tragedy of the image of "sharpening."

64 Cf. the relationship of *phrēn* to planning in *Med.* 316, *Pho.* 746, and *Supp.* 1062, discussed above.

65 For discussion of the text see Page, *ad* 37–44.

66 This adjective, φρενοβαρής, is not found elsewhere in Euripides nor in Aeschylus or Sophocles. Its meaning would be similar to the alternate text: "heavy in *phrēn.*"

67 See, e.g., *Il.* 3.45, 17.499, 20.381, 21.145; *Od.* 1.89; Hes. *Theog.* 688.

68 See *Il.* 17.573; *Od.* 3.76, 6.140. Cf. *Il.* 24.171 (θαρσέω).

69 See also *Ag.* 1302 and *Choe.* 596.

70 On *kardia* in this passage see below, chap. 6.

71 See also *Il.* 14.221; *Od.* 2.34, 15.111, 17.355, 21.157.

72 See also *Nem.* 10.29 (ἐράω).

73 See, e.g., *Il.* 13.394, 16.403; *Od.* 18.327, 22.298; Mim. 1.7 W; Pin., *Ol.* 7.30.

74 Cf. *Med.* 661, where it appears in its more usual sense of "pure" or "unsullied" with *phrenes.*

75 Cf. Fr. 1079 (Incerta), where one "confuses" (ταράσσω) *phrenes* with drink. See above under "Calm." Cf. also *Rh.* 863, where Hector says that the possibility that Odysseus has killed Dolon "distresses" (θράσσω) his *phrenes.*

76 See many examples in Homer, as e.g., *Il.* 1.555, 10.10, 15.627; *Od.* 4.825, 14.88, 24.357. See too Anac. 343.3; Pin., *Pyth.* 5.51, 9.32, *Nem.* 3.39.

77 This adjective, ἐπίσσυτος, is found only here in our extant Euripides. See also on its meaning Barrett and Halleran, *ad* 574. Cf. *Hec.* 85, where Hecuba says that her "*phrēn* has never before so shuddered (φρίσσω) and feared (ταρβέω)."

78 See the remarks of Craik, *ad* 1285–7.

79 See, e.g., *Il.* 1.362, 18.88, 24.105; *Od.* 7.219, 11.195, 18.324.

80 Cf. ὀϊζύς also at *Od.* 4.813.

81 Cf. *Med.* 55, where the Nurse says: "the affairs of masters, turning out badly, are misfortune to good slaves and they touch (ἀνθάπτω) *phrenes*." See too *Supp.* 1162, where a child says: "hearing this most distressing word, I weep; it has touched (θιγγάνω) my *phrenes*." In both instances *phrenes* are affected by sadness.

82 On *psychē* in this passage see below, chap. 8.

83 See above, n 48.

84 Cf. the reference to λύπη in Fr. 1079 (Incerta). See above under "Calm."

85 See above on *Alc.* 108 with n 81.

86 This fragment is not found in Nauck²; it is taken from Collard, Cropp, and Lee, *Selected Fragmentary Plays*, vol. 1.

87 Cf. *Rh.* 916, where the Muse speaks of her *phrēn* "touched" (ἅπτω) by grief.

88 See, e.g., *Il.* 6.481, 13.493, 19.174, 20.23; *Od.* 5.74; *H.Cer.* 232; Alcm. 7.5; Mim. 7.1 W; *Theog.* 795, 921; Bacch. 16.7, 17.131.

89 Cf. *Hcld.* 939, where Iolaus and Hyllus are described "wishing to delight" (τέρπω) the *phrēn* of Hecuba.

90 Cf. *El.* 1059, where Clytemnestra speaks of "giving delight" (ἡδύ) to Electra's *phrēn* (in a line daggered but apparently having this meaning). Cf. too *Ion* 1180, where people at a feast are to come to "pleasures" (ἡδοναί) of *phrenes*. The noun ἡδοναί is new here with *phrenes*, but the context is a traditional one.

91 Cf. *Tr.* 635 (bracketed by Diggle in the OCT), where Andromache speaks of "casting delight" (τέρψις) in the *phrēn* of Hecuba.

92 See, e.g., *Il.* 14.294; *Od.* 15.421; *H.Ven.* 38, 57; Arch. 191 W; Sa. 47, 48, 96.17; Ibyc. 286; *Theog.* 1388; Pin., *Ol.* 1.41, *Pyth.* 2.26; Bacch. 20 B8. See also my article, "Love's Effects upon Psychic Entities in Early Greek Poetry," *Eirenē* 30 (1994), 23–36.

93 See further on *psychē* in this passage in chap. 8.

94 Cf. the reference to "charms" of *phrenes* in Soph., *Tr.* 575 and, below, in *Tr.* 52 and Fr. 652 (*Protesilaus*).

95 Halleran, *ad* 1268–71, points out that ἄκαμπτος is rare, found only here and at Aesch., *Choe.* 455, where it describes "anger" (μένος).

96 Cf. *Hipp.* 969, where Theseus says that some young men prove unstable "when Cypris distresses (ταράσσω) their young (ἡβῶσα) *phrēn*." See also above, under

"Age" on this passage. Cf. too Fr. 400 (*Thyestes*), where *phrenes* are associated with Cypris, who is a "disease" (νόσημα).

97 Cf. references to a καθαρός *nous* at Theog. 89 and Scol. 901.2, in each case the adjective meaning "pure" or "holy."

98 Cf. too Sophocles' reference in Fr. 393 to "opening the locked gate of *psychē*."

99 See *Il.* 1.342, 8.360, 15.128, 24.114, 135; *Od.* 2.243; Arch. 172 W; Pin., *Pyth.* 2.26.

100 Cf. Fr. 652 (*Protesilaus*) with its reference to a "charm" (φίλτρον) of *phrēn*."

101 Cf. too *Bacc.* 359 and 1270, discussed above under "Distress," where Pentheus enters a maddened state and Agave recovers from one.

102 Cf. *Or.* 297 (discussed under "Damage" and "Fear"), where his maddened state is described by "the horror (τὸ δεινόν) and destruction (διαφθαρέν) of *phrenes*."

103 Bond, Byrde, and Wilamowitz, all *ad* 91, point out that both nouns go with *phrenes*.

104 Cf. the picture of the "maddened" (μαργάω) horses at *Hipp.* 1230. Cf. too the picture of Helen as "impassioned" (ἐκμαργόομαι) for Paris at *Tr.* 992 (discussed above under "Love").

105 See the discussion of this passage above under "Absence."

106 Cf. Fr. 640 (*Polyidos*), where *phrenes* are said to "rage (μαίνομαι) whenever they send empty feasts to the dead."

107 See *Il.* 18.430; *Od.* 19.471; Mim. 1.7 W; Sol. 4 c W; Bacch. 5.6.

108 Cf. *HF* 745, where the Chorus say that there have come to Lycus "what he never expected in his *phrēn* to suffer (πάσχω)."

109 For a discussion of the lines see Diggle, *Studies, ad* 937–31.

110 Cf. another use of the verb ἀλγέω at *IA* 1434, where Clytemnestra speaks of "paining" the *phrēn* of Iphigenia.

111 Cf. also *IA* 1580, where the Messenger describes his reaction to the death of Iphigenia: "pain (ἄλγος) not small entered my *phrēn*."

112 On *kardia* see below, chap. 6.

CHAPTER THREE

1 See, e.g., *Il.* 5.326, 14.92; *Od.* 2.231, 5.9, 8.40, 14.433, 18.216; *H.Mer.* 164; Theog. 429–34, 1008.

2 See, e.g. *Il.* 21.19, 23.176; *Od.* 8.273, 14.337, 17.66, 18.220, 23.4; Theog. 65, 161, 429–34, 733; Pin., *Pyth.* 3.13.

3 See for holiness: *Ol.* 2.57, 7.24; *Pyth.* 3.59.

4 See for justice: *Ol.* 7.47, 7.91, 8.24; *Pyth.* 2.73, 4.139; *Nem.* 10.12; Bacch. 11.124, 14.11.

5 See for prosperity: *Pyth.* 2.57; *Is.* 3.2, 3.5; Bacch. 1.162, 12.3, Fr. 1.1.

6 Theog. at 433 likewise uses this description of *phrenes*.

7 Respectively at *Ant.* 298, *Tr.* 736, and Fr. 108 (*Alcmeon*).

8 Cf. *Hel.* 501, where Menelaus refers to a man who would be "barbarous (βάρβαρος) in *phrenes*."

9 Cf. *Hel.* 732, bracketed in the *OCT*, where a slave criticizes the state of having "evil" (κακός) *phrenes*. See further on *nous* in 731 in chap. 4. Cf. too Fr. 1054 (treated above under "Love"), where love is said to live "in the most evil (κάκιστος) of *phrenes*."

10 Cf. also the reference to a "mortal" (θνητός) *phrēn* at *Pyth.* 3.59.

11 Cf. Fr. 436 (*Hippolytus*), where the wish is expressed that *Aidōs* would remove "shamelessness (τὸ ἀναίσχυντον) from *phrenes*."

12 For other passages where the verb διαφθείρω appears, see chap. 2, n 48.

13 See, e.g., *Od.* 3.266, 7.111, 11.367, 16.389; *Theog.* 429.

14 Cf. Fr. 644 (*Polyidos*), where an evil person is said to make "the *phrenes* of better (ἀμείνων) people sick."

15 Cf. Fr. 58 (*Alexander*), where "excellence (τὸ χρήσιμον) of *phrenes*" is also mentioned.

16 See also on *nous* below, chap. 4.

17 Cf. the very similar passage at *Or.* 1604, treated below.

18 See the discussion of the text in Barrett, *ad* 1448. He likewise accepts χέρα.

19 See the beginning of this chapter for examples.

20 On the meaning of this passage see Collard, *ad* 216–18.

21 The text of the end of the last line is corrupt. See *Selected Fragmentary Plays*, vol. 1, *ad Phaethon* 776.

22 Cf. *Rh.* 266, where "foolish thoughts (σκαιά) cling to the *phrēn* of shepherds." Cf. too *Rh.* 79, where another object is found in *phrēn*: "suspicion" (ὕποπτόν).

23 Both Dodds and Roux, *ad* 670–1, quote the echo of *Il.* 2.196: θυμὸς δὲ μέγας ἐστὶ διοτρεφέων βασιλήων.

24 This idea of "swiftness" is found early with *nous*. See *Il.* 15.80, where it is described as "leaping" (ἀΐσσω).

25 This too is a new use introduced by Euripides: see above, "Kinds of *Phrēn*."

26 Cf. Euripides' reference to the *phrenes* of women (γυναικεῖος) in Fr. 400 (*Thyestes*). See also chap. 2, n 96.

27 See Aesch., *Ag.* 1622, *Choe.* 746, *Eum.* 536, *Per.* 750 and Soph., *Ant.* 319, 1015.

28 See Aesch., *Ag.* 219 and *Per.* 767.

29 Halleran, *ad* 689, usefully offers examples of other references to "sharpness," namely Aesch., *Sept.* 715, Soph., *Aj.* 584 and *Or.* 1625. *Phrēn*, however, does not occur in these passages.

30 See *Choe.* 854, *Eum.* 104, and *Sept.* 25.

31 Cf. too *Rh.* 916, where, in grief, the Muse says: "you touched (ἅπτω) my *phrēn*."

32 Cf. Fr. 370K 60 (*Erechtheus*), where Poseidon "touches" (ἅπτω) the *phrenes* of Athena, also in a context of grief.

33 Neither Sophocles nor Euripides mentions *phrenes* as a location of other psychic entities. Earlier and contemporary poets frequently describe *phrenes* as such a location Aeschylus does so only once, at *Choe.* 831.

34 In contrast, Aeschylus has only 3 instances of this relationship and resembles more closely Homeric usage.

35 See Aesch., *Eum.* 158, and Soph., *Tr.* 931. Cf. the *Prometheus Bound* 361 and 881.

36 We encounter *phrēn* 160 times, *nous* 43, *thumos* 30, *kardia* 35, *kear* 3, *ētor* 1, *prapides* 3, and *psychē* 13.

37 Aeschylus: *phrēn* 104 times, *nous* 3, *thumos* 20, *kardia* 30, *kear* 7, *ētor* 1, *prapides* 3, and *psychē* 13.

38 Sophocles: *phrēn* 74 times, *nous* 38, *thumos* 35, *kardia* 6, *kear* 5, and *psychē* 35.

CHAPTER FOUR

1 In earlier and contemporary poets we usually find the form "*noos.*" In the Oxford texts Aeschylus has "*noos*" once (*Choe.* 742) and "*nous*" twice (*Sept.* 622, Fr. 393); Sophocles has "*noos*" only once, at *Ph.* 1209. In the Oxford text of Euripides we find "*nous*" in all passages. This form is found also in the fragments.

2 On *nous* in earlier and contemporary poets see Biraud, Böhme, Bona, Bremmer, Claus, von Fritz, *CPh* 38 (1943), 79–83, *CPh* 41 (1945), 223–42, Furley, Gelzer, Harrison, Jahn, Jarcho, Krafft, T. Krischer, "*Noos, noein, noema,*" *Glotta* 62 (1984), 141–9, Larock, Lesher, Marg, Meissner, 10–12, G. Nagy, "*S_ma* and *No_sis*: Some Illustrations," *Arethusa* 16 (1983), 35–55, Onians, Padel, *Mind,* 27–30, Plämbock, Russo and Simon, R. Schotlander, "Nus als Terminus," *Hermes* 64 (1929), 228–42, Snell, *Discovery, Der Weg,* Sullivan, see above, chap. 1, n 4, *Ideas,* 18–35, *Aeschylus,* chaps. 2–3, *Sophocles,* chaps. 2–3, Warden, *JHI* 32 (1971), 3–14, Webster, *JHS* 77 (1957), 149–54.

3 See *Il.* 23.590, 604; Mim. 5.8 W; Sol. 27.13 W; Theog. 629, 1267; Pin., *Pyth.* 5.110.

4 See *And.* 252, 945; *Bacc.* 252, 271; *Hel.* 731; *Hipp.* 105; *Ion* 251; *IA* 374, 1139; *Or.* 1181; *Pho.* 360, 1418; *Tr.* 652; Frs. 256, 934 (15 times). This expression is found frequently in earlier and contemporary poets and in Sophocles.

5 See *And.* 231, 667; *Hipp.* 920; Frs. 25, 212. Cf. Fr. 710 (ἔνι).

6 See above, chap. 3, "Images."

7 Kannicht, *ad* 120–2, suggests a possible echo of Epicharmus (DK 23 B12): νοῦς ὁρᾷ καὶ νοῦς ἀκούει τἄλλα κωφὰ καὶ τυφλά. Dale, *ad* 122, rejects the possibility of this echo.

8 See Mim. 5.4–8 W; Theog. 1163–4; Pin., *Pyth.* 8.67; Bacch. 5.8. See my article "*Noos* and Vision: Five Passages in the Greek Lyric Poets," *SO* 63 (1988), 7–17.

9 Cf. the reference to *phrenes* in line 732, treated above in chap. 3, under "Evil."

10 Cf. Fr. 831 (*Phrixus*), where we hear of the "more free" *phrēn* of those who are not slaves. See above, chap. 2, "Mind."

11 Cf. the reference to "swiftness" and *phrēn* in *Bacc.* 670 and Fr. 1032, new with Euripides. See chap. 3, "Euripidean Uses."

12 Both West and Willink, *ad* 906–13, reject the lines.

13 Cf. the reference to "planning" (βουλεύω) with *phrenes* at *Med.* 316. See above, chap. 2, "Planning."

14 See *Od.* 5.23, 24.479; Theog. 633.

15 See, e.g., *Od.* 3.128, 4.267, 12.211; Hes., *Theog.* 122; Theog. 1054.

16 Cf. Fr. 144 (*Andromeda*), which reads: "do not inhabit (οἰκέω) my *nous*; for I suffice."

17 Cf. the reference to *thumos* as a "possession" (κτῆμα) at [*Or.* 702].

18 Note that Kovacs in the recent Loeb places lines 251–2 after 236, coming before 237 with its reference to *nous*. Diggle in the *OCT* presents the usual order of lines, which is followed in our treatment.

19 Cf. *And.* 667, where we have another instance of *nous* as "intelligence" when Menelaus refers to its being in Peleus. Cf. too *And.* 944, where Hermione suggests that men "who have (ἔχω) *nous*" should not allow their wives to be visited by other women making evil suggestions.

20 On this passage see above, chap. 2, "Intelligence."

21 See above, chap. 3, "Euripidean Uses."

22 Cf. the effect of wine on *phrenes* that are in grief at *Alc.* 797, where its influence is seen as positive, and at Fr. 1079, where its effect is both positive and negative. See above, chap. 2, "Grief." Cf. too Aesch., Fr. 393, where wine is the "mirror of *nous*," and Soph., Fr. 929, where wine makes one "empty" (κένος) of *nous*.

23 Cf. Fr. 710 (*Telephus*), where there is a reference to "*nous* not being present" (ἔνειμι) in someone. Cf. too Fr. 934 (*Incerta*), where someone "has" (ἔχω) *nous*.

24 See, e.g., *Il.* 1.132, 363, 16.19; 18.332, 392, 24.474; Sol. 27.13 W, 34.16 W; Theog. 78, 87–92, 365, 480, 1163, 1185; Pin., *Ol.* 2.92, *Pyth.* 5.110; Fr. 213.4. See also my article "The Relationship of Speech and Psychic Entities in Early Greek Poetry," *Prometheus* 22 (1996), 1–13.

25 See, e.g., *Od.* 8.78; *H.Her.* 484; Hes., *Theog.* 37, 51; Pin., *Ol.* 1.19, 10.87, *Pyth.* 6.51.

26 See *Il.* 14.217; *H.Ven* 36; Hes., *Theog.* 122; Sa. 57.1; Theog. 89; Pin., *Nem.* 7.88.

27 On the meaning of this line see Lee, *ad* 1052.

28 See *Od.* 5.190, 6.121, 8.576, 9.176, 13.202, 20.366; *H.Her.* 393; Sol. 27.13; Theog. 74, 88–9, 698, 760, 1054; Pin., *Pyth.* 6.47.

29 See *Il.* 13.732; *Od.* 7.73; Theog. 792, 1052, 1271. Cf. Sim. 542.2.

30 See, e.g., *Il.* 10.122, 15.129; *Od.* 2.236; Hes., *W. & D.* 67, 323, 714; Arch. 124 b; Sol. 34.3; Theog. 121, 223, 580; Pin., *Pyth.* 1.95, *Nem.* 3.42.

31 See Sol. 4 c 3 W; Alc. 363.1; Theog. 379; Sim. 26 A (P).

32 Theog. 395, 397; Pin., *Pyth.* 10.68.

33 Hes., *W. & D.* 260; Sol. 4.7 W; 6.4 W.

34 For a discussion of Anaxagoras, see Sullivan, *Ideas,* 33–5, with bibliography in 33 n 46.

35 For a discussion of this passage see Dale, *ad* 1013–16, Kannicht, *ad* 1013–16, K. Mathiessen, "Zur Theonoeszene der euripideischen 'Helena,' " *Hermes* 96 (1968), 685–704; Scodel, 93–5.

36 For the ideas in this passage cf. Pin., *Ol.* 2.68–70, where a *psychē* kept from "unjust deeds" appears to escape the cycle of rebirth and to travel to the "tower of Kronus."

37 See above, n 34.

38 Contrast Sophocles' image at *O.T.* 371, where Teiresias is called "blind in *nous.*"

39 See on this subject the articles listed above in chap. 1, n 4. See also my study of Aeschylus, chap. 1.

40 See above, n 5.

41 See above, n 4. Cf. the use with *phrēn* 12 times.

42 Aeschylus, as noted above, refers to *nous* only three times.

43 On *prapides* in early literature see my article, "*Prapides* in Homer," *Glotta* 55 (1987), 182–93. See a summary of their use also in my study on Aeschylus, chap. 7, and in Meissner, 99–100, and Padel, *Mind*, 19–20.

44 Line 998 is daggered by Diggle in the *OCT* and is unclear in meaning. See on the text Dodds, *ad* 997–1010.

CHAPTER FIVE

1 On *thumos* see Biraud, Böhme, Bremmer, Caswell, Chadwick, 143–50; Cheyns, *RBPh* 61 (1983), 20–86, A. Cheyns, "Considérations sur les emplois de *thumos* dans Homère, *Iliade* 67–218," *AC* 50 (1981), 137–47, Claus, J.G. Diaz, "Sentido de 'Thymos' en la *Iliade*," *Helmantica* 27 (1976), 121–6, Dihle, *JbAC Ergzbd* 9 (1984), 9–20, Furley, R. Garland, "The Causation of Death in the *Iliad*: A Theological and Biological Investigation," *BICS* 28 (1981), 43–60, Gelzer, Harrison, Jahn, Jarcho, *Philologus* 112 (1968), 147–72, Krafft, Larock, Luck, J.P. Lynch and G.B. Miles, "In Search of *Thumos*: Toward an Understanding of a Greek Psychological Term," *Prudentia* 12 (1980), 3–9, Marg, Meissner, 100–5, Nehring, Onians, Padel, *Mind*, 27–30, Plamböck, Pelliccia, Russo and Simon, Schnaufer, Snell, *Discovery, Der Weg*, Sullivan, chap. 1, n 4, *Ideas*, 54–70, *Aeschylus*, chap. 5, *Sophocles*, chap. 6, Treu, Vivante, Webster, *JHS* 77 (1957), 149–54.

2 See, e.g., *Il.* 6.51, 9.386; *Od.* 7.258, 23.230; Hes., Fr. 22.8; Alc. 283.9; Prax. 748.

3 Cf. too his references at *Ag.* 233 and *Eum.* 738.

4 On these lines and their significance see H. Diller, "θυμὸς δὲκρείσσων τῶν ἐμῶν βουλεύματα," *Hermes* 94 (1966), 267–75; Dodds, *Greeks*, 186; D. Kovacs, "On Medea's Great Monologue (E. *Med.* 1021–80)," *CQ* 36 (1986), 343–52; J. Moline, "Euripides, Socrates and Virtue," *Hermes* 103 (1975), 45–67; Page, *ad* 1056; M.D. Reeve, "Euripides, *Medea* 1021–1080," *CQ* 22 (1972), 51–61; B. Snell, "Das früheste Zeugnis über Sokrates," *Philologus* 97 (1948), 134; *Scenes*, 48–69; Webster, *JHS* 77 (1957), 151–2.

5 See Arch. 128 W; Iby. 317 b; Theog. 213, 695, 877, 1029, 1070 a; Pin., *Ol.* 2.89, *Nem.* 3.26, Fr. 123.1, 127.4.

6 See, e.g., *Il.* 11.403, 17.90, 18.5, 20.343; *Od.* 5.285, 355, 407.

7 Contrast the reference to *thumos* at *Alc.* 829, when Heracles says that he was drinking "in spite of *thumos*."

8 See on this passage Dodds, *ad* 618–21 and Roux, *ad* 620–1.

9 This image will appear also in *IA* 125 and *Pho.* 454. Cf. too *Rh.* 786. See below, "Images."

10 See, e.g., Böhme, 23; Caswell; Furley, 3; Harrison, 66; and Redfield, 171–4.

11 This image will occur also at *IA* 919. See below, "Courage."

12 Cf. *Rh.* 786, with the picture of horses that "breathed out (πνέω) *thumos* and reared up in fear."

13 This adjective is found only here in Euripides. See Stockert, *ad* 919.

14 See, e.g., *Il.* 10.319; *Od.* 18.61; Hes., *Theog.* 641; Call. 1.1 W; Tyr. 10.17 W; Mim, 14.1 W; Theog. 1301; Pin., *Pyth.* 9.30.

15 See *Il.* 5.670; Hes., Fr. 712 (b) 2; Tyr. 12.18 W.

16 See, e.g., *Il.* 2.589, 9.177, 10.401, 12.174; *Od.* 2.248, 11.566, 15.66; Hes., *W. & D.* 381, *Theog.* 443; Sa. 1.18, 27, 5.3; Theog. 695; Pin., *Pyth.* 4.181, *Is.* 6.43.

17 On this passage see Cropp, *ad* 175–7, and Denniston, *ad* 177.

18 See, e.g., *Il.* 10.355, 12.407, 14.67, 19.328; *Od.* 3.275, 20.328, 21.126, 23.345.

19 See, e.g., *Il.* 1.196, 9.486; *Od.* 3.218–23, 18.212; *H.Aphrod.* 45, 53; Sa. 1.4, 18, 27; Alc. 283.4, 9; Theog. 1091, 1256; Pin., *Nem.* 5.31–2, Fr. 123.1. See also my article on love, above, chap. 2, n 92.

20 See, e.g., *Il.* 5.869, 6.524, 12.179, 13.86; *Od.* 1.4, 8.149, 10.78; Hes., *W. & D.* 399, Theog. 612; Arch. 128 W; Sem. 1.23 W; Sa. 1.4; Alc. 335.1, Theog. 910, 989, 1091, Pin., *Nem.* 6.57; Bacch. 1.179.

21 Namely at Sa. 42.1; Tyr. 13 W; Sim., *Ep.* 83 (b); Bacch. 1.143. Cf. too Pindar's description of Melissus as "similar in *thumos* to the daring of lions" (*Is.* 4.46).

22 See the discussion of this passage in chap. 2, "Mind."

23 See the discussion of *Med.* 110 below in chap. 8.

24 Cf. Fr. 149, where someone has "boldness more than *nous*."

25 Cf. *Hel.* 1014, where *gnōmē* is given a positive role: *nous* or death has "immortal *gnōmē*." See above, chap. 4, "Euripidean Uses."

26 Cf. also Theog. 631, where a "*noos* stronger than *thumos*" is mentioned.

27 See, e.g., *Il.* 10.69, 15.94, 23.611; *Od.* 4.694; Hes., Fr. 25.20; Sol. 13.28 W; Theog. 63, 199, 384, 444; Pin., *Nem.* 9.27; Bacch. 17.23.

28 In terms of meaning we can compare the adjective ὑπερφίαλος at *Il.* 15.94 and 23.611.

29 In these tables the adjective "Thracian" (*Hec.* 1055) has been omitted from consideration.

30 Cf. Fr. 257 (*Archelaus*), where "great *thumos*" is said "to have destroyed many mortals."

31 We have heard above in chap. 3 of a "woman's *phrēn*" (*And.* 181) and "the *phrenes* of women" (Fr. 400 [*Thyestes*]).

32 See above under *Bacc.* 620 with n 10.

33 Cf. too *Rh.* 786, where horses "breathed out *thumos.*"

34 See above, n 21.

35 For a treatment in earlier and contemporary poets see the articles listed in chap. 1, n 4.

36 On this aspect of early Greek thought, see Sullivan, *Ideas*, chap. 1.

37 Of the 18 passages in Aeschylus where *thumos* appears in a clear context, 6 are positive, 10 are negative, 2 are neutral. Of the 35 instances in Sophocles, 7 appear to be positive, 28 negative.

38 Those in positive contexts are: *Alc.* 829, *And.* 1072, *El.* 578, *IA* 919, and [*Or.* 702].

39 Those in neutral contexts are: *El.* 177, *Hipp.* 1087, 1328, and *Med.* 310.

40 See especially those discussed under "Anger," "Pain," and "Passion."

CHAPTER SIX

1 In Euripides the form *kardia* occurs except for "*kradia*" at *Hipp.* 1274, *Med.* 99, 432, and 1360. In our discussion we shall generally use the form *kardia*.

2 On the terms for "heart" see Biraud, Böhme, A. Cheyns, "Recherche sur l'emploi des synonyms *ētor, kēr,* et *kradiē* dans l'*Iliade* et l'*Odyssée*," *RBPh* 63 (1985), 15–73, Claus, Furley, Gelzer, Harrison, John, Jarcho, *Philologus* 112 (1968), 147–72, Krafft, Larock, Marg, Meissner, 39–42, 47–62, 107–25, Onians, Padel, *Mind*, 18–19, 33, Plamböck, G. Rose, "Odysseus' Barking Heart," *TAPhA* 109 (1979), 215–30, Russo and Simon, Snell, *Discovery*, Sullivan, chap. 1, n 4, *Ideas*, 70–3, *Aeschylus*, chap. 6, *Sophocles*, chap. 6, Treu, Vivante, Webster, *JHS* 77 (1957), 149–54.

3 *Ētor* is found in our extant Aeschylus only once at *Per.* 991; it is not found in our extant Sophocles.

4 In Homer we find *ētor* 101 times, *kradiē* 62 times, and *kēr* 81 times. In Hesiod we find *ētor* 8 times, *kradiē* 6 times, and *kēr* no times.

5 Lyric and elegiac poets (apart from Pindar and Bacchylides): *ētor* appears 7 times, *kradiē* or *kardiē* 13 times, *kēr* 1 time. Pindar and Bacchylides: *ētor* appears 10 times, *kradia* or *kardia* 18 times, *kēr* 11 times.

6 See, e.g., *Il.* 9.646, 10.94, 13.282, 442, 22.460; *Od.* 20.13; Sa. 31; *Theog.* 361; Pin., *Pyth.* 2.91; Bacch. Fr. 12.3.

7 In one of the three occurrences of *kear* the context is not clear, but the physical "beat" seems indicated in the description of "Pallas brandishing a spear" (*HF* 1003).

8 Cf. a use of ἄκρος with *phrēn* at Aesch., *Ag.* 805. Note at [*Bacc.* 203] the positive reference to an ἄκρος *phrēn* (see chap. 2, "Intelligence").

9 Cf. the reference at *Rh.* 770, where the Charioteer, with "thoughtful" (μελοῦσα) *kardia*, cares for the horses.

10 Cf. the praise in Fr. 412.3 (*Ino*) for one "speaking (ἐρέω) from the *kardia*."

11 See, e.g., *Il.* 9.480, 13.206, 16.585, 21.136; *Od.* 7.309, 12.376, 17.458, 22.224; Soph., *O.T.* 688.

12 On *psychē* in this passage, see below, chap. 8.

13 See *Il.* 9.646; *Od.* 20.1–24; *H.Ap.* 256; Pin., *Pyth.* 8.9.

14 Note the references in this same speech to *phrēn* in line 104, *thumos* in 108, and *psychē* in 110.

15 See, e.g., *Il.* 2.452, 11.12, 14.152, 16.266; *Od.* 4.293; Arch. 94.3 W; Mim. 14.6 W; Pin., *Pyth.* 10.44, *Nem.* 10.30.

16 "*Psychē*" here is a variant reading for χεὶρ ἐμή. Cf. also *Or.* 466 (above, "Seat of Emotion"), where the same address occurs. On *psychē*, see below, chap. 8.

17 See *Il.* 16.435 and *Od.* 4.260.

18 On the meaning and imagery in this passage see both Collard and Tierney, *ad* 1025–7.

19 See Appendix Two in the articles on *kear* (*kēr*) and *ētor* in chap. 1, n 4.

20 Barrett and Halleran, *ad* 912–13, both likewise reject these two lines as inappropriate.

21 See., e.g., *Od.* 1.353, 18.348, 20.286; *H.Cer.* 40; Hes., *W. & D.* 451; Theog. 361–2; Pin., *Pyth.* 2.91, Fr. 225; Bacch. 17.18, 18.11.

22 See *Od.* 1.341, 19.517; Pin., *Pae.* 8 A 11.

23 On *phrenes* in this passage, see above, chap. 2, "Pain."

24 On this passage see chap. 2, "Damaged."

25 See *Il.* 1.255, 13.282; Pin., Fr. 110.2.

26 Cf. the use of "melt" (τήκω) with *kardia* also at *Hec.* 433 (below, "Grief").

27 See also its use at *IT* 344 (below, "Euripidean Uses").

28 See *Il.* 10.10, 24.584; *Od.* 17.489; Hes., *Theog.* 99, 612, 623; Bacch. 11.85.

29 Cf. *Rh.* 596, when Odysseus and Diomedes are described as "stung (δάκνω) in their *kardia* with grief (λύπη)."

30 See *Od.* 4.548, 20.326; *H.Cer.* 65; Arch. 25 W; Pin., *Pyth.* 1.12, 3.96.

31 See further below, "Euripidean Images."

32 We can compare Pindar's picture of Medea in love as "burning (καίω) in her *phrenes*" (*Pyth.* 4.219).

33 The fourth passage in which Euripides relates *kardia* with love is Fr. 1063.12 (Incerta). A woman who "holds (ἔχω) her *kardia* out of doors" – i.e., lets her affections stray – is described.

34 We can compare the image of "touch" found with *phrēn* at *Alc.* 108, *Med.* 55, *Supp.* 1162, *Tr.* 1216, and Fr. 370 K 60 (*Erechtheus*). See above, chap. 3, "Euripidean Images."

35 An opposite view of direct address can be found in Meissner, 58–62, who suggests that in such cases *kardia* can stand for the "Ich." The view presented here suggests instead the separate nature of person and psychic entity.

36 Since *kear* occurs in only 2 passages with clear context (*Med.* 398, 911), we do not include it in the present discussion.

CHAPTER SEVEN

1 Note too in Appendix 4 the large number of compounds of *psychē* that occur in our extant Euripides.

2 On *psychē* see Adkins, *From the Many*, Böhme, Bremmer, J. Burnet, "The Socratic Doctrine of the Soul," *Essays and Addresses* (London 1929), 121–62, Chadwick, 311–20, Claus, Dihle, *JbAC Ergzbd* 9 (1984), 9–20, Dodds, H. Fraenkel, Furley, Garland, Gelzer, Harrison, A.G. Ingenkamp, "Inneres Selbst und Lebensträger," *RhM* 118 (1975), 48–61, Jahn, Jarcho, *Philologus* 112 (1968), 147–72, Krafft, M. McDonald, "Terms for 'Life' in Homer: An Examination of Early Concepts in Psychology," *Trans. and Stud., Coll. of Physicians of Philadelphia* 4 (1982), 26–58, Meissner, 7–10, 62–76, 107–25, Nehring, Onians, Otto, Redfield, O. Regenbogen, "*Daimonion Psychēs Phōs*" in *Kleine Schriften* (Munich 1961), 1–28, Padel, *Mind*, 30–2, Rohde, Rüsche, Schnaufer, Snell, *Discovery*, Solmsen, Sullivan, see chap. 1, n 4, *Ideas*, 76–101, *Aeschylus*, chap. 7, *Sophocles*, chap. 7, Vivante, Warden, *Phoenix* 25 (1971), 85–103, Webster, *JHS* 77 (1977), 149–54.

3 These are specifically as follows: "Life-spirit": *Ag.* 1643, *Per.* 29, 442, and 841. "Life": *Ag.* 965, 1457, 1466, *Choe.* 276, 749, and [*Sept.* 1034]. "Shade of the dead": *Ag.* 1545, *Eum.* 115, *Per.* 630.

4 On these passages, see Sullivan, *Sophocles*, chap. 7.

5 See the list under εἷς in Appendix Three.

6 See *Il.* 13.763 = 24.168; *Theog.* 568.

7 This adjective will appear also at *Hel.* 52.

8 See its appearance also in Fr. 388 (*Theseus*), treated in chap. 8.

9 Tierney, *ad* 196, accepts the reading of *psychē*. Collard, *ad* 196, accepts the OCT reading of μοίρας.

10 See above under *And.* 611.

11 See, e.g., *Il.* 5.296, 14.518, 16.563, 16.856; *Od.* 10.560, 22.444; *Theog.* 568; Sim. 553.

12 Cf. too *Rh.* 965, where the Muse says that she will ask Persephone to "release" (ἀνίημι) the *psychē* of Rhesus.

13 See *Hec.* 196, *Hel.* 946, [*Or.* 847], *Pho.* 1330, *Tr.* 900 in addition to this passage, *Hcld.* 984.

14 On the ambiguity here see Barrett, *ad* 721.

15 Cf. Fr. 360.51 (*Erechtheus*) for a similar reference to "one *psychē*" mentioned in relation to many.

16 See *Il.* 23.65; *Od.* 11.150, 471, 24.23, 35, 105, 191. Cf. Bacch. 5.77, 171.

17 For the picture given in these lines see West, *ad* 676 and Willinck, *ad* 674–6.

18 On the text see West, *ad* 1046, and Willinck, *ad* 1045–6.

19 See in particular the articles on *psychē* listed above in chap. 1, n 4.

20 Cf. too *Hel.* 1431, *Med.* 1219, and *Tr.* 1135.

21 Cf. the reference to δίδωμι also at *Hcld.* 550 and *Or.* 662. See below, "Life."

22 Cf. the reference at *Supp.* 777 (see below), where *psychē* once "paid out" cannot be retrieved.

23 See also *Od.* 18.91 and *H.Ven.* 272.

24 Cf. *Rh.* 183, where Dolon speaks of "hazarding" (προβάλλω) *psychē*. This image is a traditional one: see *Il.* 9.322; *Od.* 3.74, 9.255; *H.Ap.* 455. See also Soph., *Ag.*1270, where Ajax is described as"hazarding"(προτείνω) *psychē*.

25 See above, n 20.

26 This fragment is not in Nauck.[2] It is taken from Collard, Cropp, and Lee, *Selected Fragmentary Plays*, vol. 1.

27 See above, chap. 4, "Euripidean Uses."

28 See *Selected Fragmentary Plays*, vol. 1, *ad* 370 K71.

29 On the interpretation of this passage, see Stevens, *ad* 541.

30 Collard and Tierney, both *ad* 176, also bracket these lines.

31 We hear of *psychē* being "saved" (σώζω) also at *Alc.* 929 and [*Or.* 644].

32 Contrast the reference to "loving" (φιλέω) *psychē* at *Alc.* 704 (treated above under "Life-Spirit".

33 Note that Tyrtaeus uses the verb φιλοψυχέω in 10.18 to imply cowardice. This quality is absent also in Iolaus.

34 The verb δίδωμι appears here at *Hcld.* 550 and also at *Or.* 662 (see below) and *Pho.* 998 (see "Life-Spirit").

35 See Bond, *ad* 452, who also rejects the line because of its "strange language."

36 Cf. τάλας with *kardia*, introduced by Sophocles (*Tr.* 651) and Euripides (*Or.* 466, Fr. 908.6).

37 See, e.g., *Il.* 1.3, 22.257, 24.754; *Od.* 22.444.

38 West, *ad* 644, does not bracket these lines; Willinck, *ad* 644–5, questions the authenticity of 644.

39 On the meaning of these lines, see West, *ad* 644.

40 Cf. *Or.* 662, where Orestes asks Menelaus to "give" (δίδωμι) his "life" (*psychē*). Line 663, bracketed in the OCT, may refer also to the *psychē* of Electra: Menelaus is to give "that of my sister." Here, as at *Hcld.* 550 and *Pho.* 998, we find the verb δίδωμι with *psychē*.

41 Biehl and West do not bracket these lines; Willinck does.

42 Cf. also the expression "about *psychē*" at *Od.* 9.423 and 22.245. See above, n 13, for instances of περί in Euripides.

43 See on [*Or.* 847] for passages in earlier poetry. See also Mastronarde, *ad* 1330, on the image.

44 See *Il.* 11.334 (χάζω); *Od.* 9.523–4 (εὖνιν ποιέω), 21.154, 171 (χάζω).

45 The meaning of "life" is prominent in Aesch., *Choe.* 276, 749, and in Soph., *Aj.* 559, *O.T.* 893, Fr. 941.

CHAPTER EIGHT

1 For a discussion of this change see the articles on *psychē* listed above in chap. 1, n 4, and chap. 7, n 1, and Sullivan, *Ideas*, 76–101.

2 For this view see W. Jaeger, *The Theology of Early Greek Philosophers* (Oxford 1947), 81–3; Harrison, 77; Meissner, 62–76; Warden, *Phoenix* 25 (1971), 85–103.

3 *Il.* 23.65–106; *Od.* 11.51, 24.1–15.

4 *Od.* 11.155–234.

5 This role of *psychē* in Plato and later authors has been frequently noted. See in particular Adkins, *From the Many*, 62–4; Claus, 1–7; Furley, 1; Guthrie, vol. 3, 467–9; Havelock, *History* 197–200; F. Solmsen, "Plato and the Concept of the Soul (*Psychē*): Some Historical Perspectives," *JHI* 44 (1983), 355–67; Snell, *Discovery*, 14.

6 See other examples in my article in *SIFC* 6 (1988), 172–3.

7 See Sullivan, *Aeschylus*, chap. 7.

8 See Sullivan, *Sophocles*, chap. 7.

9 In *Toward the Soul* Claus questions whether the use of *psychē* in expanded ways after Homer shows "new ideas about the nature of the psychological self" (60). He argues that the basic meaning of *psychē* as "life-spirit" was already present in Homer and for the most part continued. He offers a "life-spirit model" (29) and argues that uses of *psychē* in the fifth century follow it, except for those instances in periphrastic constructions. As mentioned in chap. 1, Claus does not focus in particular on Euripides but interprets various passages where *psychē* occurs.

Our interpretation of Euripides differs in suggesting that *psychē* gradually becomes a psychological agent in the living person, absorbing more and more functions often ascribed to other psychological entities. These functions include those that are intellectual, emotional, and moral.

For assessments of the approach of Claus see my review in *Phoenix* 36 (1982), 272–5, and the reviews of Renehan, *CPh* 79 (1984), 200–5, and Wright, *CR* 33 (1983), 52–3.

10 We find another reference to a "willing" (ἑκοῦσα) *psychē* at Fr. 360.44 (*Erechtheus*): "there is not anyone who will cast out the ancient laws of parents without my *psychē* being willing."

11 Cf. her assertion at 550 that she will "give up *psychē*" for her brothers "willingly" (ἑκοῦσα). See above, chap. 7, "Life."

12 The vocative of *psychē* appears here at *Ion* 859, and at *Alc.* 837, *IT* 838, 882, *Or.* 466, Fr. 308.1 (*Bellerophontes*), and Fr. 924 (Incerta).

13 *Psychē* is associated with speech here at *IT* 838 and also at *Hec.* 87, *Ion* 859, and Fr. 924 (Incerta). Cf. also *Rh.* 345.

14 Cf. in meaning his use of τάλας at [*HF* 452]. See above, chap. 7.

15 See Platenauer, *ad* 882.

16 Cf. another direct address to *psychē* at Fr. 308.1 (*Bellerophontes*): "hasten, o *psychē*."

17 On *kardia*, see above, chap. 6.

18 See above, chap. 4, "Evil."

19 See above, n 13.

20 See, e.g., *Il.* 23.65, 106; *Od.* 11.471, 541, 24.23; Bacch. 5.77, 171.

21 See *Ant.* 227, *O.C.* 999, *O.T.* 64, *Ph.* 1014–15, and *Tr.* 1260–3.

22 Cf. the connection of *psychē* with speech at *Rh.* 345: "I will speak what is dear (προσφιλές) to *psychē* to say (λέγω)."

23 On this passage see Webster, *JHS* 77 (1957), 151.

24 On the meaning of these lines see Barlow and Lee, both *ad* 1171–2.

25 See above, n 13.

26 See above the discussion of these passages in chaps. 2, 5, and 6.

27 We follow here Diggle in the *OCT* in taking "quivering" with "spear," not with "*psychai*." On this passage see Mastronarde, *ad* 1297–8.

28 Contrast the reference to Aegisthus' *psychē* as "cowardly" (κακός) at *Ag.* 1643.

29 On *kardia* in this passage, see above, chap. 6.

30 On the literal meaning of these lines see Barlow and Lee, both *ad* 182.

31 See *Od.* 11.387, 541; 24.20.

32 On *phrenes* see above, chap. 2, "Grief."

33 On this passage see Webster, *JHS* 77 (1957), 151, and Sullivan, *Sophocles*, chap. 7, "Distress."

34 For the image see Conacher, *ad* 354.

35 Cf. the use of this verb τήκω with *kardia* at *Hec.* 433. See above, chap. 6, "Grief." See also *Hcld.* 645, below.

36 For example see my article, "Love's Effects on Psychic Entities," *Eirene* 29 (1994), 23–36.

37 On *phrenes*, see chap. 2, "Love."

38 Note that ἄκρος in this passage means "deep." See Barrett and Halleran, both *ad* 255.

39 On the image see Barrett and Halleran, both *ad* 503–6.

40 Cf. *Supp.* 1103 (treated above under "Courage"), where the *psychai* of men are described as "greater but less sweet (γλυκύς) for caresses (θώπευμα)." The *psychai* of daughters are more "sweet" in showing affection.

41 See above, chap. 2, "Mind."

42 Cf. too the description of Pentheus at 214: "ὡς ἐπτόηται." See Seaford, *ad* 1268, on the significance of this verb.

43 See above, "Grief," for examples from Homer.

44 Cf. Euripides' use of this adjective of Orestes at *IT* 882.

45 Bond, *ad* 1366, questions the exclusion.

46 Cf. too the Nurse's description of her at 110 as "bitten in *psychē* by evils."

47 Cf. the references to "weight" of *psychē* at *Alc.* 354 and *Hipp.* 259.

48 See Barlow, *ad* 640, for this interpretation. The genitive of εὐπραξία is taken here as one of "cause." Another interpretation would take this genitive as one of "separation": "he wanders from his former good fortune" (see Lee, *ad* 640).

49 See above on this fragment, chap. 4, "Fear."

50 See above on this passage, chap. 6, "Fear."

51 Cf. the reference to one "wandering in *psychē*" at *Tr.* 640.

52 On these two references, see above, chap. 2, "Mind," and chap. 4, "Mind."

53 Cf. too Theog. 910 and Soph., *Ant.* 317.

54 See above, chap. 7, "Life-Spirit."

55 This fragment also occurs as Fr. 684 (*Phaedra*) of Sophocles. See above, "Love."

56 See Appendix Three for details on these words.

57 Cf. the reference to a "contest" (ἀγών) in Fr. 67 (*Alcmeon*).

58 See my studies on *psychē* listed above, chap. 1, n 4.

59 See the list of occurrences above in n 12.

60 Fr. 308 (*Bellerophontes*) is not clear but is probably a case of self-address: "hasten, o *psychē*."

61 See also Meissner, 68–76, 107–25, who suggests that in certain passages *psychē* has come to represent the person.

CHAPTER NINE

1 In our extant Euripides we do not find references to *ētor*.

2 See *Hipp.* 926, *Bacc.* 670, and Fr. 1032 (Incerta).

3 See examples above, chap. 4, n 4.

4 See [*Hel.* 122] and Fr. 909.6.

5 *Prapides* occur rarely in Aeschylus (3 times) and not at all in our extant Sophocles.

6 See *Or.* 1180, *Tr.* 1171, Fr. 220 (*Antiope*), Fr. 924 (Incerta).

7 See Fr. 831 (*Phrixus*) for *phrēn*, [*Hel.* 731] for *nous*.

8 We do not include possessive adjectives in our comparison.

9 See *Bacc.* 203 for *phrēn*; *Hec.* 242 for *kardia*.

10 *Phrēn*: *Hipp.* 1419, 1454; *psychē*: *And.* 611, Fr. 388 (*Theseus*).

11 *Phrēn*: *HF* 212, *Hipp.* 1298; *psychē*: Fr. 388 (*Theseus*).

12 *Phrēn*: *Hcld.* 540; *psychē*: *Hec.* 87.

13 *Phrēn*: *Hipp.* 936; *psychē*: *Supp.* 777.

14 *Kardia*: *IT* 344, *Or.* 466, Fr. 908.6 (Incerta); *psychē*: [*HF* 452].

15 *Kardia*: *Hec.* 1026; *psychē*: *Or.* 1034.

16 See, e.g., *phrenes* as location of *thumos* (*Il.* 23.600; *Od.* 20.38), *kēr* (*Od.* 18.345), *noos* (*Il.* 18.419), and *ētor* (*Il.* 17.111). See also Hes., *Theog.* 239, 549, *W. & D.* 381 (*thumos*); Tyr. 10.17 W (*thumos*); Sol. 4 c 1 W, Theog. 122 (*ētor*); Bacch. 17.22 (*thumos*).

17 Cf. too *Choe.* 831–2: "*kardia* is in *phrenes*," and *Choe.* 997: "*kear* is near *phrenes*."

18 Cf. too *O.T.* 982–3, where "weapons of *thumos*" seem able to "harm" *psychē*.

19 See, e.g., *nous*: *Hipp.* 920, *IA* 1139; *thumos*: *IA* 125, *Med.* 1152, *Supp.* 556.

20 Cf. Meissner, 68–76, 107–25, who likewise points out that *psychē* can stand for the person.

APPENDIX E

1 On these terms see especially Jarcho, 176–7, Meissner, 17–32, Onians, 84–9, Padel, *Mind*, 13–19, and de Romilly, 28–31.

2 Passages are: *El.* 688; *Hel.* 983; *H.F.* 979, 1149; *Hipp.* 1070; *I.T.* 1370; *Med.* 40, 379; *Or.* 1063; *Pho.* 1421; *Supp.* 919; Fr. 495.29 (*Melanippe Des.*), 979.1 (Incerta).

3 Cf. Aeschylus' association of *hēpar* with grief at *Ag.* 432 and 492.

4 Passages are: *El.* 828, 838; *Supp.* 212; Fr. 403.4 (*Ino*).

5 This usage is similar to references that Aeschylus and Sophocles make to *splanchna* at *Ag.* 995, *Choe.* 413, and *Aj.* 995.

Selected Bibliography

SOURCES AND NUMBERING
OF FRAGMENTS [N]

HOMER

Allen, T.W. *Homer's Odyssey*². 2 vols. Oxford 1917. [N]
Allen, T.W., W.R. Halliday, and E.E. Sikes. *The Homeric Hymns*². Oxford 1936. [N]
Munro, D.B., and T.W. Allen. *Homer's Iliad*³. 2 vols. Oxford 1920. [N]

HESIOD

Merkelbach, R., and M.L. West. *Fragmenta Hesiodea*. Oxford 1967.
Solmsen, F., ed. *Hesiodi Theogonia, Opera et Dies, Scutum*³. With R. Merkelbach and
    M.L. West, eds. *Fragmenta Selecta*. Oxford 1990. [N]

LYRIC AND ELEGIAC POETS

Davies, M. *Poetarum Melicorum Graecorum Fragmenta*. Vol. 1. Oxford 1991. [N]
Gentili, B., and C. Prato, eds. *Poetarum Elegiacorum Testimonia et Fragmenta*. 2 vols.
    Leipzig 1979, 1985.
Page, D.L. *Poetae Melici Graeci*. Oxford 1962. [N]
– *Supplementum Lyricis Graecis*. Oxford 1974. [N]
– *Epigrammata Graeca*. Oxford 1975.
Voigt, E.-M., ed. *Sappho et Alcaeus Fragmenta*. Amsterdam 1971. [N]
West, M.L., ed. *Iambi et Elegi Graeci*. Vol. 1². Oxford 1989. Vol. 2². Oxford 1992. [N]

PINDAR AND BACCHYLIDES

Maehler, H., ed. *Bacchylidis Carmina cum Fragmentis*. Leipzig 1970. [N]
– post B. Snell. *Pindari Carmina cum Fragmentis*. Part 1. Leipzig 1971. [N]
– post B. Snell. *Die Lieder des Bakchylides*. Parts 1 and 2. Leiden 1982.
– *Pindari Carmina cum Fragmentis*. Part 2. Leipzig 1989. [N]

EURIPIDES

Bibliography
Collard, C. *Euripides, Greece and Rome Surveys*, 14. Oxford 1981.
Looy, H. van. "Les Fragments d'Euripide." *AC* 32 (1963): 162–99, 607–8.
– "Tragica 2." *AC* 39 (1970): 528–62.
– "Tragica 4." *AC* 53 (1984): 306–32.
Mette, H.J. "Euripides (Bruchstücke) 1939–1967." *Lustrum* 12 (1967): 5–288; 13 (1968): 289–403.
– "Euripides (Bruchstücke) 1968–1975." *Lustrum* 17 (1973): 5–26.
Miller, H.W. "Euripidean Drama 1955–1965." *CW* 60 (1967): 177–87, 218–20.
Saïd, S. "Bibliographie Tragique, 1900–1988." *Metis* 3 (1988): 408–512.

Lexicon
Allen, J.T., and G. Italie. *A Concordance to Euripides*. Berkeley 1954, repr. Groningen 1971.
Collard, C. *Supplement to the Allen and Italie Concordance to Euripides*. Groningen 1971.

Texts
Diggle, J. *Euripidis Fabulae*. 3 vols. Oxford 1981–94. [N]
Kovacs, D. *Euripides*. 2 vols. Cambridge, Mass., 1994–95.

Commentaries:
Alcestis
Conacher, D.J. *Euripides, Alcestis*. Warminster 1988.
Dale, A.M. *Euripides, Alcestis*. Oxford 1954.
Lennep, D. van. *Euripides, Selected Plays: The Alcestis*. Leiden 1949.
Paduano, G. *Euripide, Alcesti*. Firenze 1969.

Andromache
Brassi, D. *Euripides, Andromache*. Milan 1933.
Lloyd, M. *Euripides, Andromache*. Warminster 1994.
Stevens, P.T. *Euripides, Andromache*. Oxford 1971.

Bacchae

Dodds, E.R. *Euripides, Bacchae*². Oxford 1960.

Kirk, G.S. *The Bacchae of Euripides*. Englewood Cliffs, NJ, 1970, repr. Cambridge 1979.

Lacroix, M. *Les Bacchantes d'Euripide*. Paris 1976.

Roux, J. *Euripide, Les Bacchantes I, II*. 2 vols. Lyons 1970–72.

Seaford, R. *Euripides, Bacchae*. Warminster 1996.

Electra

Cropp, M.J. *Euripides, Electra*. Warminster 1988.

Denniston, J.D. *Euripides' Electra*. Oxford 1939, repr. 1954.

Hecuba

Biehl, W. *Textkritik und Formanalyse zur euripideischen Hekabe*. Heidelberg 1997.

Collard, C. *Euripides, Hecuba*. Warminster 1991.

Garzya, A. *Euripide, Ecuba*. Rome 1955.

Tierney, M. *Euripides' Hecuba*. Dublin 1946, repr. Bristol 1979.

Helen

Barone, C. *Euripides, Elena*. Firenze 1995.

Dale, A.M. *Euripides, Helena*. Oxford 1967.

Kannicht, R. *Euripides, Helena*. 2 vols. Heidelberg 1969.

Pearson, A.C. *Euripides, Helen*. Cambridge 1903.

Heraclidae

Garzya, A. *Euripide, Eraclidi*. Rome and Naples 1958.

Pearson, A.C. *Euripides, Heraclidae*. Cambridge 1907.

Wilkins, J. *Euripides, Heraclidae*. Oxford 1993.

Hercules Furens

Bond, G.W. *Euripides, Heracles, with Introduction and Commentary*. Oxford 1981.

Byrde, O.R.A. *Euripides, Heracles*. Oxford 1914.

Collard, C. *Euripides, Heracles*. Warminster 1996.

Gray, A., and J.T. Hutchinson. *The Hercules Furens of Euripides*. Cambridge 1917.

Wilamowitz-Moellendorf, U. von. *Euripides, Herakles*. 2 vols. Berlin 1895, repr. Darmstadt 1959.

Hippolytus

Barrett, W.S. *Euripides, Hippolytos*. Oxford 1964.

Halleran, M. *Euripides, Hippolytus*. Warminster 1995.

Ion
Burian, P. *Euripides, Ion.* New York 1996.
Lee, K.H. *Euripides, Ion.* Warminster 1997.
Owen, A.S. *Euripides, Ion.* Oxford 1939.
Willamowitz-Moellendorf, U. von. *Ion.* Berlin 1926, repr. 1969.

Iphigenia at Aulis
Stockert, W. *Euripides, Ipheginie in Aulis.* 2 vols. Vienna 1992.

Iphigenia at Tauris
Platnauer, M. *Euripides' Iphiginia in Tauris.* Oxford 1938, repr. 1952.
Strohm, H. *Euripides' Iphigenie im Tauerland.* Munich 1949.

Medea
Elliott, A. *Euripides, Medea.* Oxford 1969.
Flacelière, R. *Euripide, Médée.* Paris 1970.
Page, D.L. *Euripides' Medea.* Oxford 1938.

Orestes
Benedetto, V. di. *Euripidis Orestes.* Firenze 1965.
Biehl, W. *Euripides' Orestes.* Berlin 1965.
West, M.L. *Euripides, Orestes.* Warminster 1987.
Willink, C.W. *Euripides, Orestes.* Oxford 1986.

Phoencian Women
Craik, E. *Euripides, Phoenician Women.* Warminster 1988.
Mastronade, D. *Euripides, Phoenissae.* Cambridge 1994.
Pearson, A.C. *The Phoenissae of Euripides.* London 1909, repr. New York 1979.
Powell, J.U. *The Phoenissae of Euripides.* London 1911, repr. New York 1979.

Suppliant Women
Collard, C. *Euripides, Supplices.* 2 vols. Groningen 1975.

Trojan Women
Barlow, S.H. *Euripides, Trojan Women.* Warminster 1986.
Lee, K.H. *Euripides, Troades.* London 1976.
Schiassi, G. *Le Troiane.* Firenze 1953.

Fragments
Austin, C. *Nova Fragmenta Euripidea in Papyris Reperta.* Berlin 1967.
Bond, G.W. *Euripides, Hypsipyle.* Oxford 1963.
Bubel, F. *Euripides, Andromeda.* Stuttgart 1991.
Carrara, P. *Euripide, Eretteo.* Firenze 1977.

Collard, C., M.J. Cropp, and K.H. Lee. *Selected Fragmentary Plays*. Vol. 1. Warminster 1995. Vol. 2 in preparation.

Diggle, J. *Euripides, Phaethon*. Cambridge 1970.

Donovan, B.E. *Euripides Papyri 1: Texts from Oxyrhynchos*. New Haven 1969.

Harder, A. *Euripides, Kresphontes and Archelaos*. Leiden 1985.

Jouan, F., and H. van Looy. *Euripides, Fragments (Aigeus – Autolykos)*. Paris 1998.

Kambitsis, J. *L'Antiope d'Euripide*. Athens 1972.

Looy, H. van. *Zes verloren Tragedie van Euripides*. Brussels 1964.

Nauck, A. *Tragicorum Graecorum Fragmenta*[2]. With a supplement by B. Snell. Hildesheim 1964. [N]

GENERAL CRITICISM

Adkins, A.W.H. *From the Many to the One*. London 1970.

– *Poetic Craft in the Early Greek Elegists*. Chicago 1985.

Aélion, R. *Euripide, Heritier d'Eschyle*. 2 vols. Paris 1983.

Assmann, M.M. *Mens et Animus*. Diss. Amsterdam 1917.

Austin, N. *Archery at the Dark of the Moon*. Berkeley 1975, 1982.

Barlow, S.A. *The Imagery of Euripides*[2]. Bristol 1986.

Basta-Donizelli, G. *Studio sull' Elettra di Euripide*. Catania 1978.

Biraud, M. "La Conception psychologique à l'époque d'Homère: les 'organs mentaux'. Études lexicale de *kēr, kradiē, thumos, phrenes*." *Cratyle* 1 (1984): 27–49; 2 (1984): 1–23.

Böhme, J. *Die Seele und das Ich im Homerischen Epos*. Leipzig and Berlin 1929.

Bona, G. *Il noos e i nooi nell' Odissea*. Torino 1959.

Bowra, C.M. *Greek Lyric Poetry*[2]. Oxford 1961.

– *Pindar*. Oxford 1964.

Bremmer, J. *The Early Greek Concept of the Soul*. Princeton 1983.

Burian, P., ed. *Directions in Euripidean Criticism: A Collection of Essays*. Durham, NC, 1985.

Burn, A.R. *The Lyric Age of Greece*. London 1960.

Burnett, A.P. *Catastrophe Survived: Euripides' Plays of Mixed Reversal*. Oxford 1971.

– *Three Archaic Poets*. Cambridge, Mass., 1983.

Campbell, D.A. *Greek Lyric*. 4 vols. Cambridge, Mass., 1982–92.

– *The Golden Lyre: The Themes of the Greek Lyric Poets*. London 1983.

Caswell, C.P. *A Study of Thumos in Early Greek Epic*. Leiden and New York 1990. *Mnem. Suppl.* 114.

Chadwick, J. *Lexicographica Graeca*. Oxford 1996.

Cheyns, A. "La Notion de *phrenes* dans l'*Iliade* et l'*Odysée*, 1." *Cah. Inst. Ling. de Louvain* 6 (1980): 121–202.

– "Le *thumos* et la conception de l'homme dans l'épopée homérique." *RBPh* 61 (1983): 20–86.

Claus, D.B. *Toward the Soul: An Inquiry into the Meaning of Psychē before Plato.* New Haven and London 1981.

Clay, D.M. *A Formal Analysis of the Vocabularies of Aeschylus, Sophocles and Euripides.* Part 1. Minneapolis 1960. Part 2. Athens 1958.

Conacher, D.J. *Euripidean Drama: Myth, Theme and Structure.* Toronto 1967.

– *Euripides and the Sophists.* London 1998.

Croally, N.T. *Euripidean Polemic: The Trojan Women and the Function of Tragedy.* Cambridge 1994.

Cropp, M., E. Fantham, and G.E. Scully, eds. *Greek Tragedy and Its Legacy: Essays Presented to D.J. Conacher.* Calgary 1986.

Crotty, K. *Song and Action: Odes of Pindar.* Baltimore 1982.

Dale, A.M. *Collected Papers.* Ed. T.B.L. Webster and E.G. Turner. Cambridge 1969.

Darcus, S.M. "*Noos* Precedes *Phrēn* in Greek Lyric Poetry." *AC* 46 (1977): 41–51.

Davison, M.A. *From Archilochus to Pindar.* London 1968.

Dawe, R.D., J. Diggle, and P.E. Easterling. *Dionysiaca, Studies Page.* Cambridge 1978.

de Jong, I. *Narrative in Drama: The Art of the Euripidean Messenger Speech.* Leiden 1991. *Mnem. Suppl.* 116.

Diggle, J. *Studies on the Text of Euripides.* Oxford 1981.

– *Euripides: Collected Essays.* Oxford 1994.

Dihle, A. *The Theory of Will in Classical Antiquity.* Berkeley 1982.

– "Totenglaube und Seelenvorstellung im 7. Jahrhundert vor Christus." In T. Klauser, E. Dassmann, and K. Thraede, eds., *Jenseitsvorstellungen in Antike und Christentum, JbAC Ergzbd* 9 (1984): 9–20.

Dodds, E.R. *The Greeks and the Irrational.* Berkeley 1951.

– *The Ancient Concept of Progress.* Oxford 1973.

Duchemin, J. *Pindare, Poète et Prophète.* Paris 1955.

Erbse, H. *Studien zum Prolog der euripideischen Tragödie.* Berlin 1984.

Frame, D. *The Myth of Return in Early Greek Epic.* New Haven 1978.

Fränkel, H. *Dichtung und Philosophie des frühen Griechentums².* Munich 1962. *Early Greek Poetry and Philosophy.* Trans. M. Hadas and J. Willis. Oxford 1975.

Friis Johansen, H. *General Reflection in Tragic Rhesis: A Study of Form.* Copenhagen 1959.

Fritz, K. von. "*Nous, Noein* in the Homeric Poems." *CPh* 38 (1943): 79–93.

– "*Nous, Noein* and Their Derivatives in Presocratic Philosophy (excluding Anaxagoras)." *CPh* 41 (1945): 223–42.

Furley, D.J. "The Early History of the Concept of the Soul." *BICS* 3 (1956): 1–16.

Garland, R. "The Causation of Death in the *Iliad.*" *BICS* 28 (1981): 43–60.

Garner, R.K. *From Homer to Tragedy: The Art of Allusion in Greek Poetry.* London and New York 1990.

Gelzer, T. "How To Express Emotions of the Soul and Operations of the Mind in a Language That Has No Words for Them." *CHS* 55 (1988): 1–49.

Gerber, D.E., ed. *Greek Poetry and Philosophy, Studies Woodbury.* Chico, Calif., 1984.

Gill, C. *Personality in Greek Epic, Tragedy, and Philosophy: The Self in Dialogue.* New York 1996.

Greenwood, L.H.G. *Aspects of Euripidean Tragedy.* Cambridge 1953.

Gregory, J. *Euripides and the Instruction of the Athenians.* Ann Arbor 1991.

Griffiths, A., ed. *Stage Directions, Studies Handley.* London 1995.

Grube, G.M. *The Drama of Euripides².* London 1961.

Guthrie, W.K.C. *A History of Greek Philosophy.* 3 vols. Cambridge 1962–69.

Harrison, E.L. "Notes on Homeric Psychology." *Phoenix* 14 (1960): 63–80.

Havelock, E.A. *A History of the Greek Mind.* Vol. 1. *A Preface to Plato².* Oxford 1978.

Headlam, W. "Metaphor." *CR* 16 (1902): 434–42.

Heath, M. *The Poetics of Greek Tragedy.* London 1987.

Hose, M. *Studien zum Chor bei Euripides.* 2 vols. Stuttgart 1990.

Hubbard, T.K. *The Pindaric Mind.* Leiden 1985.

Imhof, M. *Euripides' Ion: Eine literarische Studie.* Bern 1966.

Irwin, E. *Colour Terms in Greek Poetry.* Toronto 1974.

Irwin, T.H. "Euripides and Socrates." *CPh* 78 (1983): 183–97.

Jaeger, W. *Paideia: The Ideals of Greek Culture.* Trans G. Highet. 2 vols. Oxford 1945.

Jahn, T. *Zum Wortfeld "Seele-Geist" in der Sprache Homers.* Munich 1987. *Zetemata* 83.

Jarcho, V.N. "Zum Menschenbild der nachhomerischen Dichtung." *Philologus* 112 (1968): 147–72.

Jaynes, J. *The Origin of Consciousness in the Breakdown of the Bicameral Mind.* Boston 1976.

Kirkwood, G.M. *Early Greek Monody.* Ithaca, NY, 1974.

– *Selections from Pindar.* Chico, Calif., 1982.

Kitto, H.D.F. *Form and Meaning in Drama.* London 1960.

– *Greek Tragedy: A Literary Study³.* London 1961.

Knox, B.M.W. *Word and Action.* Baltimore 1979.

Kovacs, D. *Euripidea.* Leiden 1994.

Krafft, F. *Vergleichende Untersuchungen zu Homer und Hesiod.* Göttingen 1963. *Hypomnemata* 6.

Kranz, W. *Untersuchungen zu Form und Gehalt der griechischen Tragödie.* Berlin 1933.

Kurtz, E. *Die bildliche Ausdrucksweise in den Tragödien des Euripides.* Amsterdam 1985.

Larock, V. "Les Premières Conceptions psychologiques des Grecs." *RBPh* 9 (1930): 377–406.

Lattimore, R. *The Poetry of Greek Tragedy.* Oxford 1958.

– *Story Patterns in Greek Tragedy.* London 1964.

Lesher, J.H. "Perceiving and Knowing in the *Iliad* and the *Odyssey*." *Phronesis* 26 (1981): 2–24.

Lesky, A. "Psychologie bei Euripides." In O. Reverdin, ed., *Euripide*. Geneva 1960. 123–68.

– "Zur Problematik des Psychologischen in der Tragödie des Euripides." *Gymnasium* 67 (1966): 10–26.

– *Greek Tragedy*². Trans. H.A. Frankfurt. London 1967.

– *Greek Tragic Poetry*. Trans. M. Dillon. New Haven 1983.

Lloyd, M. *The Agon in Euripides*. Oxford 1992.

Lloyd-Jones, H. *Greek Comedy, Hellenistic Literature, Greek Religion and Miscellanea: The Academic Papers of Sir Hugh Lloyd-Jones*. Oxford 1990.

– *Greek Epic, Lyric, and Tragedy: The Academic Papers of Sir Hugh Lloyd-Jones*. Oxford 1990.

Luck, G. "Der Mensch in der frühgriechischen Elegie." In G. Kurz, O. Muller, and W. Nicholai, eds., *Gnomosyne, Festschrift Marg*. Munich 1981. 167–76.

Luschnig, C.A.E. *The Gorgon's Severed Head: Studies in Alcestis, Electra, and Phoenissae*. Leiden 1995. *Mnem. Suppl.* 153.

Lynch, J.P., and G.B. Miles. "In Search of *Thumos*: Toward an Understanding of a Greek Psychological Term." *Prudentia* 12 (1980): 3–9.

McDonald, M. *Terms for Happiness in Euripides*. Göttingen 1978. *Hypomnemata* 54.

Marg, W. *Der Charakter in der Sprache der frühgriechischen Dichtung*. Wurzburg 1938, repr. Darmstadt 1967.

Mastronarde, D. *Contact and Discontinuity: Some Conventions of Speech and Action on the Greek Tragic Stage*. Berkeley 1979.

Meissner, B. *Mythisches und Rationales in der Psychologie der euripideischen Tragödie*. Diss. Göttingen 1951.

Melchinger, S. *Euripides*. Hannover 1967.

Mellert-Hoffmann, G. *Untersuchungen zur "Iphigenie in Aulis" des Euripides*. Heidelberg 1969.

Michelini, A.N. *Euripides and the Tragic Tradition*. Madison 1987.

Mossman, J. *Wild Justice: A Study of Euripides' Hecuba*. Oxford 1995.

Mueller-Goldingen, C. *Untersuchungen zu den Phönissen des Euripides*. Stuttgart 1985.

Murray, G. *Euripides and His Age*². London 1965.

Nagy, G. *Pindar's Homer: The Lyric Possession of an Epic Past*. Baltimore and London 1990.

Nehring, A. "Homer's Descriptions of Syncopes." *CPh* 42 (1947): 106–21.

Neumann, V. *Gegenwart und mythische Vergangenheit bei Euripides*. Stuttgart 1995.

North, H. *Sophrosyne*. Ithaca, NY, 1966.

Nussbaum, M. *The Fragility of Goodness: Luck and Ethics in Greek Tragedy and Philosophy*. Cambridge 1986.

Onians, R.B. *The Origins of European Thought*². Cambridge 1954.

Ostenfeld, E. *Ancient Greek Psychology and the Modern Mind-Body Debate*. Aarhus, Denmark, 1987.

Otto, W.F. *Die Manen*². Darmstadt 1962.

Padel, R. *In and Out of Mind: Greek Images of the Tragic Self*. Princeton 1992.

– *Whom Gods Destroy: Elements of Greek and Tragic Madness*. Princeton 1995.

Parry, H. *The Lyric Poems of Greek Tragedy*. Toronto 1978.

Pelliccia, H. *Mind, Body, and Speech in Homer and Pindar*. Göttingen 1995. *Hypomnemata* 107.

Plämbock, G. *Erfassen, Gegenwartigen, Innesein, Aspekte homerischer Psychologie*. Kiel 1959.

Podlecki, A.J. *The Early Greek Poets and Their Times*. Vancouver 1984.

Pohlenz, M. *Die greichische Tragödie*. 2 vols. Göttingen 1954.

Porter, J.R. *Studies in Euripides' Orestes*. Leiden 1994. *Mnem. Suppl.* 128.

Redfield, J.M. *Nature and Culture in The Iliad: The Tragedy of Hector*. Chicago 1975.

Reverdin, O., ed. *Euripide. Entretiens sur l'antiquité classique* 6. Geneva 1960.

Rivier, A. *Essai sur le tragique d'Euripide*². Paris 1975.

Rodley, L., ed. *Papers given at a Colloquium on Greek Drama*. London 1987.

Rohde, E. *Psyche*⁸. Trans. W.B. Hillis. London 1925.

Rohdich, H. *Die euripideische Tragödie*. Heidelberg 1968.

Romilly, J. de. *"Patience, mon coeur." L'essor de la psychologie dans la littérature grecque classique*. Paris 1984.

– *La Modernité d'Euripide*. Paris 1986.

Rosenmeyer, T.C. *The Masks of Tragedy*. New York 1971.

Rüsche, F. *Blut, Leben und Seele*. Paderborn 1930.

Russo, J., and B. Simon. "Homeric Psychology and the Oral Epic Tradition." *JHI* 29 (1968): 483–98.

Saïd, S. *La Faute tragique*. Paris 1978.

Sansone, D. *Aeschylean Metaphors for Intellectual Activity*. Wiesbaden 1975.

Schmitt, A. *Selbständigkeit und Abhängigkeit menschlichen Handelns bei Homer*. Mainz 1990.

Schnaufer, A. *Frühgriechischen Totenglaube*. Hildesheim 1970. *Spudasmata* 20.

Schwinge, E.R., ed. *Euripides*. Darmstadt 1968. *Wege der Forschung* 89.

Scodel, R. *The Trojan Trilogy of Euripides*. Göttingen 1980. *Hypomnemata* 60.

Segal, C. *Dionysiac Poetics and Euripides' Bacchae*. Princeton 1982.

– *Interpreting Greek Tragedy: Myth, Poetry, Text*. Ithaca 1986.

– *Euripides and the Poetics of Sorrow*. Durham and London 1993.

Segal, E., ed. *Euripides: A Collection of Critical Essays*. Englewood Cliffs, NJ, 1968.

Segal, E. *Greek Tragedy: Modern Essays in Criticism*. New York 1983.

Snell, B. *The Discovery of Mind*. Trans. T.G. Rosenmeyer. Oxford 1953.

– *Scenes from Greek Drama*. Berkeley and Los Angeles 1964.

– *Der Weg zum Denken und zur Wahrheit*. Göttingen 1978. *Hypomnemata* 57.

Snell, B., and others. *Lexikon des frühgriechischen Epos*. Göttingen 1955–.

Solmsen, F. *Hesiod and Aeschylus*. Ithaca, NY, 1949, repr. 1967.

– "Plato and the Concept of the Soul (*Psychē*), Some Historical Perspectives." *JHI* 44 (1983): 355–67.

– *"Phrēn, Kardia, Psychē* in Greek Tragedy." In *Greek Poetry and Philosophy, Studies Woodbury.* Chico, Calif., 1984. 265–74.

Stanford, W.B. *Greek Metaphor.* Oxford 1936.

– *Greek Tragedy and the Emotions: An Introductory Study.* London 1983.

Stevens, P.T. *Colloquial Expressions in Euripides.* Wiesbaden 1976.

Stinton, T.C.W. *Collected Papers on Greek Tragedy.* Oxford 1990.

Strohm, H. *Euripides: Interpretationen zur dramatischen Form.* Munich 1957. *Zetemata* 15.

Sullivan, S.D. *Psychological Activity in Homer: A Study of Phrēn.* Ottawa 1988.

– *Psychological and Ethical Ideas: What Early Greeks Say.* Leiden 1995. *Mnem. Suppl.* 144.

– *Aeschylus' Use of Psychological Terminology: Traditional and New.* Montreal 1997.

– *Sophocles' Use of Psychological Terminology: Old and New.* Ottawa 1999.

Taplin, O. *Greek Tragedy in Action.* London 1978.

Tarrant, D. "Greek Metaphors of Light." *CQ* 10 (1960): 181–7.

Thalmann, W.G. *Conventions of Form and Thought in Early Greek Epic Poetry.* Baltimore and London 1984.

Treu, M. *Von Homer zur Lyrik².* Munich 1968.

Valk, M. van der. *Studies in Euripides: Phoenissae and Andromache.* Amsterdam 1985.

Velacott, P. *Ironic Drama: A Study of Euripides' Method and Meaning.* Cambridge 1976.

Verdenius, W.J. *Commentaries on Pindar.* Leiden 1987, 1988. *Mnem. Suppl.* 97 and 101, vols. 1 and 2.

Vickers, B. *Towards Greek Tragedy: Drama, Myth, Society.* London 1973.

Vivante, P. "Sulle designazione Omeriche della realtà psichica." *AGI* 41 (1956): 113–38.

Warden, J. "The Mind of Zeus." *JHI* 32 (1971): 3–14.

– *"Psychē* in Homeric Death-Descriptions." *Phoenix* 25 (1971): 85–103.

Webster, T.B.L. "Some Psychological Terms in Greek Tragedy." *JHS* 77 (1957): 149–54.

– *The Tragedies of Euripides.* London 1967.

– *Greek Tragedy.* Oxford 1971.

West, M.L. *Studies in Greek Elegy and Iambus.* Berlin 1974.

– "Tragica IV." *BICS* 27 (1980): 9–22.

– "Tragica V." *BICS* 28 (1981): 61–78.

Whitman, C.H. *Euripides and the Full Circle of Myth.* Cambridge, Mass., 1974.

Wilson, J.R., ed. *Twentieth Century Interpretations of Euripides' Alcestis: A Collection of Critical Essays.* Englewood Cliffs, NJ, 1968.

Winnington-Ingram, R.P. *Euripides and Dionysius, and Interpretation of the Bacchae.* Cambridge 1948.

– "Euripides: *Poiētēs Sophos." Arethusa* 2 (1969): 127–42.

Zuntz, G. *The Political Plays of Euripides².* Manchester 1963.

Zürcher, W. *Die Darstellung des Menschen im Drama des Euripides.* Basel 1947.

Index of Passages Discussed

General Index

Entries in bold indicate chief discussions.